IMAGES
*of America*

# HIGH BRIDGE GLENS OF CUYAHOGA FALLS

**On the Cover:** Springfield, Ohio, photographer J.A. Baumgardner toured picturesque areas of northeast Ohio, including the High Bridge Glens, in 1894. While at the Glens, he recorded this scene, which he titled, "Three Cuyahoga Boys." (David Neuhardt collection.)

IMAGES
*of America*

# HIGH BRIDGE GLENS OF CUYAHOGA FALLS

Mary L. McClure

ARCADIA
PUBLISHING

ISBN 978-0-7385-9361-6

Published by Arcadia Publishing
Charleston, South Carolina

Printed in the United States of America

Library of Congress Control Number: 2011938906

For all general information, please contact Arcadia Publishing:
Telephone 843-853-2070
Fax 843-853-0044
E-mail sales@arcadiapublishing.com
For customer service and orders:
Toll-Free 1-888-313-2665

Visit us on the Internet at www.arcadiapublishing.com

*To the city of Cuyahoga Falls, Ohio, which celebrates its bicentennial in 2012, and to the Cuyahoga Falls Historical Society, which promotes and preserves local history.*

# Contents

# ACKNOWLEDGMENTS

This book would not have been possible without the love, encouragement, and support of many friends, family members, fellow historians, and knowledgeable collectors, and I would like to acknowledge their contributions here. While it is impossible to recognize each and every person, my deepest gratitude goes to:

My boyfriend, Jeff, who was the first person to encourage me to take all the information I had gathered on the High Bridge Glens and develop it into a book. He generously gave me the time I needed to work on the manuscript—and he was a marvelous sounding board, offering many suggestions for bringing the Glens story to life. Everyone should have someone so caring and supportive in their lives.

My best friend, Lauren Wentz-Middleton, who patiently and meticulously reviewed early drafts of the book and provided wonderful insights. Writers know that everyone needs an editor, and she is a marvelous reviewer and wonderful friend.

My brother Don and sister Marilyn, who always encouraged me to follow my dreams.

The Cuyahoga Falls Historical Society—including Pres. Dick Horn, curator Liz Cross, and museum staff members Mary Lou Atleson, Babette Robinson, Irene Metz, and Amy Stahl—who shared their knowledge of local history and provided access to key research materials. This organization (and their museum) is one of the true gems of the community. Special thanks go to Liz Cross, who is passionate about preserving local history, especially that of the Glens. Her tremendous knowledge of this area and infectious sense of humor made this research project a true joy.

The local history/special collections departments of the Akron-Summit County Public Library, Cuyahoga Falls Library, and Stow-Munroe Falls Public Library, whose staffs helped point me toward materials and artifacts that were a vital part of my research.

Local experts John Waldsmith, David Neuhardt, Pete Mellinger, Eric Thompson, and John Phillips, who generously shared rare images of the park from their private collections.

The City of Cuyahoga Falls, whose mayor and economic development team have diligently worked to create a new park on the site of the original Glens, as well as to preserve the heritage of the original park.

# INTRODUCTION

In the 1870s, enterprising Cuyahoga Falls, Ohio, hardware store owner L.W. Loomis had a bold idea. Seeing the success of other area summer resorts, including nearby Silver Lake Park and Gaylord's Grove, Loomis—one of the town's leading business owners—proposed creating a new park along the picturesque banks of the Cuyahoga River at Front and Prospect Streets.

The advance and retreat of glaciers during the last ice age and related geological events created stunning scenery along that portion of the Cuyahoga River, including cascades and waterfalls, towering cliffs, mysterious caves, and curiously shaped rock formations. These features, combined with the lush vegetation along the riverbanks, were just the type of wild natural beauty that Victorians loved to behold.

As Loomis began to envision the new park, he planned a resort that would span both sides of the Cuyahoga River, beginning at the present-day intersection of Front and Prospect Streets. The park would then extend south for approximately one mile to the future site of the former Gorge Power Plant at Front Street and Howe Avenue. On the western half (Front Street side) of the park, Loomis pictured a large dining hall and dance pavilion featuring some of the best meals and musical entertainment available. He also foresaw a network of trails leading visitors to scenic nooks and overlooks, eventually reaching river level. On the park's eastern half, he planned additional trails leading past tall cliffs, the remains of an abandoned water race (known as the Chuckery), and special features constructed for children.

However, before Loomis could make his dream a reality, he had to overcome several obstacles. First, he needed a partner to help create and manage the park. He found the perfect collaborator right under his own roof at Loomis Hardware—his sales agent, the prophetically named Harvey Parks. Because Parks's position at the hardware store required him to travel extensively, he was the ideal person to help promote the new park to neighboring communities and book excursion parties.

The next obstacle was slightly more difficult. To make the park economically viable, Loomis needed to find a way for out-of-town visitors, who would arrive by the various railway lines bordering the Glens' eastern side, to easily cross the river to reach the park's entrance on the western side of the river. That problem was solved in the late 1870s, when the Summit County commissioners approved construction of a high iron bridge crossing the Cuyahoga River at Front and Prospect Streets. The new bridge, capable of accommodating pedestrian and horse-and-buggy traffic, essentially joined the two halves of the future park. Additionally, the bridge, which stood approximately 100 feet above the Cuyahoga River, offered a perfect vantage point for enjoying the park's stunning scenery.

With the bridge and partnership issues resolved, Loomis began negotiating leases with various individuals who owned property within the confines of the future park. By early 1879, work was underway on the park's pavilion, trails, and other attractions. In June 1879, the High Bridge Glens and Caves park opened for its first public event. According to historians, first-day receipts at the Glens were approximately $2,500—an impressive sum, considering admission was 5¢.

According to park brochures, the High Bridge Glens became so popular that within one year of opening, the park had far outgrown its original pavilion. For the 1880 season, the owners added a new Grand Pavilion that was twice the size of the original building. To accommodate the growing throng of out-of-town visitors, the owners also purchased a nearby home and converted it into the Glen House hotel. Loomis and Parks also added a new partner—H.H. Hoover, formerly of New Jersey—to help run the Glen House and the park.

During the first several years the park was in business, Loomis and his partners worked to keep the Glens exciting. They hired some of the area's leading bands to play at the Grand Pavilion. They organized some of the largest Fourth of July fireworks shows around and set up nighttime bonfire illuminations of the Glens. They hosted balloon ascensions and hired the DaComa Brothers, a troupe of acrobats who had performed at the Crystal Palace in London and the Cirque Fernando in Paris, to present a daring bicycle and trapeze exhibition on a cable strung 100 feet over the Glens. These promotional efforts appeared to have paid off, as thousands of visitors came to the Glens during the summer season, including 60 trainloads arriving daily from out of town. Many well-known Ohioans frequented the park, including Gov. Charles Foster and Congressman (and future US president) William McKinley.

In 1884, the park debuted one of its most thrilling attractions—an early version of the roller coaster known as the circular gravity railway. Some local history books have indicated that the Glens roller coaster was the first in the United States. The claim is difficult to prove or disprove, as roller-coaster historians themselves do not always seem to agree on what device constitutes the first true roller coaster or who invented it. Based on 1884 *Cuyahoga Falls Reporter* accounts, it appears the Glens coaster made its debut close to the time LaMarcus Thompson's switchback railway, which is sometimes credited as being the first true roller coaster in the United States, began operating at New York's Coney Island.

While the Glens coaster may or may not have been first in the country, it appears to be one of the first in the area. Although some local historians have indicated that Chippewa Lake Park had a crude version of an early coaster, the High Bridge Glens had a roller coaster before many local parks, including Geauga Lake Park, Congress Lake, Meyers Lake, Silver Lake Park, or Turkeyfoot Lake. For Victorians, who had not seen a mechanical ride of this type before, a ride on the coaster was a real thrill. Enjoying the fact that a spin around the track occasionally caused their dates to bump against them, local boys nicknamed the Glens coaster the "hug me closer." Charles Henry and Samuel Miller of Akron owned the Glens coaster.

For the first five years the park was in operation, it enjoyed increasing popularity. Local newspapers quoted area residents and business owners as being extremely proud of Cuyahoga Falls' growing status as one of the state's leading tourist destinations. However, for reasons that were never explained, by 1883, Parks and Hoover were no longer partners in the park. And by 1884, Loomis himself was advertising the Glens as being available for rent to new operators.

Soon thereafter, Cleveland, Akron & Columbus Railway auditor C.W. Schaap announced that he would be proprietor of the High Bridge Glens starting in the 1885 season. To assist with the park's day-to-day operations, he hired F.W. Fuchs as manager. Like the previous owners, Schaap brought exciting attractions to the park. He continued to hold grand fireworks displays and hired popular local bands to perform at the pavilion. He also installed new attractions, including an aerial swing known as the Mikado Swing. At one point, he even advertised that he was looking for an acrobat willing to dive off the High Bridge into a net stretched just above the Cuyahoga River; it does not appear that he found anyone willing to attempt the feat.

By 1887, the High Bridge Glens boasted its highest attendance figures ever—more than 8,500 visitors in one day; however, if 1887 was a banner year at the Glens, 1888 was an entirely different proposition. While the park traditionally opened around the Decoration Day (now Memorial Day) holiday, in 1888 the park did not really get rolling until about the Fourth of July. Local residents, including the editor of the *Cuyahoga Falls Reporter*, were mystified by the change in fortune at the Glens. The newspaper described the park as being "as deserted as an old bird's nest" and wondered who could explain the Glens' declining popularity.

It was not just tourists who lost interest in the Glens. Harry Veon, who helped Schaap manage the park after Fuchs left, also departed, announcing plans to open a store in Akron. In 1889,

Schaap announced that he too would be leaving the Glens, as he planned to retire from the railroad and return to his native country of Holland.

Nearly a decade after he first opened High Bridge Glens, L.W. Loomis stepped back in as proprietor of the park in 1889—much to the delight and approval of Cuyahoga Falls residents. He formed a "stock company" to run the park, with investors including some of the town's leading businessmen. Investors included R.H. Lodge (owner of Silver Lake Park), Judge C.R. Grant, Charles F. Thomas (grocer), George Marvin (hotel proprietor), Minor H. Howe (partner in a local mill), Robert Adams (livery stable and coal), S. McGrew (agent for the Pittsburgh & Western Railroad), Eugene O. Knox (editor of the local newspaper), Towler & Inskeep (dry goods), A.L. Gilbert (owner of a livery stable), Heath & Co. (drugstore), George Estey, W.O. Beebe (dry goods), D.H. Jones (confectioner), George Paul (civil engineer), J.F. Weidner (cooper), S.D. Tifft (merchant), Henry Wetmore, Orlando Wilcox (attorney), W.C. Hall (American Express agent), J.H. Insande (coal dealer), W.M. Taylor, A.D. Alexander, J.M Beyery, D.A. Holcomb (grocer), George Sackett, E. Sill, William Weaver, and the Wills brothers.

Though the new park underwent numerous improvements and enjoyed some renewed popularity, its success was short-lived. By 1892, Loomis was again advertising the Glens as being available to rent to new operators. Newspapers from the era shed little light on the cause of the change in fortune at the Glens; however, a major "financial panic" around 1893 may have caused business owners to scale back operations.

In addition to the financial panic of 1893, another event that year cast a dark shadow over the Glens. In fact, it became a major news story that made headlines across the country. On May 8, 1893, a young couple named Martha Kline and Gustave Schuler took a moonlight buggy ride across the Glens Bridge (also known as the High Bridge), at Front and Prospect Streets, on their way to visit friends in nearby Kent, Ohio. Unfortunately, unknown to the young couple, the bridge was in the process of being adapted to accommodate streetcar traffic. As such, a number of the floorboards on the bridge had been removed. Although some accounts indicate that barriers had been erected, they apparently failed to stop the horse and buggy from starting to cross the bridge.

Within seconds, the horse fell through an open space in the bridge floor, causing the buggy to break apart and tip Kline and Schuler into the Cuyahoga River, 90 feet below. Nearby residents, hearing a crash, ran to the scene. Seeing the horse—which had miraculously landed, unharmed, on a rock ledge approximately 15 feet below—and the broken buggy, onlookers quickly sent for help. Armed with torches, local residents searched the riverbanks for any trace of survivors.

Kline's lifeless body was not found until about three weeks later, downstream in the Gorge a few miles south of the Glens Bridge. While Schuler's coat, pants, suspenders, and hat were found in the same vicinity, his remains were still missing. Area residents continued to search for Schuler, but, given the condition of Kline's remains, most believed that Schuler's body would probably never be found. All that changed in the spring of 1897. Approximately four years after sensational headlines first announced the Glens Bridge tragedy, the banners of Akron newspapers once again screamed in large black type, "A GHASTLY FIND." In March, a young man fishing along the banks of the Cuyahoga River near Old Maid's Kitchen found a large thighbone near the edge of the water. Doctors later identified it as belonging to Schuler. Sometime later, Schuler's skull was found.

While no references to the Glens' 1893 or 1894 seasons have been found in newspapers, in 1895 the fate of it became much clearer. In April, Loomis announced that the Glens would not be reopened for the 1895 season. The High Bridge Glens was officially closed as a place of formal entertainment.

In the spring of 1895, workers began demolition of the original pavilion. Several weeks later, an auction was held to dispose of various items, ranging from tables, chairs, coolers, and cutlery to lamps, crockery, a bowling alley, and iron swings. Later, Thomas F. Walsh, who was building a competing attraction named Randolph Park (next door to Silver Lake Park), bought the Glens' Grand Pavilion and had it dismantled and moved to his park.

What made the Glens fall out of favor with the public? In its later years, the High Bridge Glens and Caves suffered a series of blows from which it never recovered—including increasing reports of drunkenness and disorderly behavior at the park, which gave it a bad reputation, and growing competition from newer parks including Lakeside (Summit Beach), Blue Pond, Long Lake, and others.

Another event that helped the Glens fade from memory occurred several years after the park closed. Around 1912, the local power company (then known as Northern Ohio Traction and Light) built a dam downstream from the Glens, at the Gorge, to generate power for its trolley car system as well as to provide electricity for growing Akron businesses and neighborhoods. The building of the dam also created a small lake that served as a cooling pond for the electric company's power plant.

According to historians, construction of the dam backed up the level of the Cuyahoga River several feet, flooding the Glens and covering many of the former park's caves, trails, and other features. It also caused the "Big Falls" (in the Gorge)—for which Cuyahoga Falls was named—to vanish from sight.

After the High Bridge Glens closed as a place of formal entertainment, area residents continued to visit the former park and hike the trails. Some news accounts indicate that an individual or company charged a small admission to the Glens and sold refreshments.

In subsequent decades, the former park property at Front and Prospect Streets underwent a number of uses. For several years, homes were built on the site. Later, the property was adapted for manufacturing uses. Everything changed in 2002, when the City of Cuyahoga Falls targeted the South Front Street site of the former High Bridge Glens for redevelopment. As part of those efforts, the city later created a new two-acre urban park, also known as High Bridge Glens, on the site of the original park. The park was officially dedicated in October 2009. In 2010, the park won a Scenic Ohio award.

Completion of the park opens an exciting new chapter in the history of High Bridge Glens and reconnects residents with the river that so enthralled previous generations of visitors to Cuyahoga Falls. After more than a century, the city of Cuyahoga Falls is again seeing the many possibilities created by the beautiful scenery along the river. L.W. Loomis and his partners at the original High Bridge Glens would approve.

# *One*

# Birth of the Glens
## From Manufacturing Center to Tourist Destination

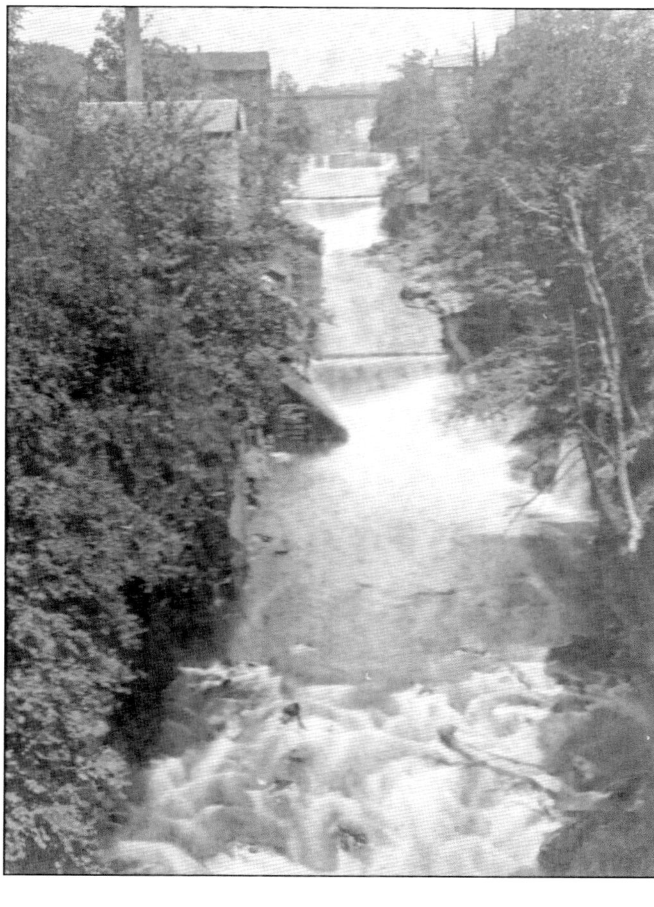

The city of Cuyahoga Falls, Ohio, located north of Akron along the banks of the Cuyahoga River, was founded in 1812. Early settlers from the East were attracted to the community by the many commercial opportunities available to those who could harness the power of the river. According to one advertising tract, the Cuyahoga River had a descent of 150 to 200 feet over a two-mile stretch, including numerous rapids and waterfalls, making it an ideal source for powering mills. This view of the cascading Cuyahoga River, looking north from the Prospect Street Bridge, or "High Bridge," shows several of the early dams constructed along the riverbanks. In the far distance is a covered wooden bridge. This is the original Broad Boulevard, which is now one of the city's busiest thoroughfares. (Author's collection.)

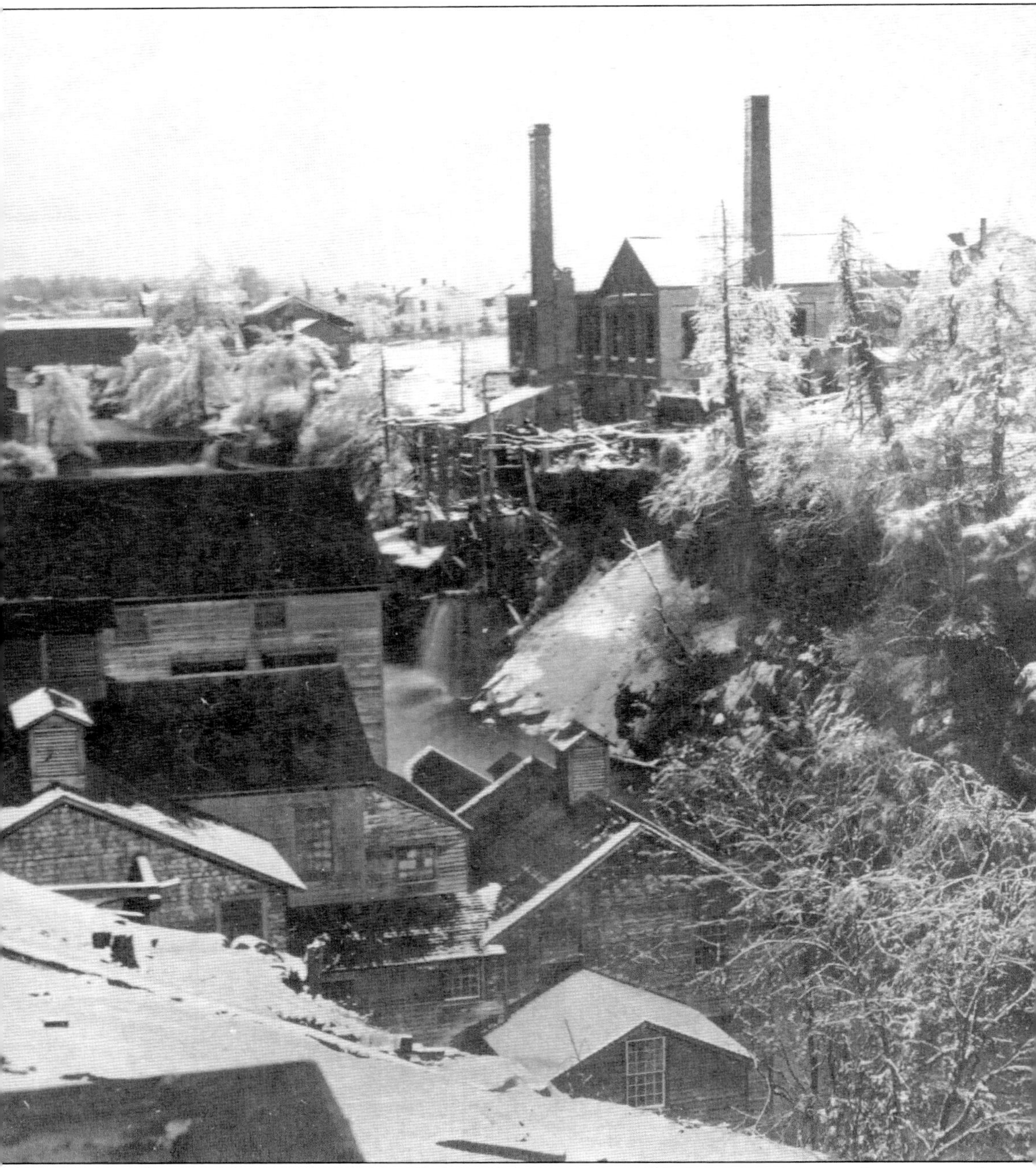

Cuyahoga Falls was originally called Manchester, reportedly because of its similarities to other manufacturing centers of the same name. In later years, the name was changed at the request of the post office, which noted that there were already several other Manchesters in the state; the town became known as Cuyahoga Falls. It was named for the Big Falls of the Cuyahoga, which were located south of the manufacturing district. By the latter half of the 19th century, at least five dams had been constructed along the section of the Cuyahoga River depicted here, and the area's sawmills, gristmills, and linseed oil mills were soon flourishing. (Eric Thompson collection.)

One of the largest manufacturing enterprises in Cuyahoga Falls in the late 1800s was The Falls Rivet Company, which produced Norway iron rivets, washers, and riveting burrs. The factory was located on the east side of the Cuyahoga River north of Portage Street (now Portage Trail). Note the Cleveland, Pittsburgh & Wheeling train car in the left foreground. (Eric Thompson collection.)

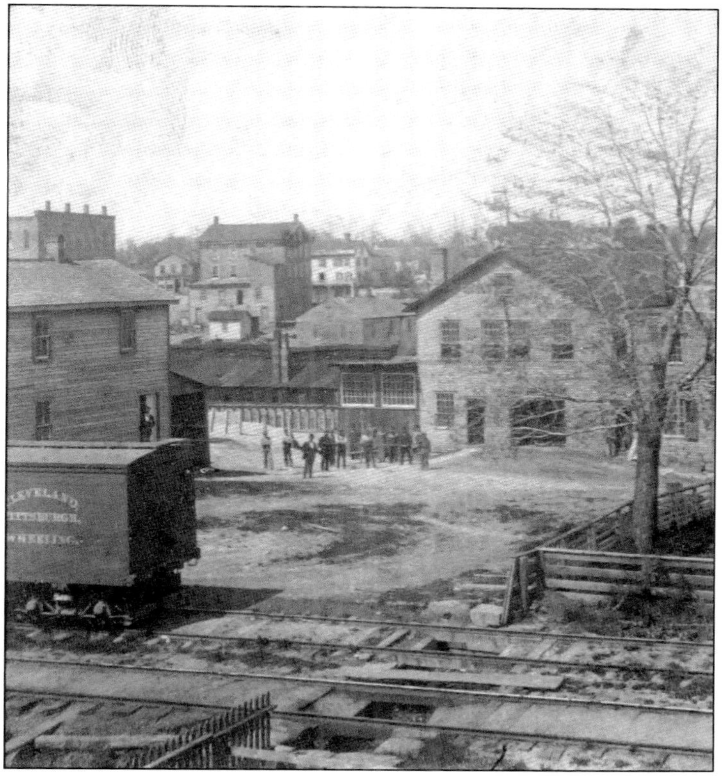

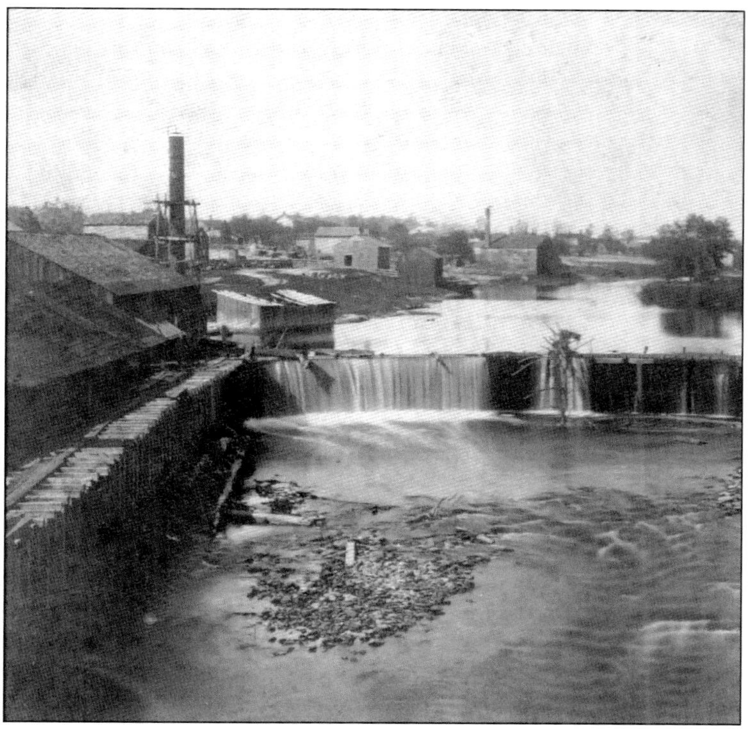

This scene is believed to be located up the river from the stone bridge at Portage Trail. This area contained booming enterprises such as flour mills, tanneries, and firms that produced machine-forged nuts and rivets. As Cuyahoga Falls grew in commercial appeal, so did its population. By 1870, the town boasted 1,860 residents. (Eric Thompson collection.)

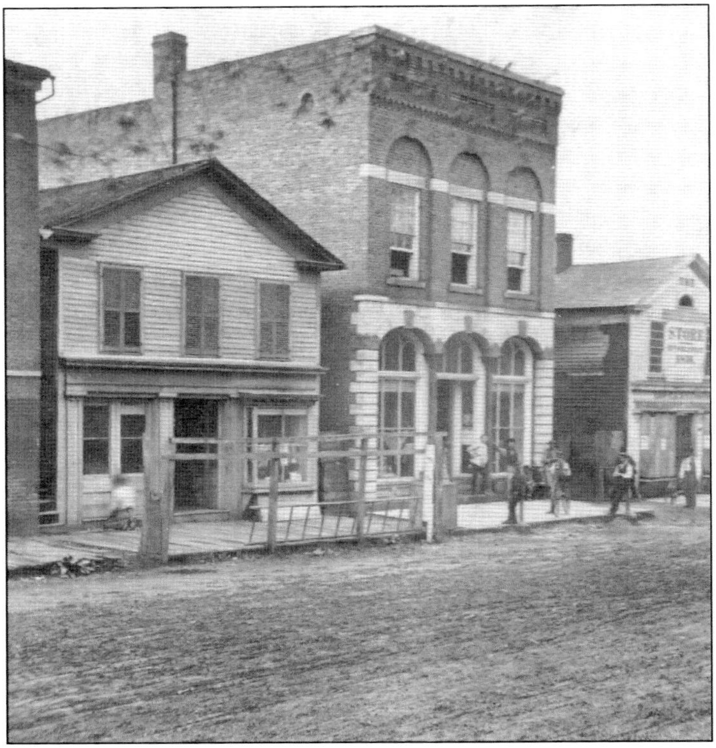

As the manufacturing base expanded in Cuyahoga Falls, the nearby Front Street area soon bustled with stores and other businesses. One of the most successful business owners was Ezra Comstock. According to *Fifty Years and Over of Akron and Summit County* by Samuel Lane, Comstock originally considered locating his business in Chicago but later concluded after a visit to the Windy City that the falls "was more of a business place than Chicago and always would be." His general store was established in 1836. (Eric Thompson collection.)

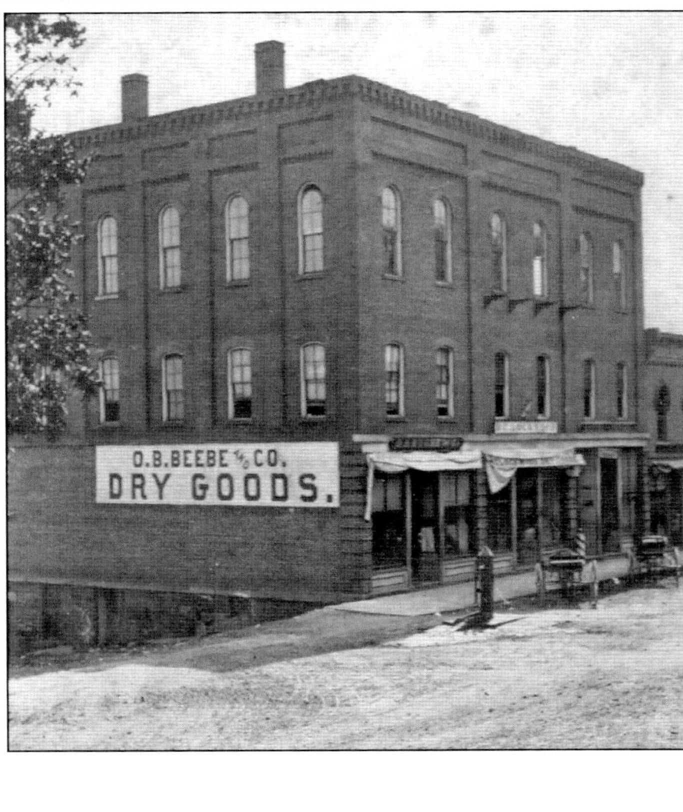


Oliver B. and William O. Beebe operated a dry goods store in the James Block, which—like Comstock's store—was located on the east side of Front Street south of Portage Trail. Note the water pump in front of the store. (Eric Thompson collection.)

Horse-and-buggy rigs line Front Street, which was a dirt road in the 1800s. The store at center left in this image belonged to George Parks. Other nearby businesses included a shoe store, book dealer, undertaker, and newspaper office. (Eric Thompson collection.)

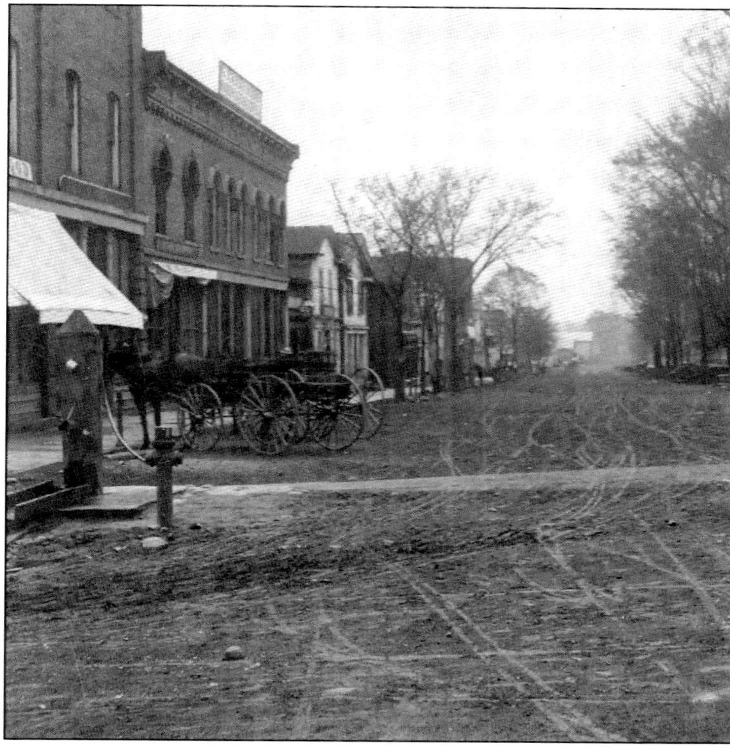

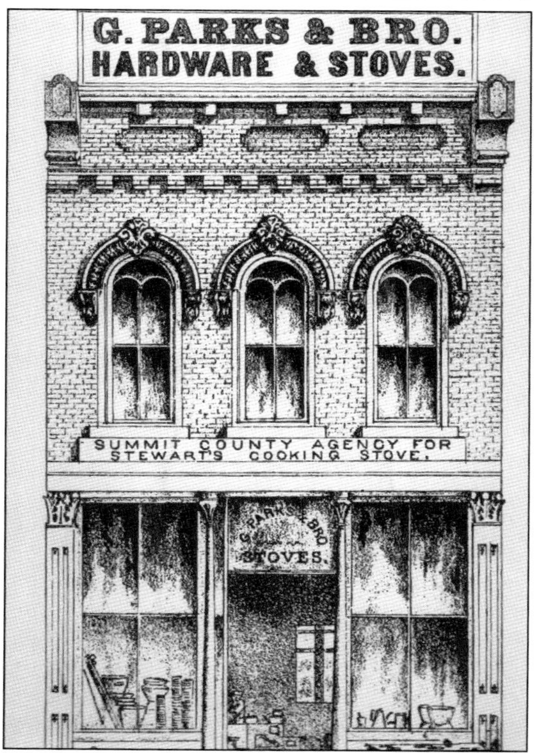


George Parks was a purveyor of hardware, stoves, and farming implements. He also sold insurance and served as the town's justice of the peace. His prosperous store was depicted in this scene from an 1874 Summit County, Ohio, atlas. (Cuyahoga Falls Historical Society Museum.)

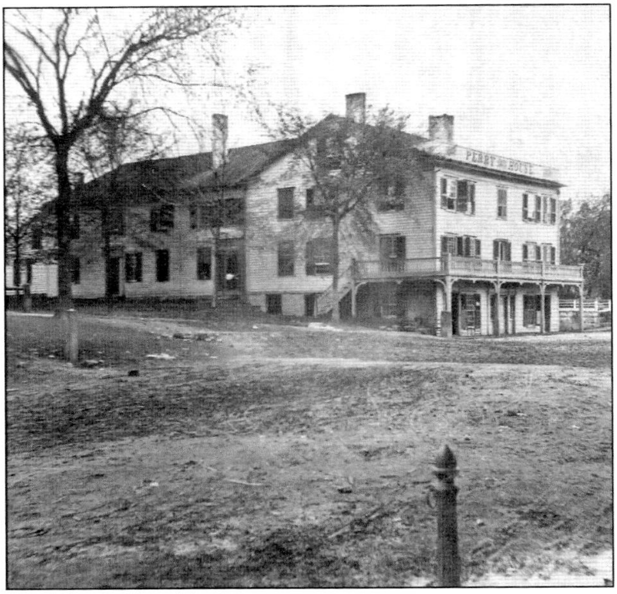

To accommodate the growing number of visitors, a hotel was erected on the northwest corner of Front Street and Portage Trail. This establishment had a variety of different owners and names. At the time this photograph was taken, the hotel was known as the Perry House. (Eric Thompson collection.)

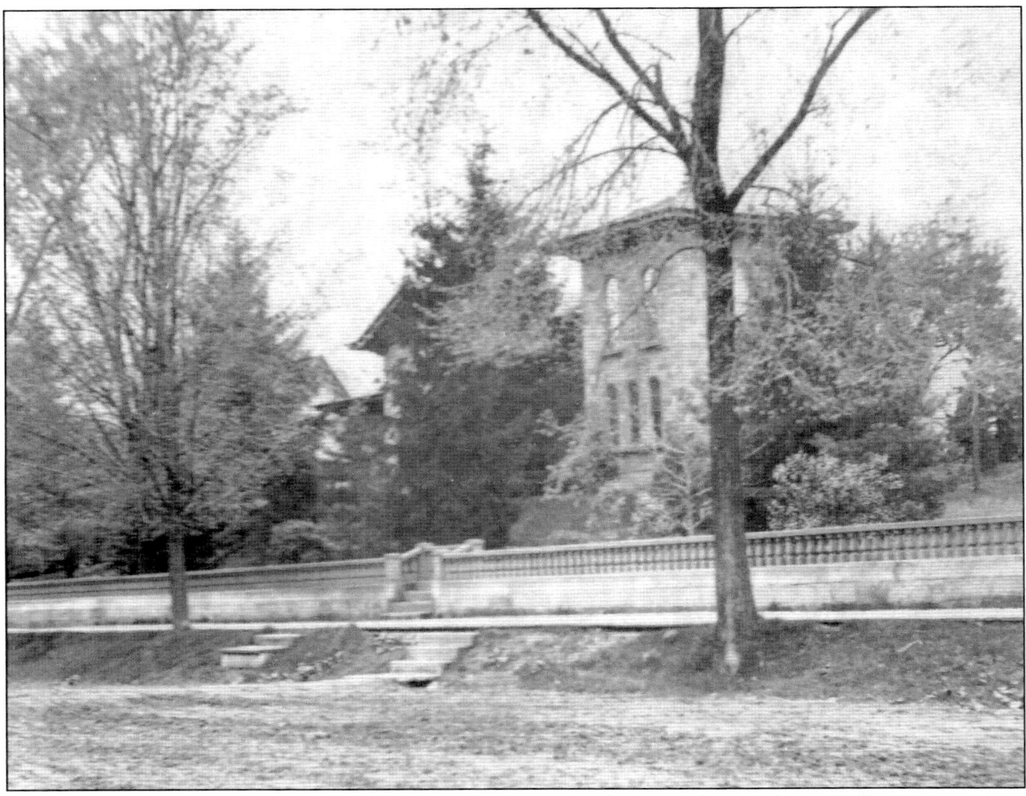

In addition to its expanding manufacturing and business base, early Cuyahoga Falls was noted for its educated, genteel citizenry. According to early historian Samuel Lane, the town's population was "unsurpassed for intelligence and enterprise." This elegant home on Front Street belonged to E.N. Sill, uncle of nationally known poet Edward Rowland Sill. (Eric Thompson collection.)

The area near the Sill mansion, lovely in summer, was equally charming when draped in snow. This scene was taken during an ice storm in the 1870s. (Eric Thompson collection.)

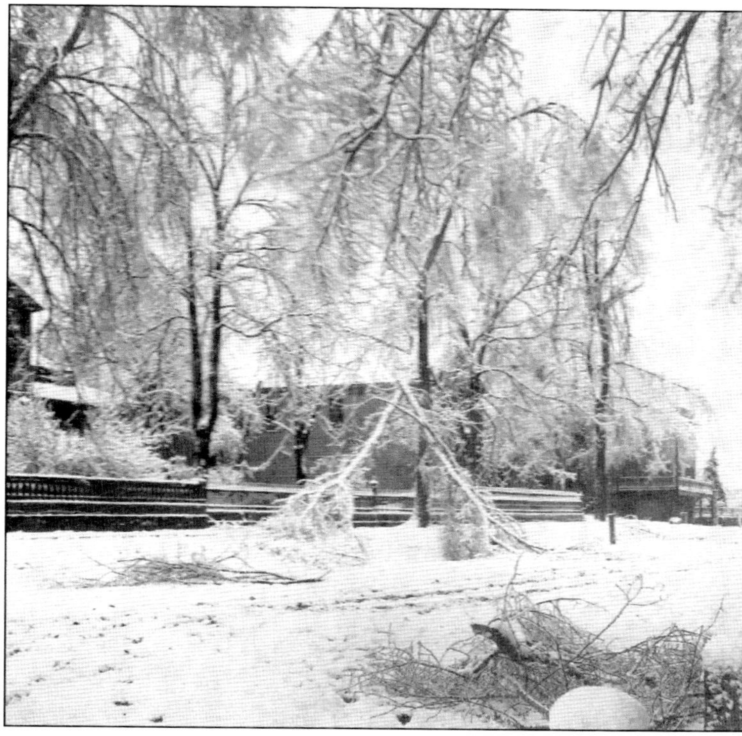

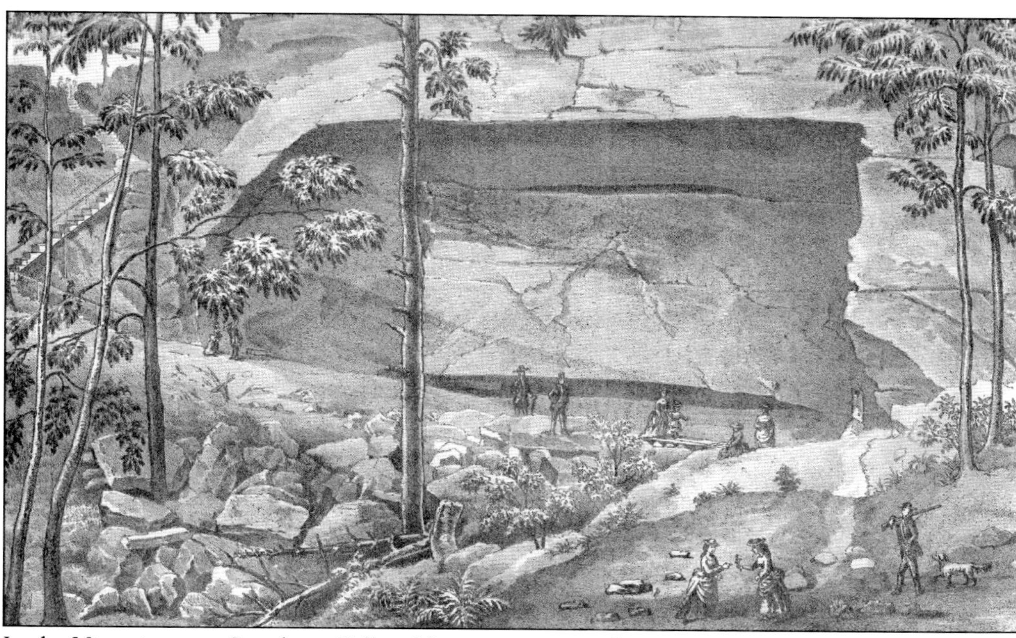

In the Victorian era, Cuyahoga Falls—like many surrounding communities—began establishing parks where visitors could swim, picnic, or commune with nature. One of the earliest of these areas was located approximately one mile south of town, along the Cuyahoga River, in an area known as the Gorge. It included a large cavern originally called Old Maid's Kitchen. (Author's collection.)

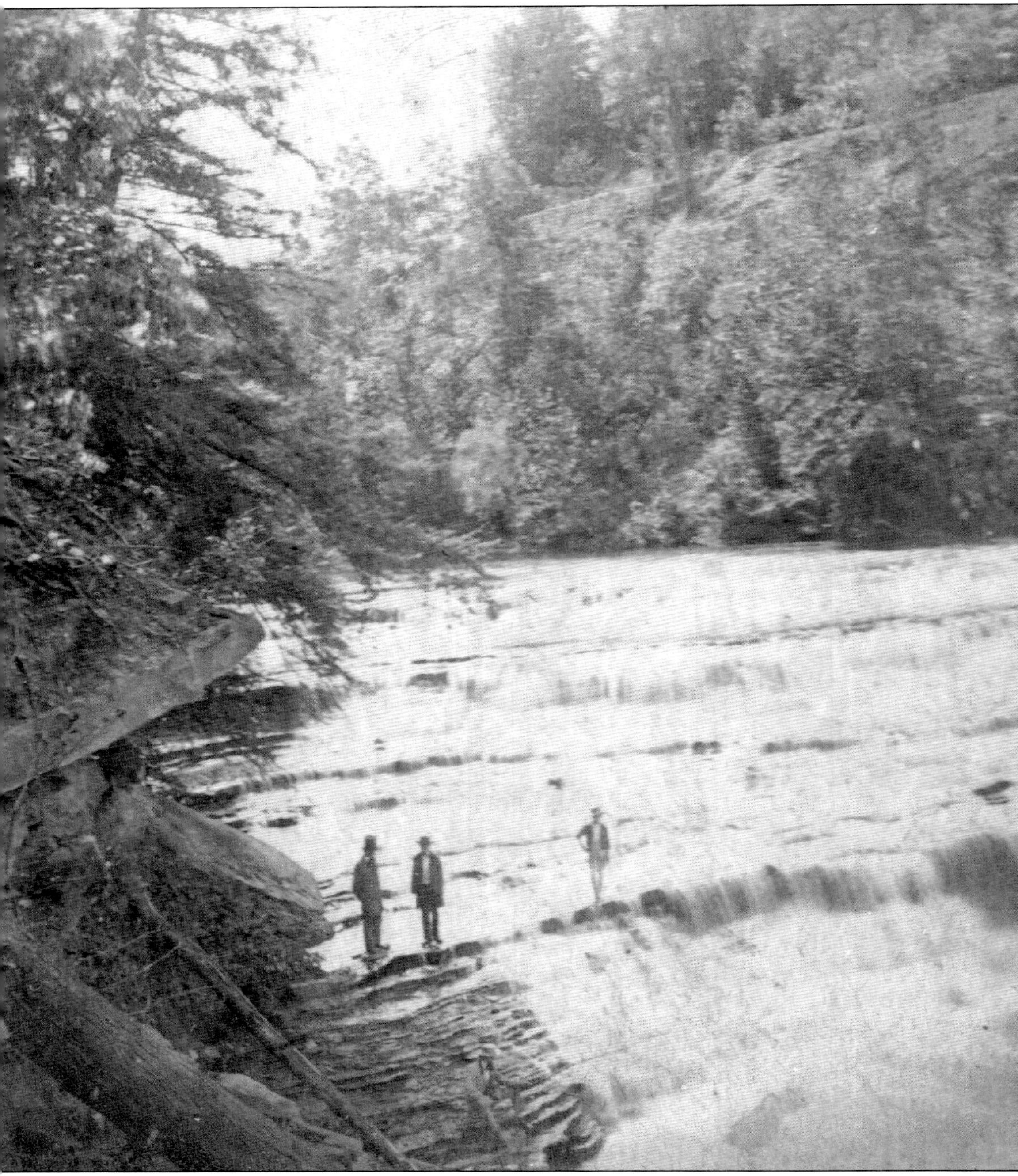

Victorian visitors thrilled to the rushing waters of the Big Falls in the Gorge. To provide accommodations for the many tourists who visited the area, the Fosdick family built a large hotel at street level above Old Maid's Kitchen. A set of steps led from the hotel down to the cave and river. This area had been a popular picnic spot since the Civil War era. Photographers traveled many miles to record the beauty of the waterfalls for which the town of Cuyahoga Falls was named. (Author's collection.)

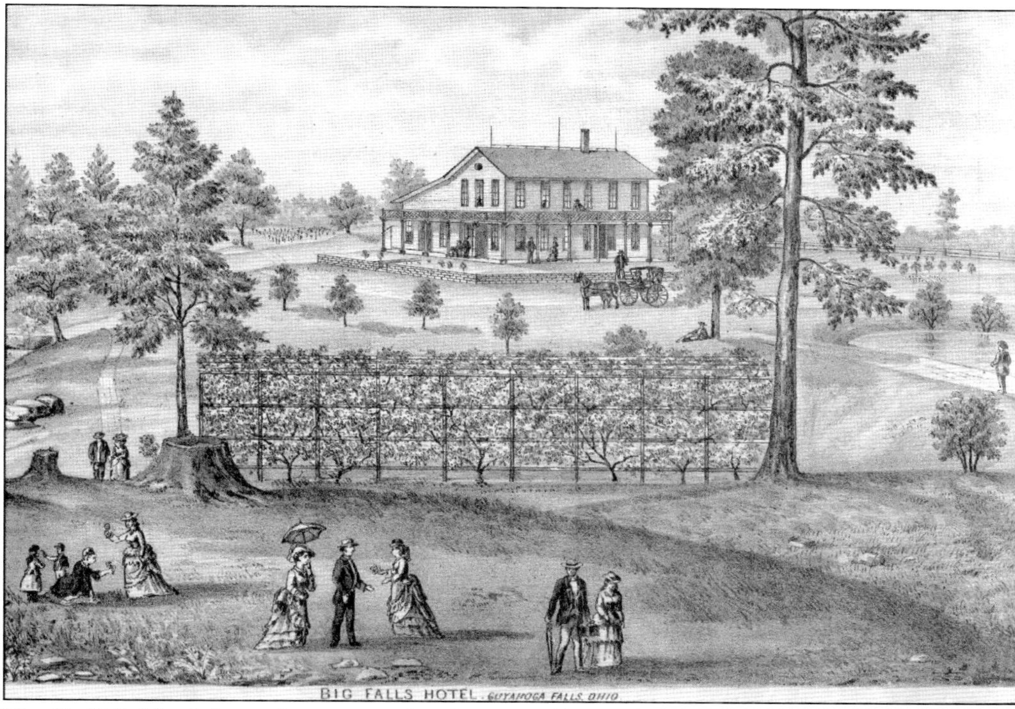


The Big Falls Hotel, located on a street then known as Resort Avenue, drew visitors from throughout Ohio. The hotel was particularly well known for the delicious chicken dinners served by Mary Fosdick. (Author's collection.)

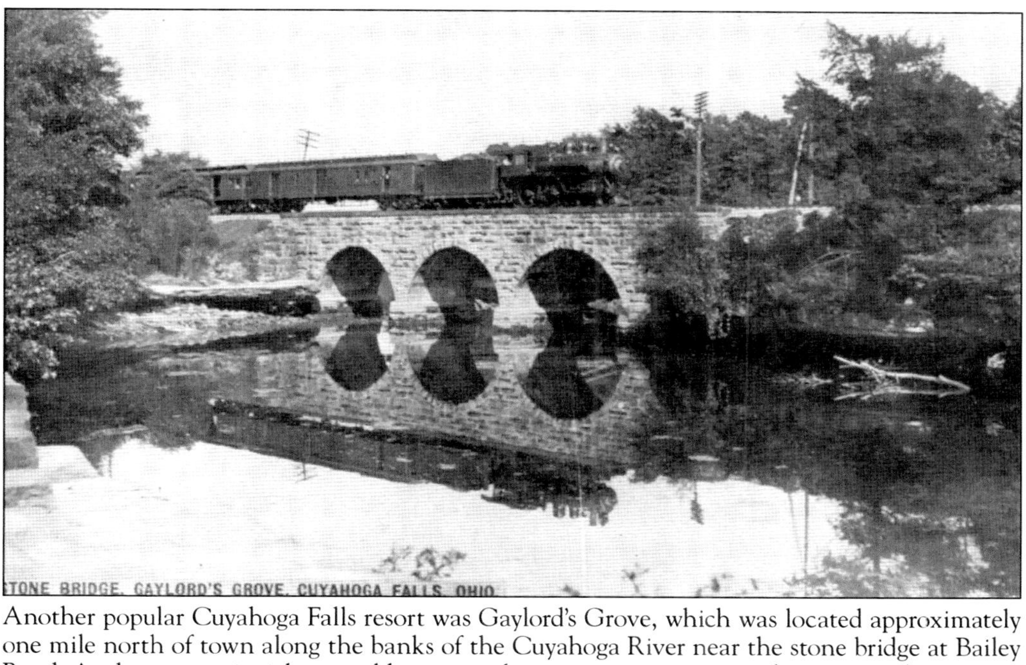


Another popular Cuyahoga Falls resort was Gaylord's Grove, which was located approximately one mile north of town along the banks of the Cuyahoga River near the stone bridge at Bailey Road. At the grove, picnickers could enjoy rowboat or steamer trips on the river or play croquet or baseball. (Author's collection.)

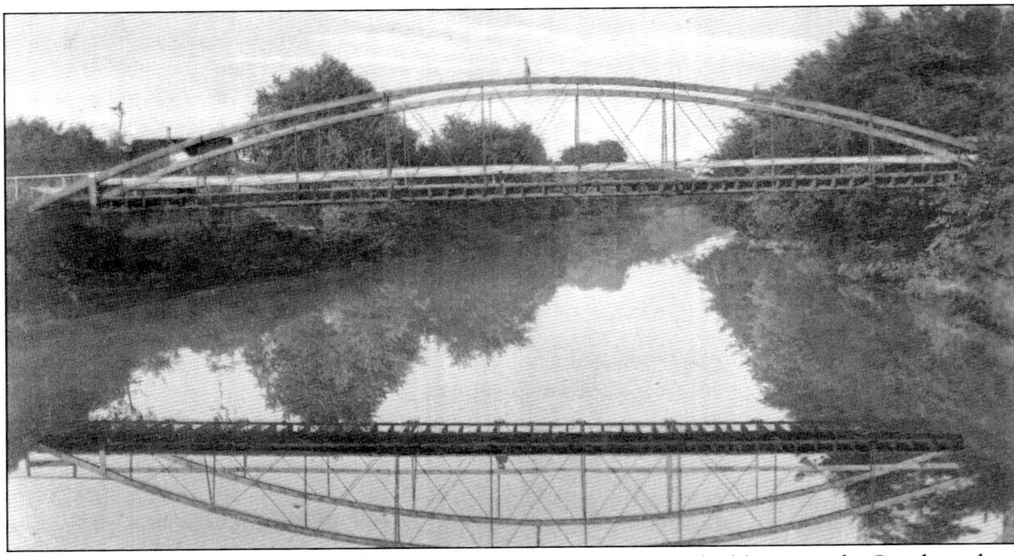

The tree-lined banks of the river by Gaylord's Grove made it an ideal location for Sunday school picnics or excursions. Mr. Hobart managed the park for a number of years. One of the park's steamers reportedly traveled from the grove to the neighboring community of Munroe Falls. This is a small wagon or footbridge near the grove. (Author's collection.)

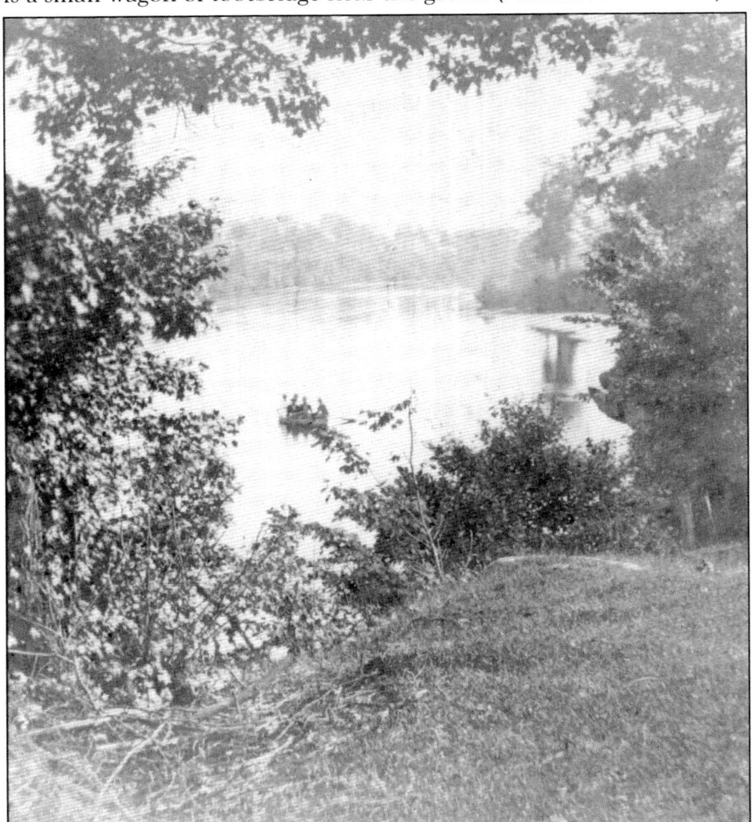

Within walking distance just north of Gaylord's Grove was a beautiful body of water known as Stow Pond, or Silver Lake. Around 1875, Ralph H. Lodge established a picnic resort along the lake. Initially, the park was known for picnicking, swimming, or boating. (Author's collection.)

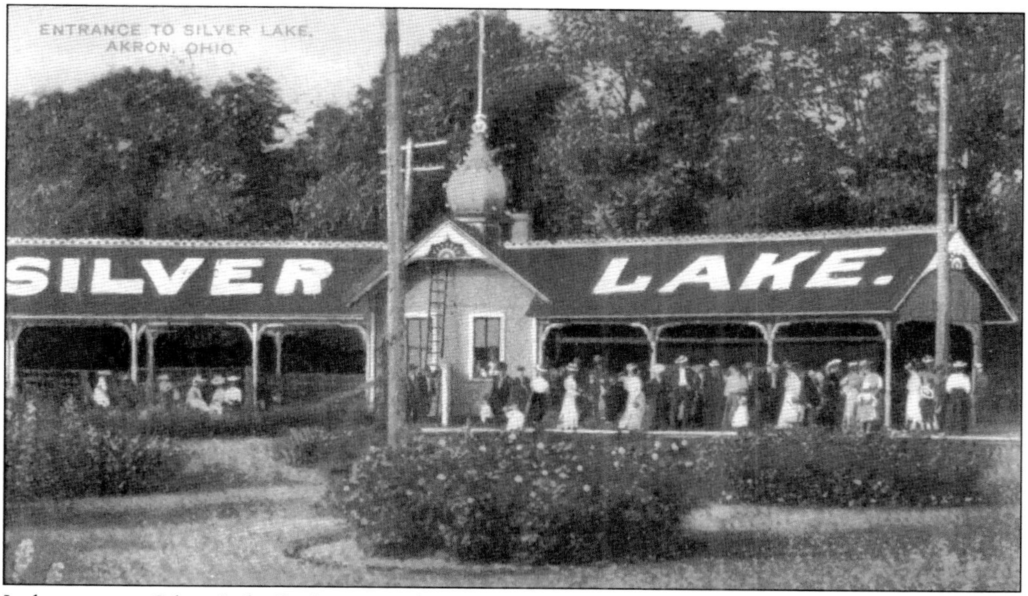


In later years, Silver Lake Park grew to become one of the premier amusement parks in the state. Several reporters nicknamed it the "Coney Island of the West." Later attractions included roller coasters, a merry-go-round, water toboggans, miniature railroads, a menagerie, the state's first aquarium, pony rides, and other thrilling attractions. (Author's collection.)

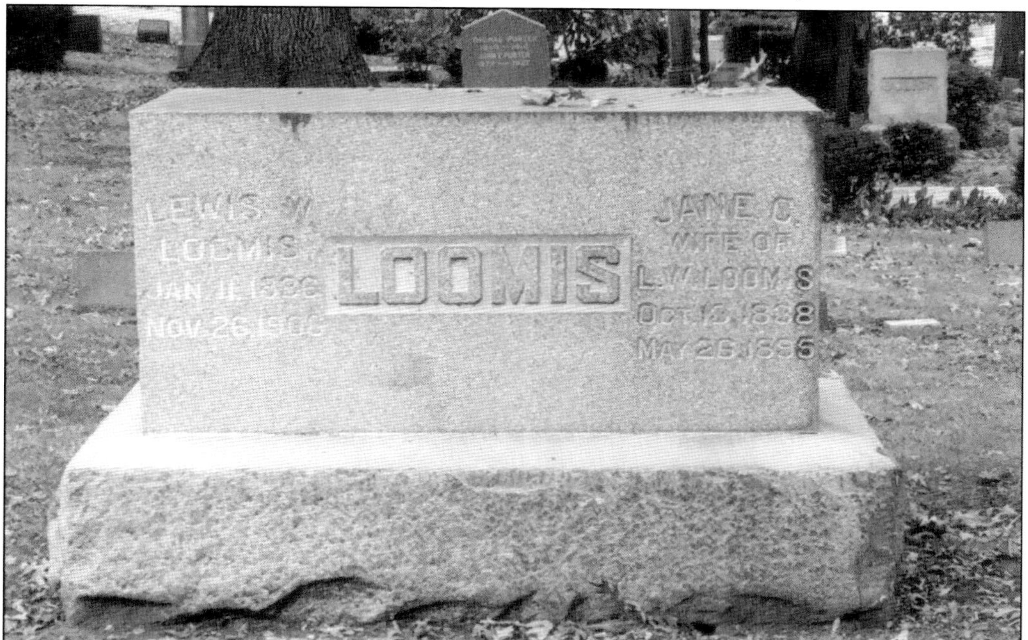


Although Cuyahoga Falls had many charming picnic spots, enterprising hardware store owner L.W. Loomis believed there was room for one more. He proposed creating a park along the banks of the Cuyahoga River at Front and Prospect Streets south of the main manufacturing district. His modest tombstone at Oakwood Cemetery does not even begin to convey the important role he played in the community. (Author's collection.)

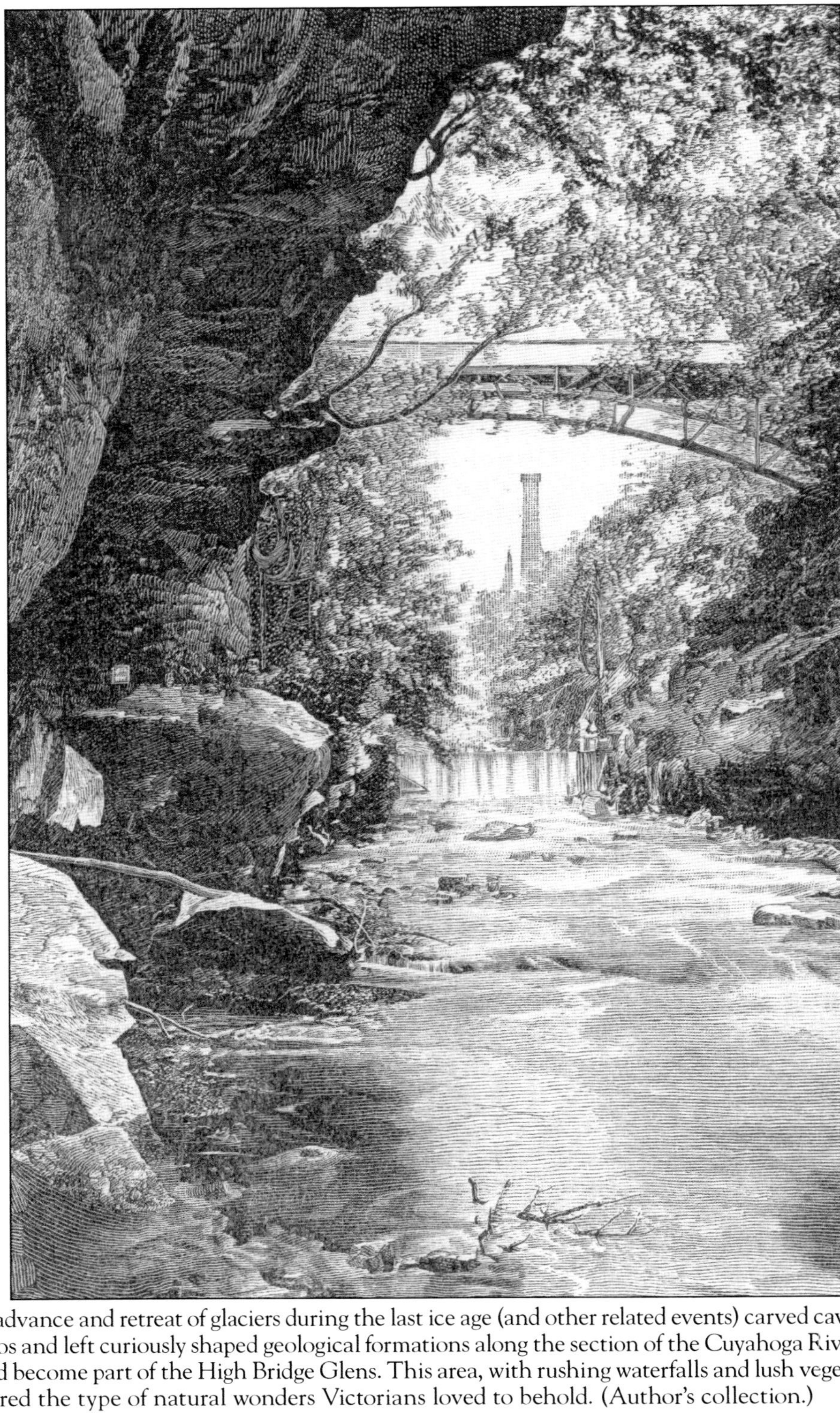

The advance and retreat of glaciers during the last ice age (and other related events) carved caves and grottos and left curiously shaped geological formations along the section of the Cuyahoga River that would become part of the High Bridge Glens. This area, with rushing waterfalls and lush vegetation, featured the type of natural wonders Victorians loved to behold. (Author's collection.)

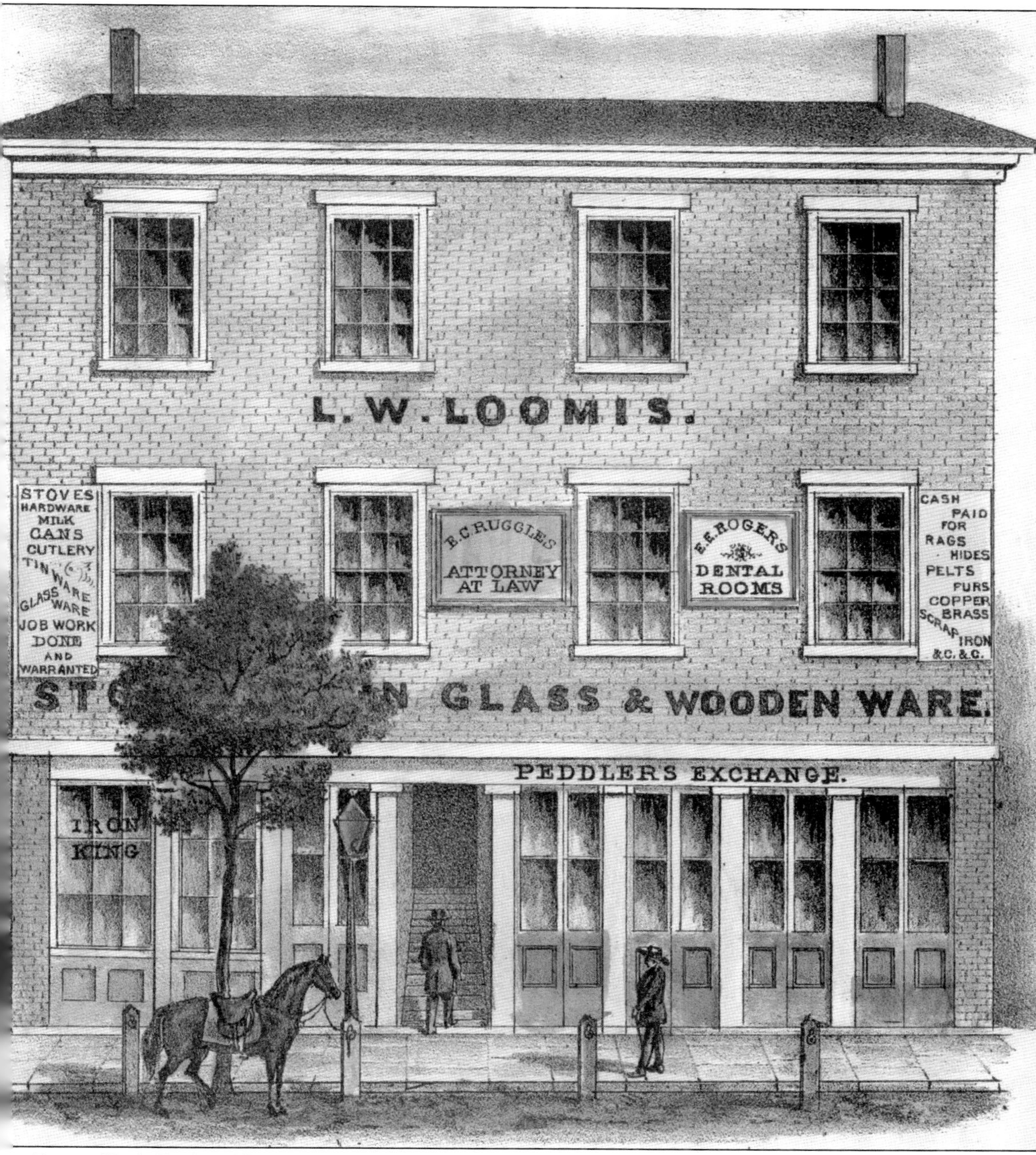


Future High Bridge Glens owner L.W. Loomis came to Cuyahoga Falls from New York state in 1864 and established what would become one of the town's longest-running businesses, Loomis Hardware. His store was located on the northeast corner of Front Street and Portage Trail. Active in civic affairs, Loomis also served as a village trustee (the equivalent of a city council member) and president of Falls Savings and Loan. In later years, he and his wife operated Hotel Warren on Front Street. (Author's collection.)

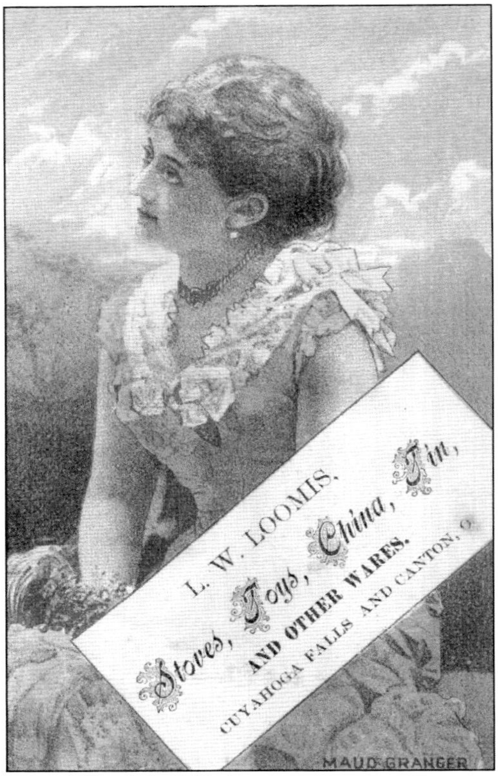


According to this trade card, Loomis also had a successful store in nearby Canton, Ohio. His primary sales representative in Cuyahoga Falls was H.E. (Harvey Ethelbert) Parks, who later became his partner in the High Bridge Glens. The agent for the Canton store, located in the Commercial Block of Public Square, was G.F. Kent. (Author's collection.)

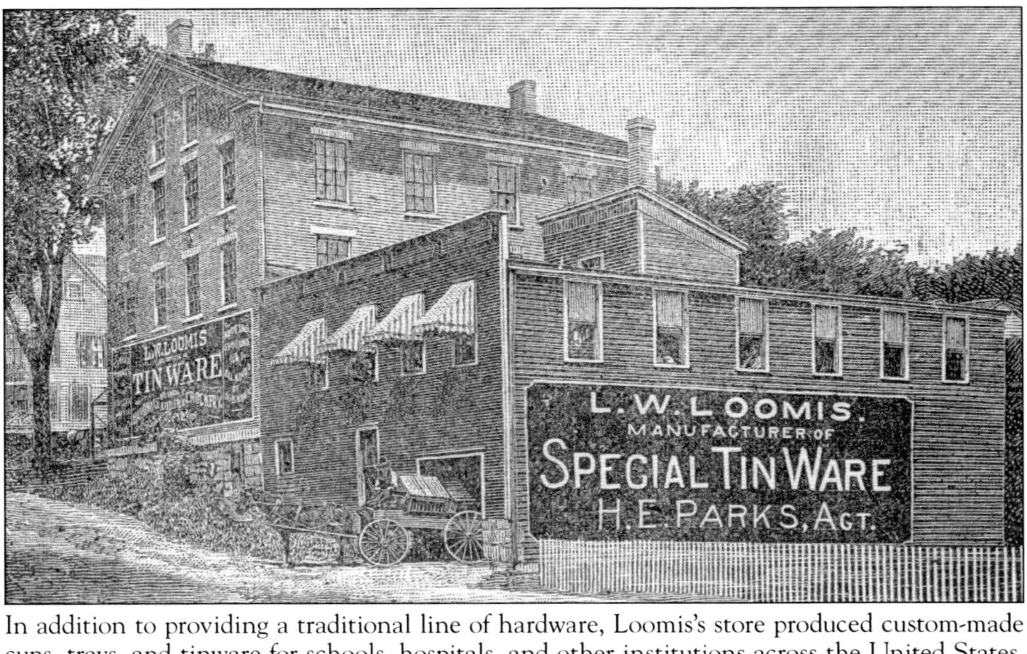


In addition to providing a traditional line of hardware, Loomis's store produced custom-made cups, trays, and tinware for schools, hospitals, and other institutions across the United States. Eventually, Loomis's store took up three buildings. His inventory expanded to include stoves, china, lamps, roller skates, and other assorted merchandise. (Author's collection.)

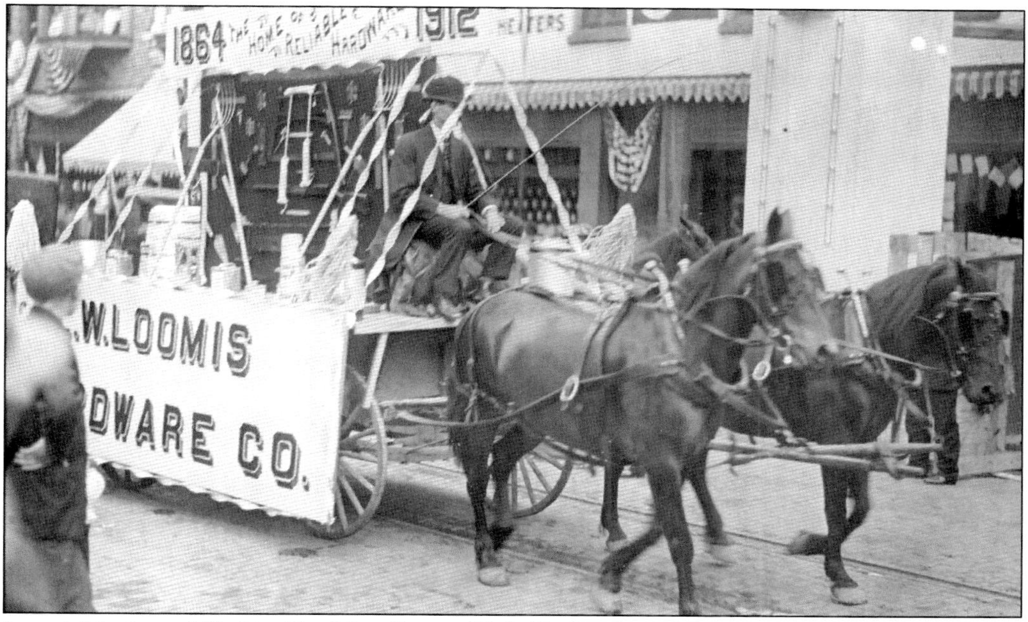

Loomis Hardware billed itself as "The Home of Reliable Hardware." During a community celebration, the store sponsored this horse-drawn display of its wares. In later years, Loomis's children Byron, Irving, and Lillian joined him in running the business. (Author's collection.)

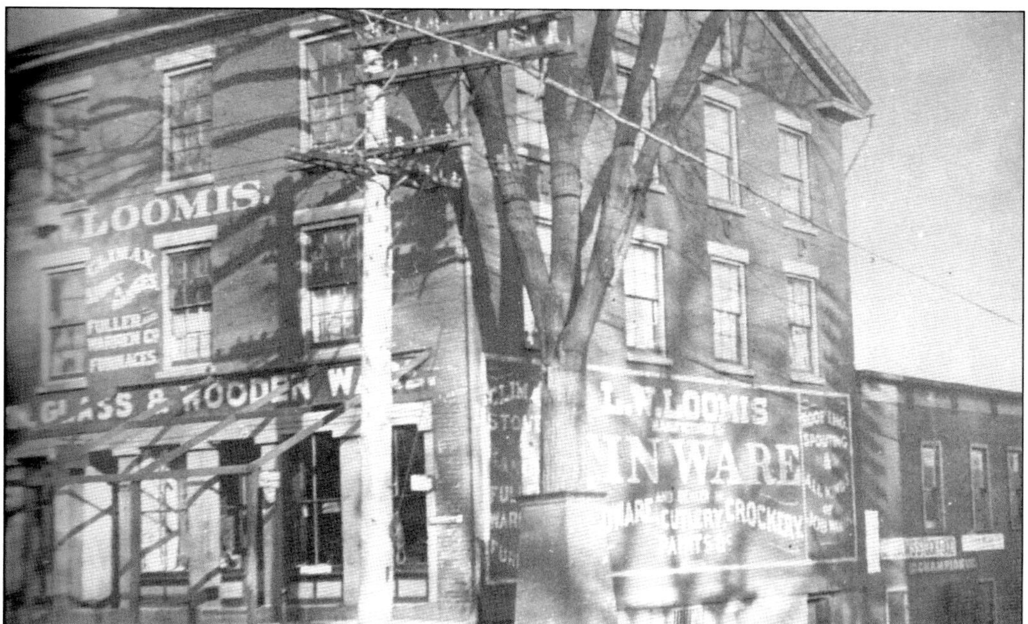

The store was a landmark on Front Street for many years. In 1905, fire destroyed a portion of the structure, but after a hastily organized fire sale, Loomis quickly made repairs and resumed business. Falls Hardware later occupied this site. (Cuyahoga Falls Historical Society.)

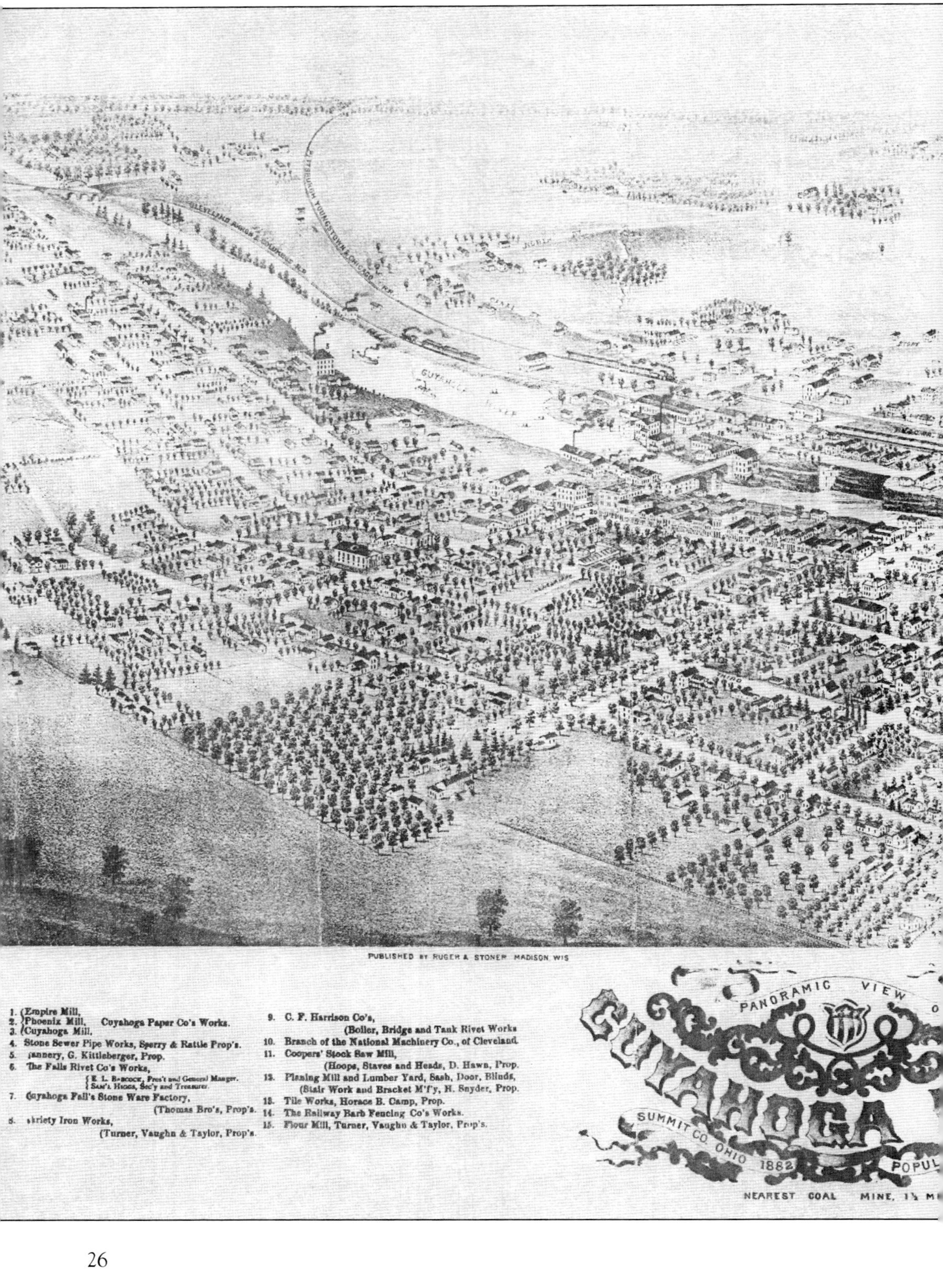

PUBLISHED BY RUGER & STONER MADISON, WIS
1. Empire Mill,
2. Phoenix Mill, Cuyahoga Paper Co's Works.
3. Cuyahoga Mill,
4. Stone Sewer Pipe Works, Sperry & Rattle Prop's.
5. Tannery, G. Kittleberger, Prop.
6. The Falls Rivet Co's Works,
E. L. Babcock, Pres't and General Manager. Sam'l Higgs, Sec'y and Treasurer.
7. Cuyahoga Fall's Stone Ware Factory, (Thomas Bro's, Prop's.
8. Variety Iron Works, (Turner, Vaughn & Taylor, Prop's.
9. C. F. Harrison Co's, (Boiler, Bridge and Tank Rivet Works
10. Branch of the National Machinery Co., of Cleveland.
11. Coopers' Stock Saw Mill, (Hoops, Staves and Heads, D. Hawn, Prop.
12. Planing Mill and Lumber Yard, Sash, Door, Blinds, (Stair Work and Bracket M'f'y, H. Snyder, Prop.
13. Tile Works, Horace B. Camp, Prop.
14. The Railway Barb Fencing Co's Works.
15. Flour Mill, Turner, Vaughn & Taylor, Prop's.
PANORAMIC VIEW O
CUYAHOGA
SUMMIT CO. OHIO 1882
POPUL
NEAREST COAL MINE, 1½ MI

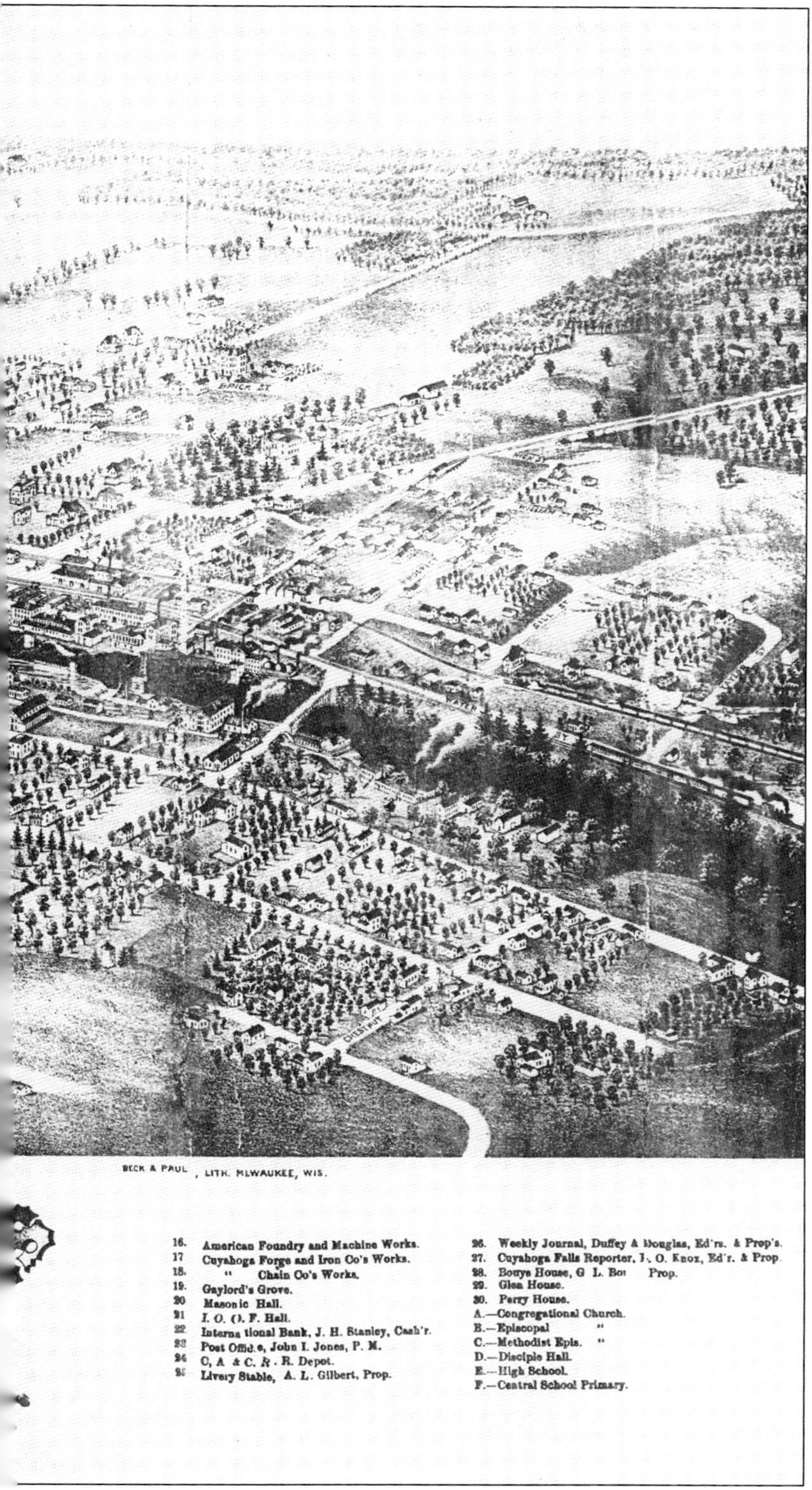


This bird's-eye-view map depicts Cuyahoga Falls around 1882. The sole bridge shown on page 27 crossed the Cuyahoga River at Front and Prospect Streets and marked the entrance to the High Bridge Glens park. The park's pavilion was located to the right of the bridge on the Front Street side of the Glens. The two bridges depicted on the inner third of page 26 are the stone bridge at Portage Trail and the former covered bridge at Broad Boulevard. Note the steamers on the river (left) and the trains steaming toward town. (Cuyahoga Falls Historical Society.)

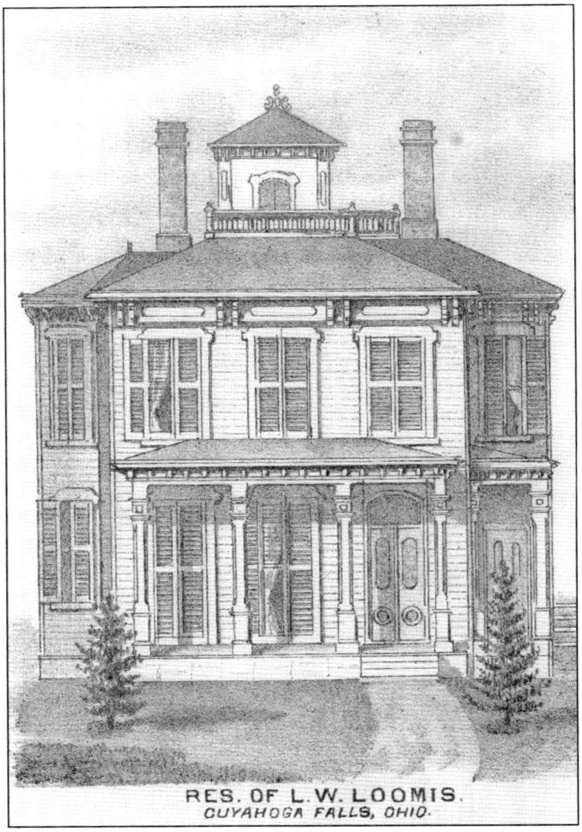


Both Loomis Hardware and Loomis's impressive southern Italianate-style home on Newberry Street were located close to the future site of the High Bridge Glens. As a result, Loomis was quite aware of the great natural beauty to be found along the banks of the Cuyahoga River. In 1879, he hired workers to construct a network of trails throughout the Glens, as well as scenic overlooks, a suspension bridge, and dance pavilion. (Author's collection.)

By June 1879, the Glens was ready for its first official event: a private picnic party hosted by Eunice Pendleton, wife of J.H. Pendleton. This photograph depicts Mrs. Pendleton (second row, far right) with a group of faculty members and guests of Buchtel College (now the University of Akron) at nearby Old Maid's Kitchen in the Gorge. The first full day the Glens was open, receipts reportedly totaled $2,500. Within a few short weeks, visitors began arriving from as far away as Cleveland. (Author's collection.)

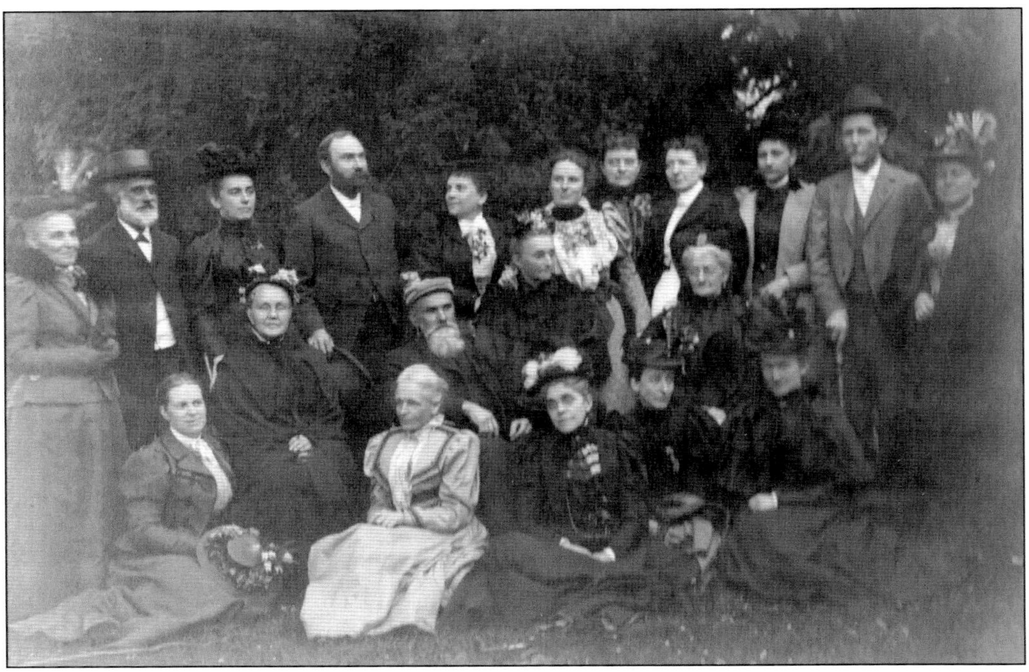

# *Two*

# A Walk in the Glens

## Touring the West Side of the Park

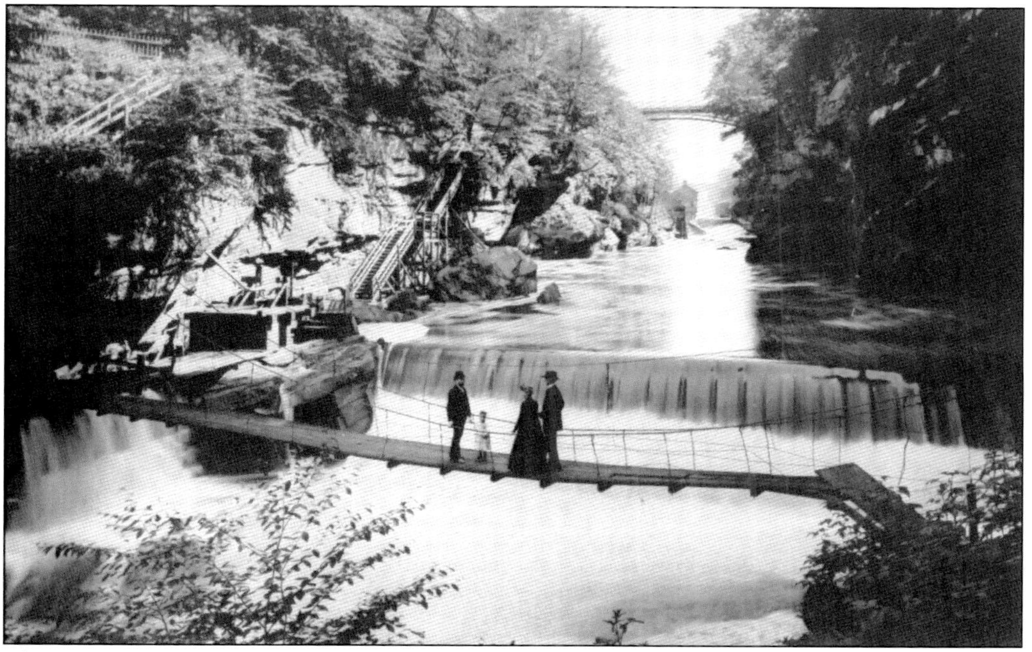

The entrance to the High Bridge Glens was located at Front and Prospect Streets. The park's High Bridge is visible in the background of this image. The pavilion was located slightly west of the bridge. The Grand Staircase is on the left, and the suspension bridge is in the foreground. Traditionally, visitors began their tours at the top of the Glens on the park's west (Front Street) side and eventually descended a set of diagonal stairways, taking them closer to the caves and footbridge located near river level. They would then cross the river to enjoy the features on the eastern side. (Author's collection.)

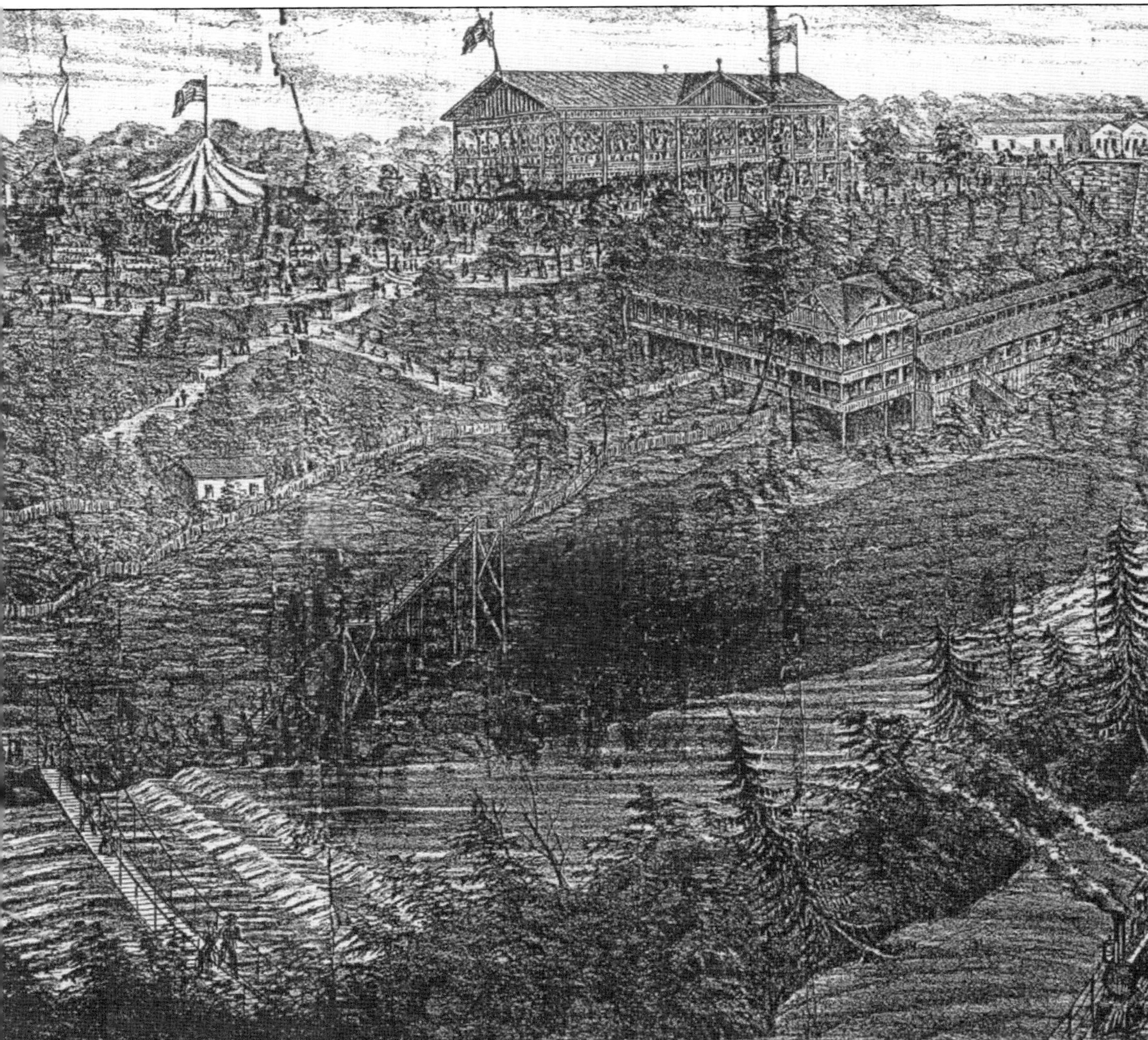

# HIGH BRIDGE GLENS AN

## CUYAHOGA FALLS, O

**Most Romantic and Convenient Place in Ohio for Picnics and Excursion Parties. Two large Pavilions with s**

S ON C. A. & C. AND P. & W. R. R. STOP WITHIN 10 RODS OF ENTRANCE TO CAVE AND GLEN. . . . . . 2 MILES FROM SILVER LAKE, 4 FRO

HACK LINE BETWEEN GLEN AND LAKE.

BUSS, Passenger Agent, 101 St. Clair Street (Telephone 27), Cleveland, Ohio.
DUNHAM, General Passenger Agent C. A. & C. R. R., Columbus, Ohio.

C. W. BASSETT, General
J. B. CAVEN, General Pass

HIGH BRIDGE GLENS CO. Cuyahoga Falls

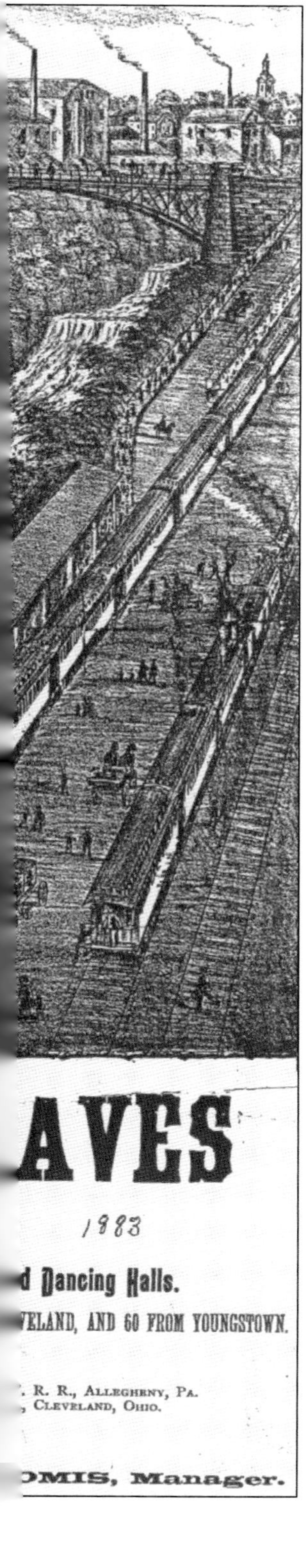


This 1883 artifact is the only known poster from the park. The Cuyahoga Falls Historical Society found this poster in the home of the late Charles Boyd, a well-known dance instructor and avid local collector. The Glens extended along both sides of the Cuyahoga River as far south as the former Gorge Power Plant at Front Street and Howe Avenue. During the Victorian era, the park was bounded on the west side by Front Street and on the east side by several railway lines. Note the Cleveland, Akron & Columbus Railway platform on the right side of the poster. The two large buildings depicted on page 30 are the park's original pavilion and dining hall and the Grand Pavilion. (Cuyahoga Falls Historical Society.)

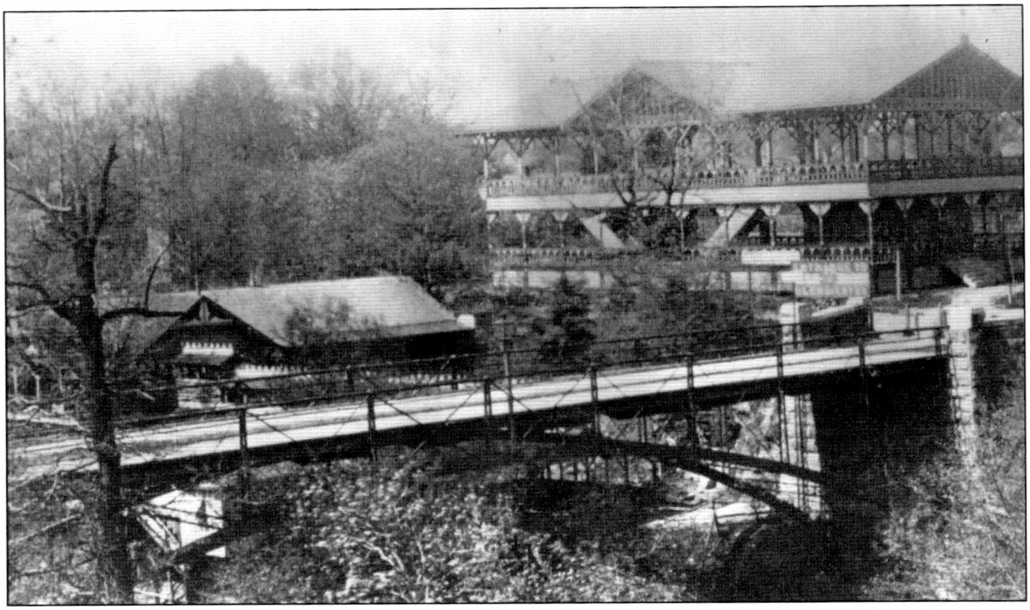

This image shows the entrance to the High Bridge Glens as seen from the railroad tracks on the eastern side of the park. According to the *Akron Beacon and Republican*, the High Bridge was built by the King Iron Bridge Company of Cleveland. (Cuyahoga Falls Library.)

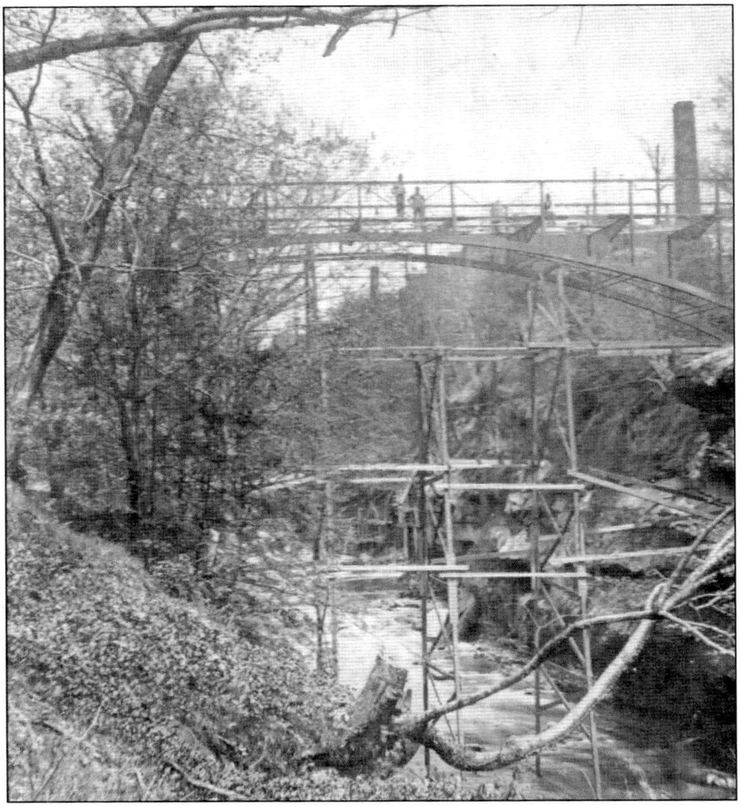

The High Bridge Glens and Caves park was named, in part, for the high iron bridge at the entrance. While these men posing on the bridge's open framework show no hesitation, the *Akron City Times* reported that one local crew took one look at the river rushing 90 feet below and nearly fainted. (Eric Thompson collection.)

Once completed, the High Bridge offered a perfect vantage point for enjoying the scenic vistas along the Cuyahoga River. Here, several Victorian women stare into the swirling waters below. Note how park visitors wore their Sunday best to the High Bridge Glens. (Author's collection.)

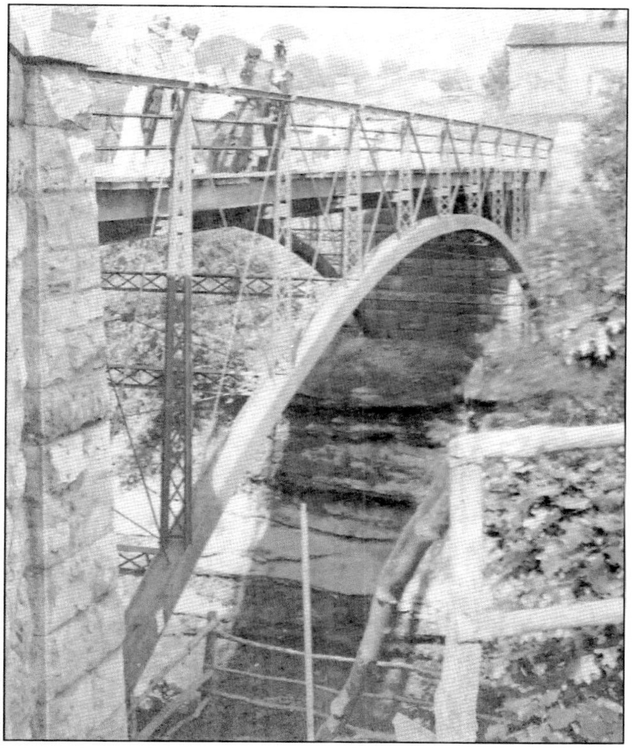

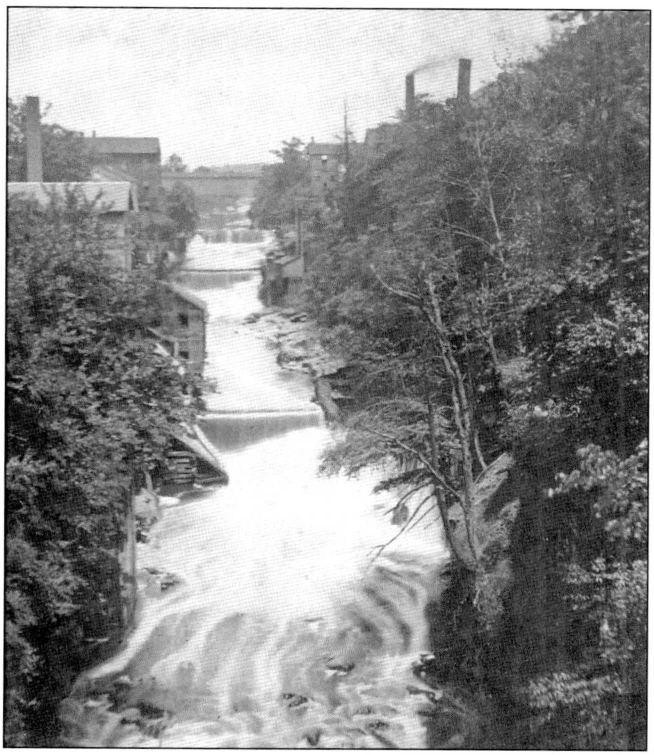

Looking north from the High Bridge toward the present-day location of Broad Boulevard, visitors could see numerous businesses and man-made dams along the river. Today, to enhance the water quality of the Cuyahoga River, the City of Cuyahoga Falls and the Environmental Protection Agency are planning to remove several early dams. (Eric Thompson collection.)

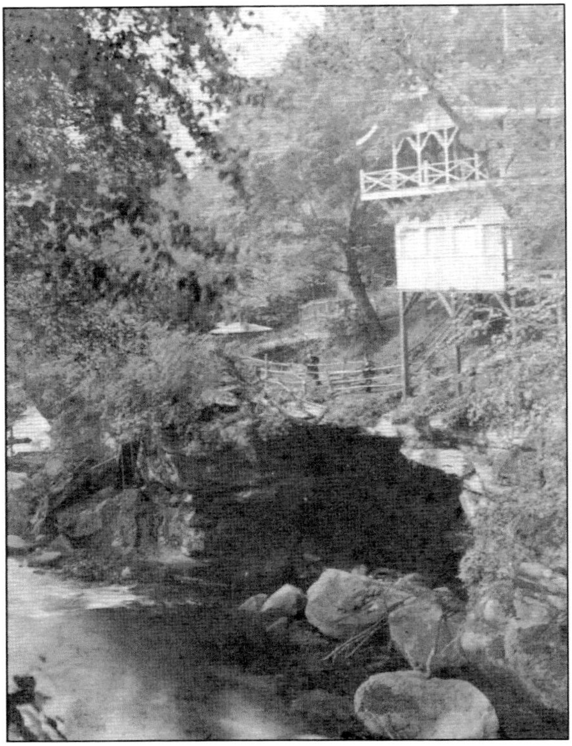

Looking south from the bridge toward the Glens, visitors could see the park's main pavilion overlooking a rocky cavern, thick vegetation, and the cascades of the Cuyahoga River. An *Akron Daily Beacon* reporter who visited the park predicted that its breathtaking scenery would make the Glens internationally famous. (Author's collection.)

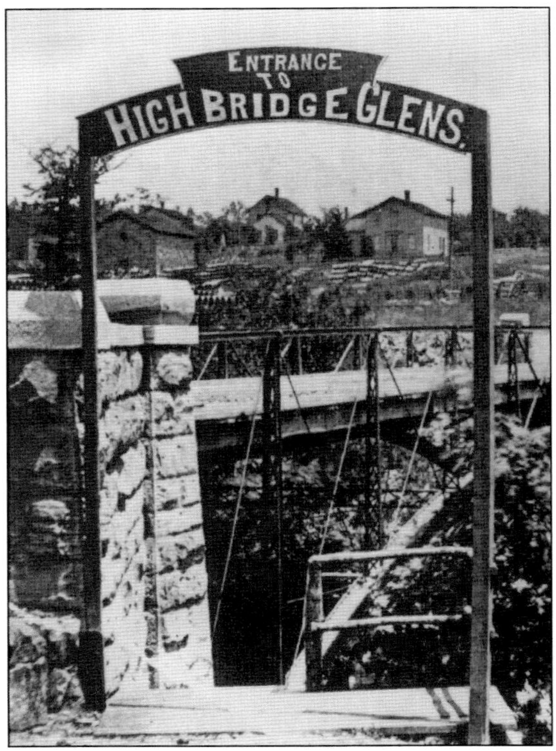


After enjoying the scenery from the High Bridge, visitors passed underneath this high, arching entrance sign. The modest sign belied the grand scenery of the park. (Cuyahoga Falls Library.)

The park's original sign was later replaced by a larger, more elaborate one. A streetlamp was also erected in the center of the northern side of the bridge. (Author's collection.)

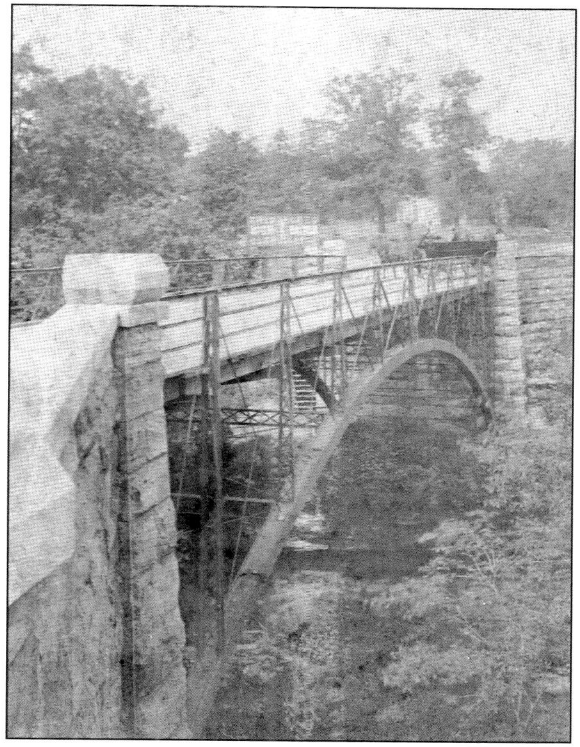

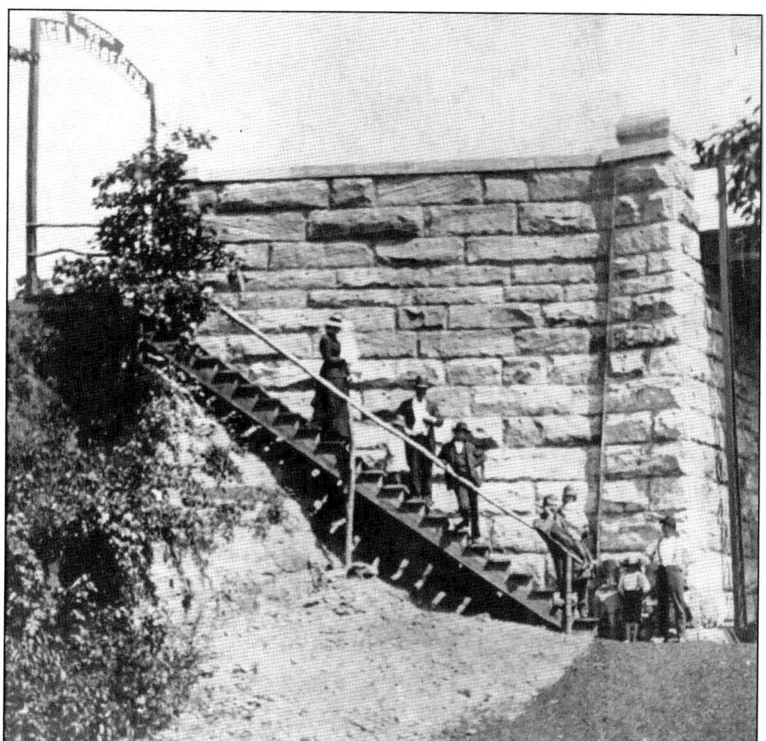

After passing through the entrance, visitors descended a set of wooden steps leading to a broad plateau area. Here, a group pauses for a photograph before viewing the Glens' various attractions. (Cuyahoga Falls Historical Society.)

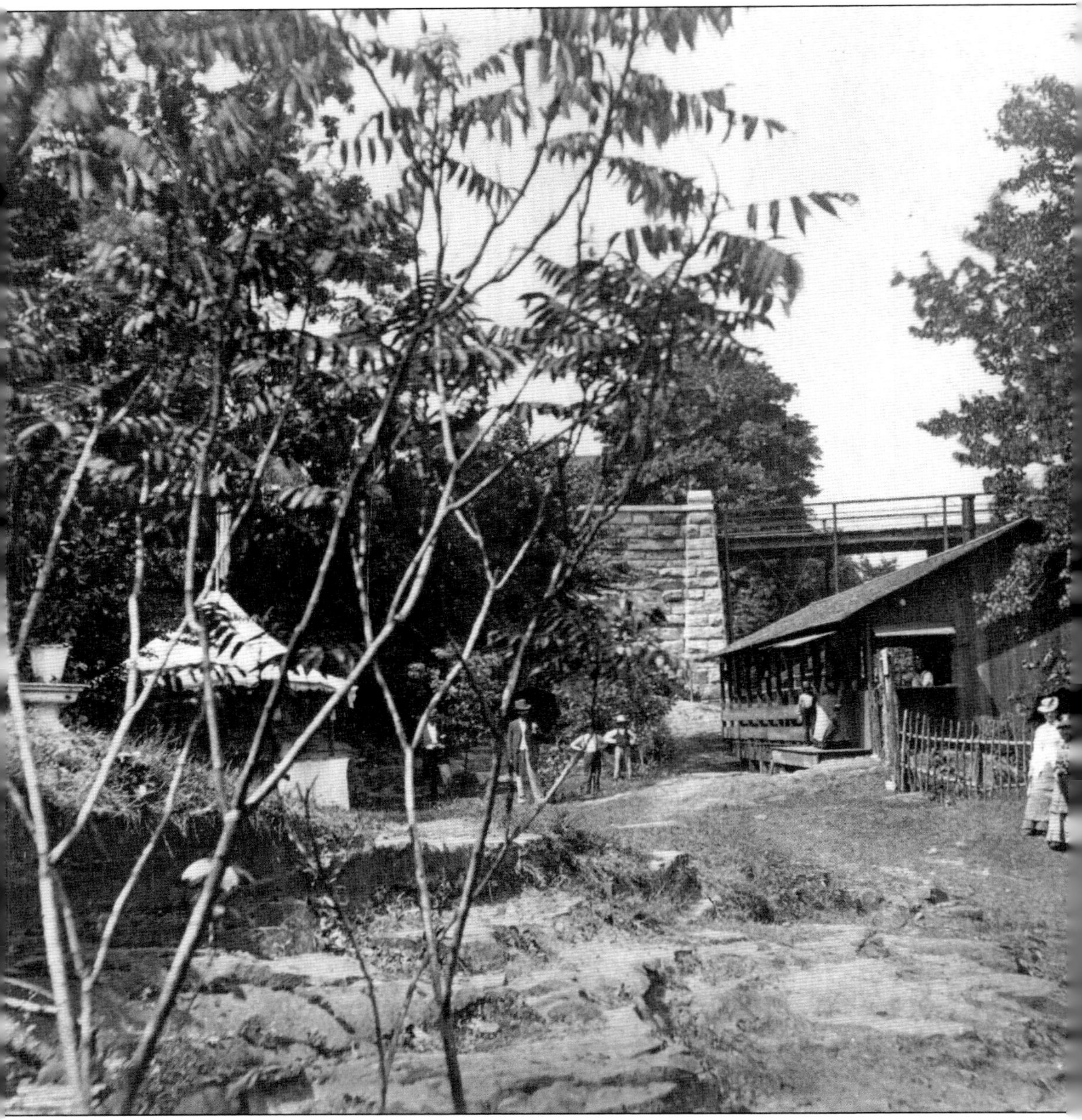

At the bottom of the steps was a small area with an outdoor dining hall (right), which was bordered by rustic stick fences to blend in with the park's natural features. The small roofed structure (left) is believed to be a souvenir or refreshment stand. (Cuyahoga Falls Library.)

At the park's dining hall, visitors could stash picnic baskets or enjoy a meal in the fresh air. The park's croquet grounds were located just south of the hall; croquet was a very popular Victorian pastime. (Eric Thompson collection.)

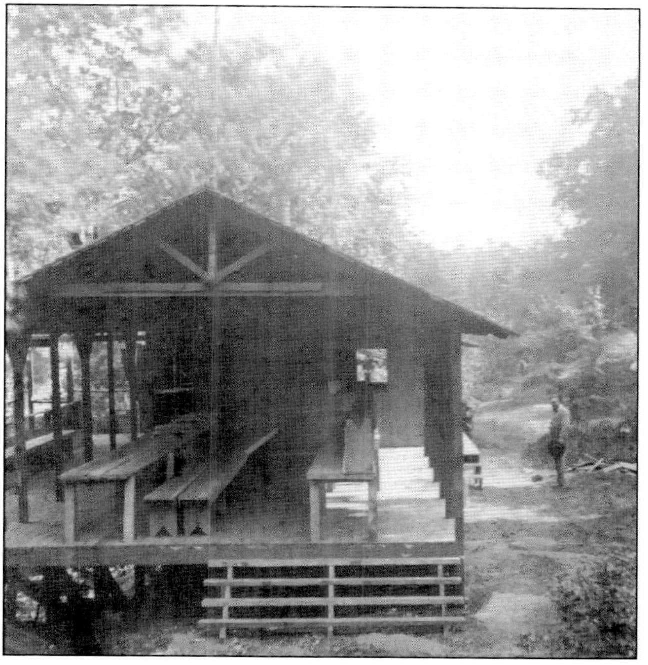

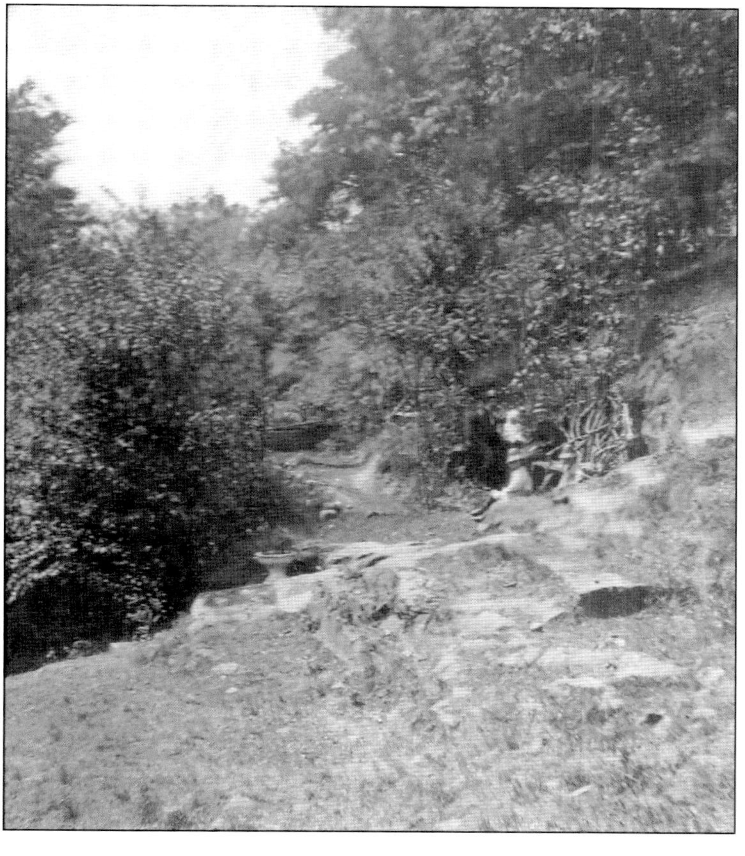

Looking south from the dining hall, visitors could see winding paths, croquet courts, and rustic urns and vases. Note the people to the right of the path. In later years, additional games were available at the park, including a bowling alley (near the roller coaster) and a 10-pin game (in the pavilion). (Eric Thompson collection.)

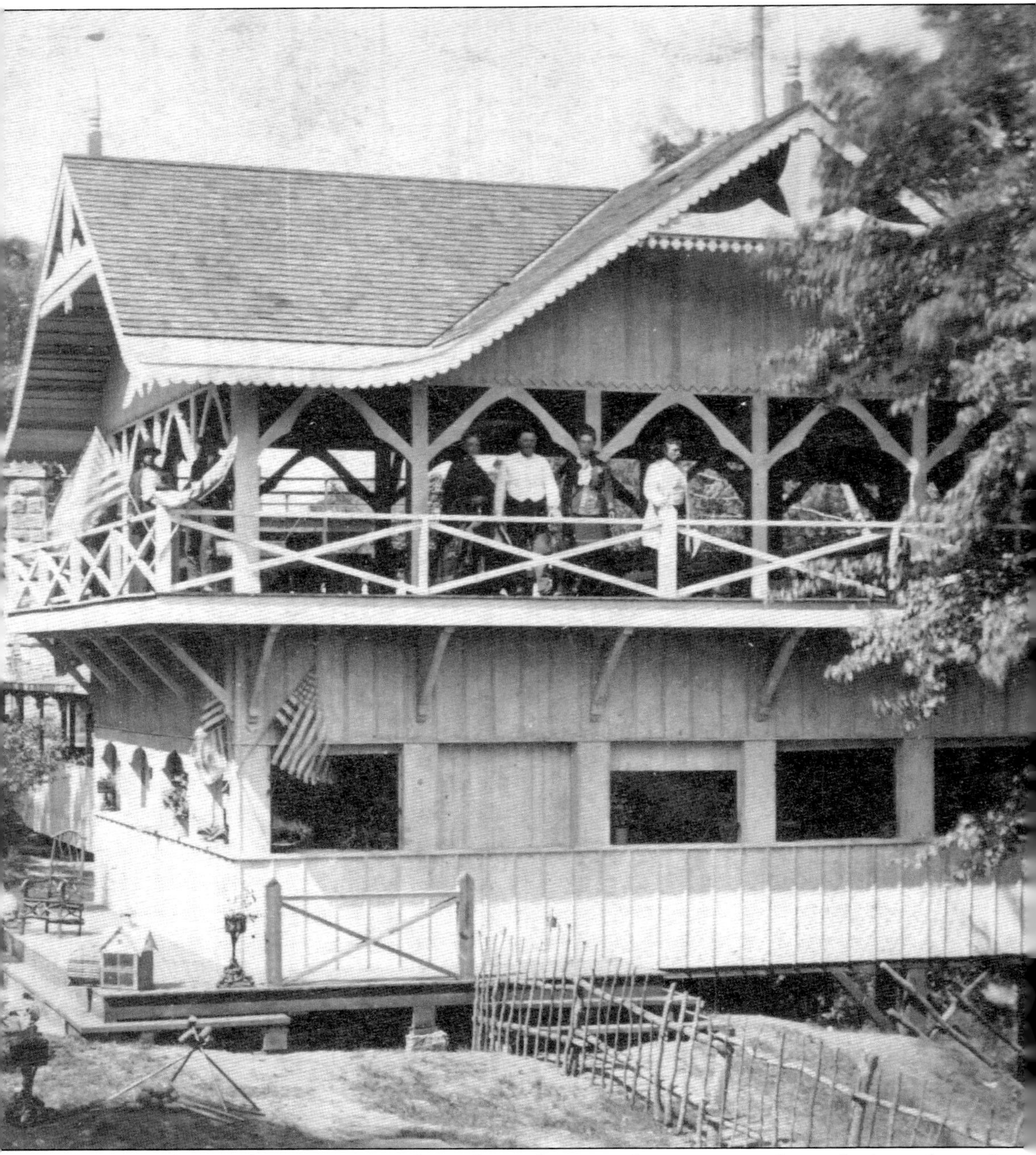

One of the grandest structures at the park was the original two-story pavilion, which was located near the park's entrance. The first floor of the pavilion housed a restaurant and dining area. In the evening, the second floor was used for dances. Although modern generations might imagine Victorians to be rather "stuffy" by today's standards, newspaper accounts indicate that some of the dances at the park lasted until 1:00 a.m. In keeping with the morals of the time, no dances were held on Sundays. Loomis took great offense when a newspaper mistakenly reported that he earned a tidy sum from holding a dance on the Sabbath. (Author's collection.)

High Bridge Glens management hired some of the area's top musical acts to perform at the park, including the 20-piece Hessian Rifle Battalion Band, Morey's Orchestra, Mustill's Orchestra, and the Eighth Regiment Band. Here, visitors pose at the park's pavilion with a group of musical performers. The banner underneath the pavilion's awning advertises park admission as costing a nickel. (Cuyahoga Falls Library.)

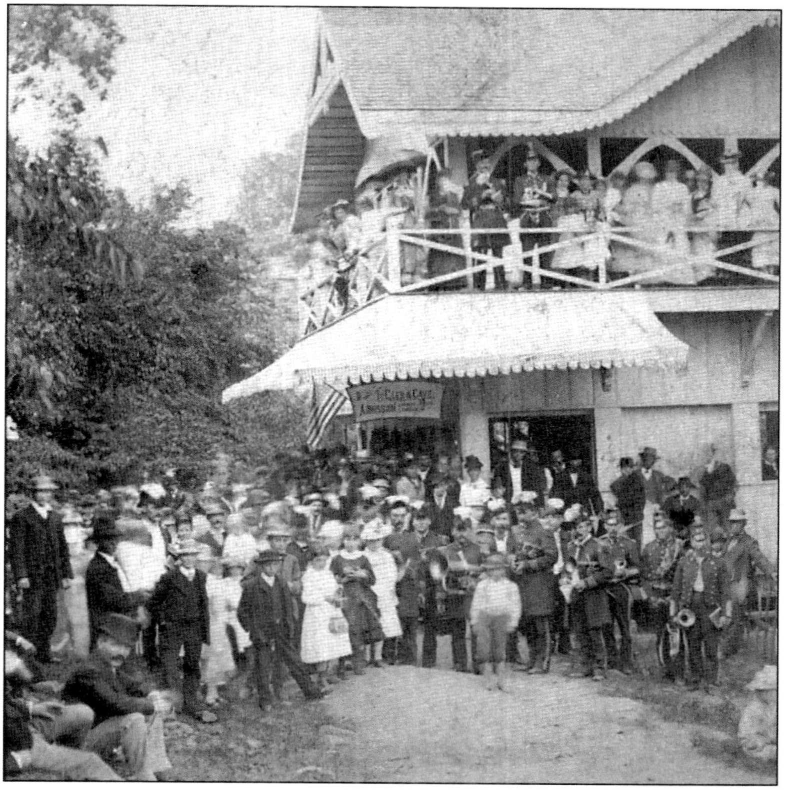

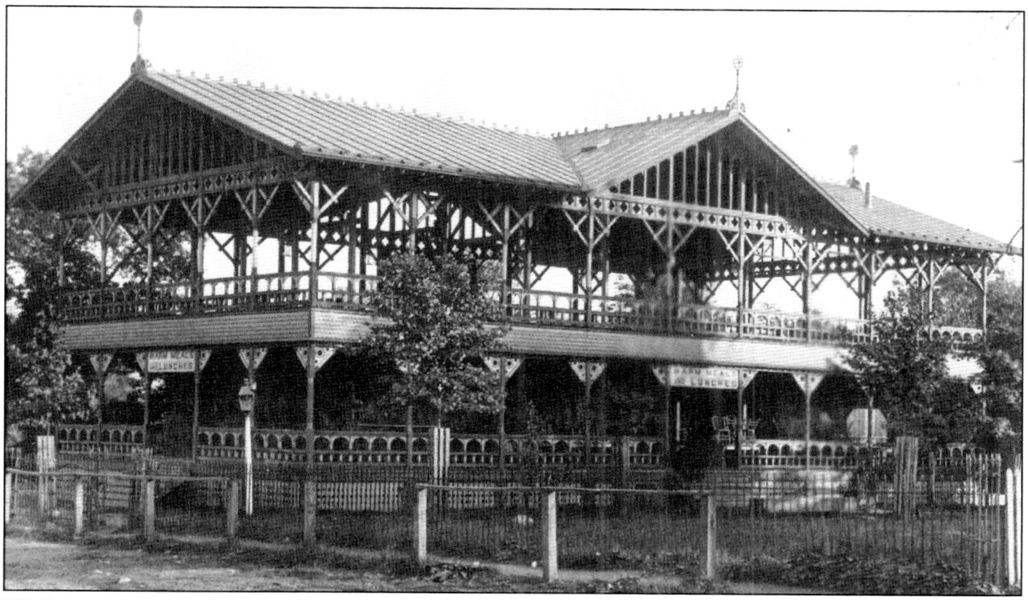

Within one year of the park's opening, the Glens had become so popular that it required the addition of a second, larger pavilion. In 1880, the Grand Pavilion made its debut. The new building was approximately twice the size of the original pavilion and was constructed at a cost of $3,500—quite a sum of money at the time. (Cuyahoga Falls Library.)

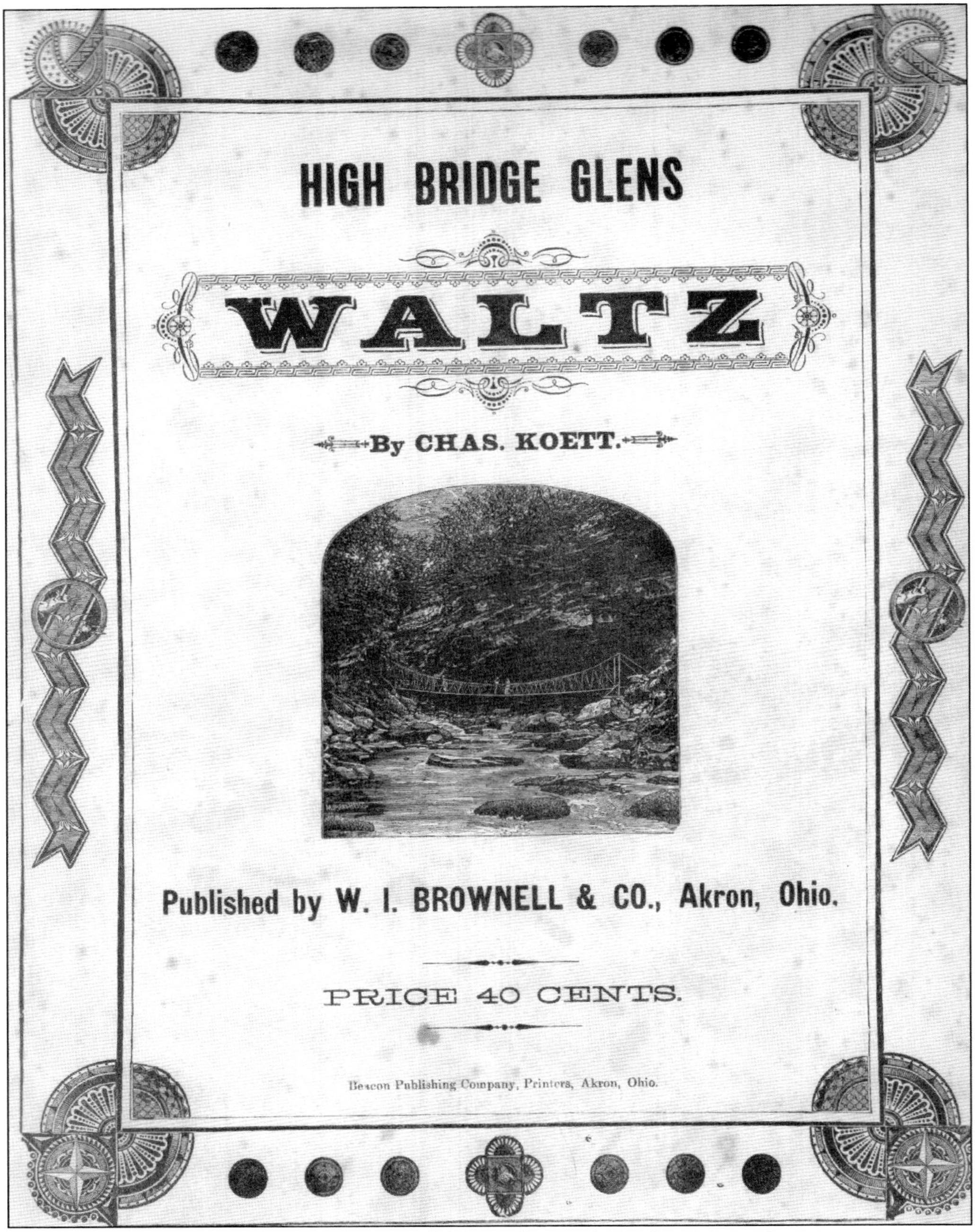


Music was such an integral part of social life at the High Bridge Glens that two pieces were specifically composed for the park: the "High Bridge Glens Waltz," by Charles Koett, and the "High Bridge Glens March," by J.N. Goodman. Both pieces of sheet music were available for purchase in local music stores and at the park. (Author's collection.)

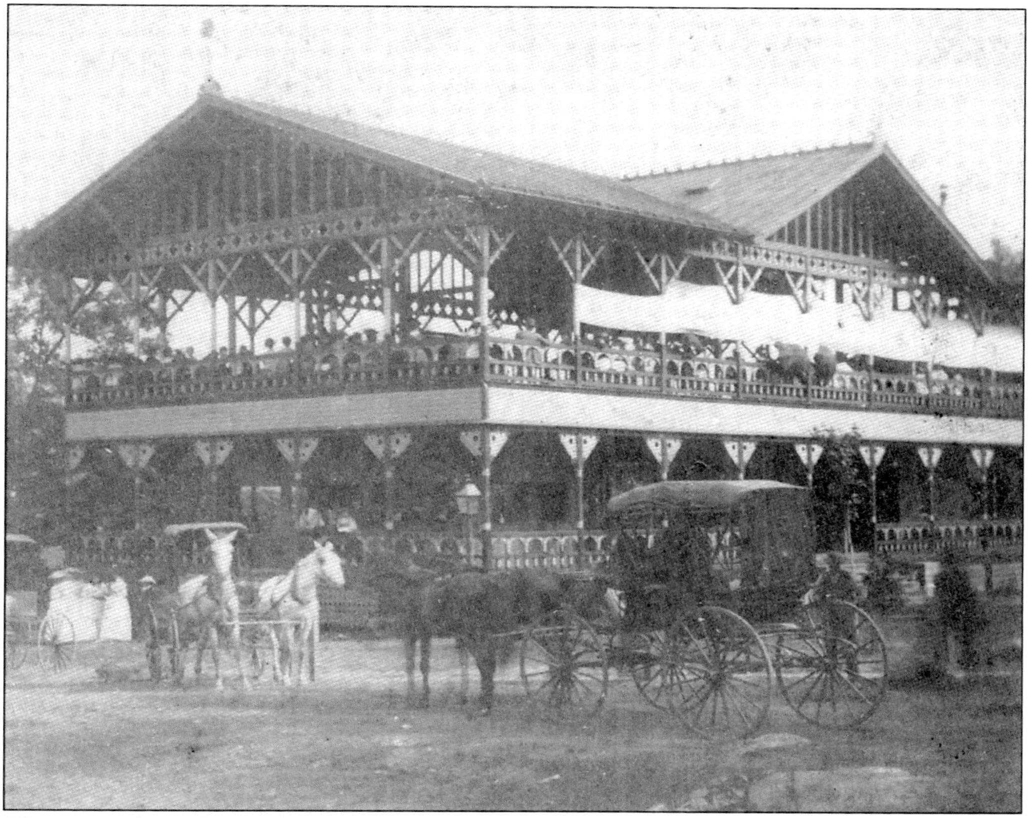

The owners hosted special events, including balloon ascensions and a grand dance, to celebrate the many park improvements made for the 1880 season, including the addition of the Grand Pavilion. The owners also initiated a "hack" line between Akron and Cuyahoga Falls, with round-trip fare costing 50¢. (Author's collection.)

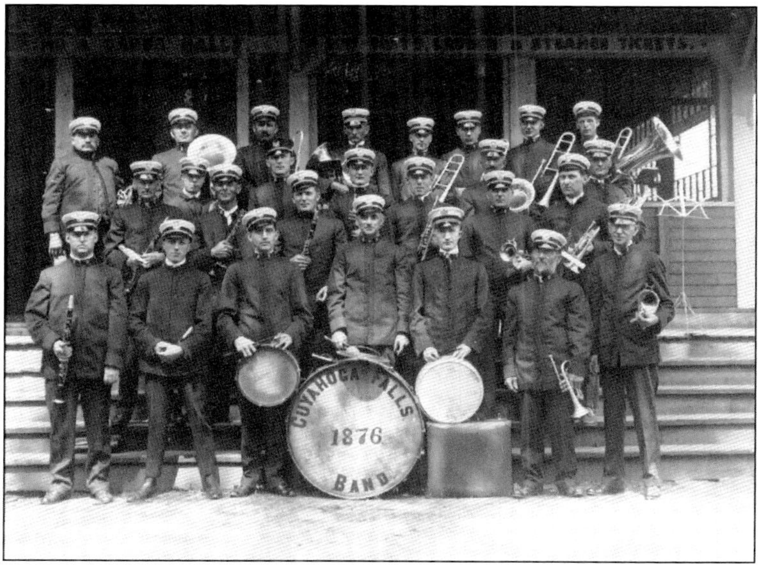


The Cuyahoga Falls Band performed regularly at the High Bridge Glens. The band was also much in demand and played at venues throughout northeast Ohio, including nearby Silver Lake Park. One of the band's most prestigious "gigs" was playing at the opening of the Pennsylvania and Ohio Canal in 1840. (Cuyahoga Falls Historical Society.)

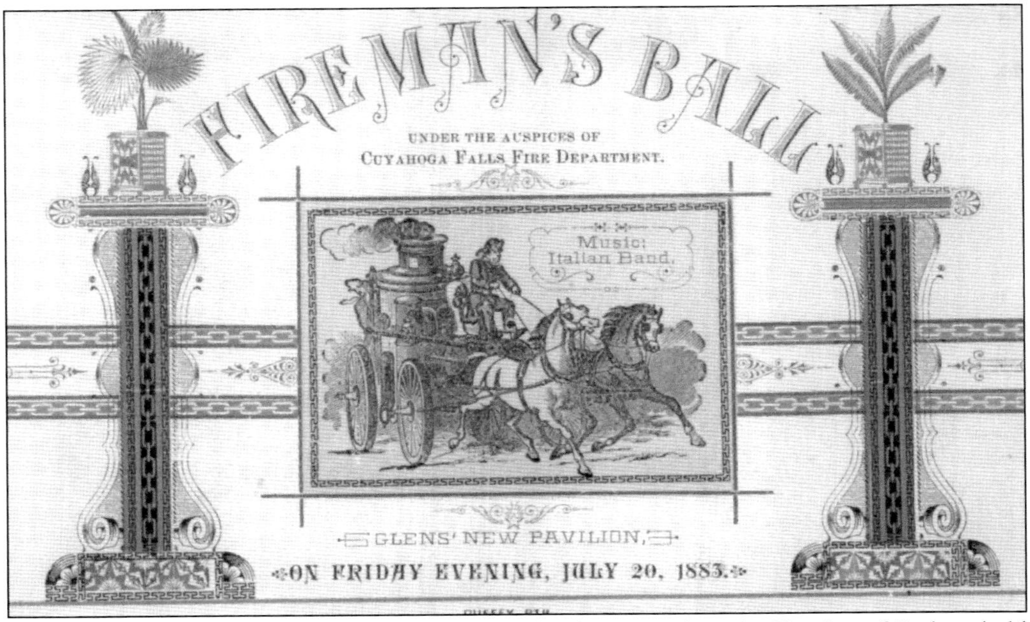


The Grand Pavilion was the scene of many popular dances. When the Knights of Pythias held its annual convention in Akron, approximately 300 to 400 couples traveled to Cuyahoga Falls to attend an evening dance at the Glens. In 1883, the local fire department hosted its annual ball at the Grand Pavilion. Victorians not only danced into the wee hours at the pavilion, they sometimes danced until they dropped. On one occasion, a young woman mysteriously passed out at a Glens dance. After a doctor examined her, he quickly identified the cause of her fainting spell: her corset had been laced too tightly, making it difficult for her to catch her breath during the high-spirited dances. (Pete Mellinger collection.)

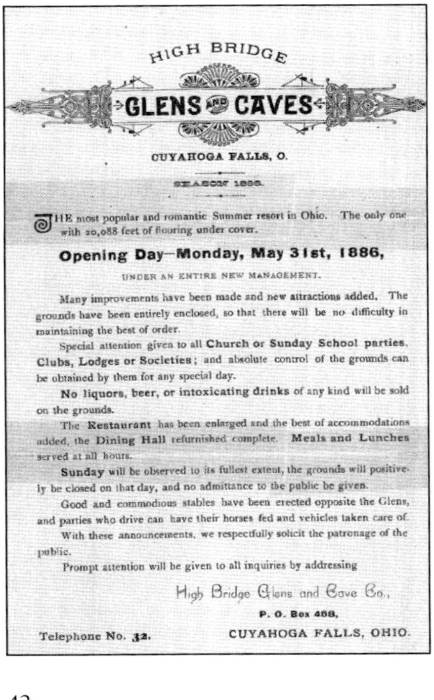

HIGH BRIDGE

GLENS AND CAVES

CUYAHOGA FALLS, O.

SEASON 1886.

THE most popular and romantic Summer resort in Ohio. The only one with 20,088 feet of flooring under cover.

**Opening Day—Monday, May 31st, 1886,**

UNDER AN ENTIRE NEW MANAGEMENT.

Many improvements have been made and new attractions added. The grounds have been entirely enclosed, so that there will be no difficulty in maintaining the best of order.

Special attention given to all **Church or Sunday School parties, Clubs, Lodges or Societies**; and absolute control of the grounds can be obtained by them for any special day.

**No liquors, beer, or intoxicating drinks** of any kind will be sold on the grounds.

The **Restaurant** has been enlarged and the best of accommodations added, the **Dining Hall** refurnished complete. **Meals and Lunches** served at all hours.

**Sunday** will be observed to its fullest extent, the grounds will positively be closed on that day, and no admittance to the public be given.

Good and commodious stables have been erected opposite the Glens, and parties who drive can have their horses fed and vehicles taken care of.

With these announcements, we respectfully solicit the patronage of the public.

Prompt attention will be given to all inquiries by addressing

High Bridge Glens and Cave Co.,
P. O. Box 488,
Telephone No. 32. CUYAHOGA FALLS, OHIO.

The High Bridge Glens had a variety of owners throughout its history. Around 1885, Cleveland, Akron & Columbus Railroad auditor C.W. Schaap assumed management of the park. After an earlier misstep in which an unnamed individual installed a bar at the Glens, Schaap tightened the reins and announced that—with a few special exceptions—no alcohol would be served at the park. Like his predecessors, Schaap worked to bring thrilling attractions to the park. He advertised his interest in hiring an acrobat to leap from the High Bridge into a net stretched above the Cuyahoga River, but it appears that he never found anyone willing to perform the stunt. (Cuyahoga Falls Library.)

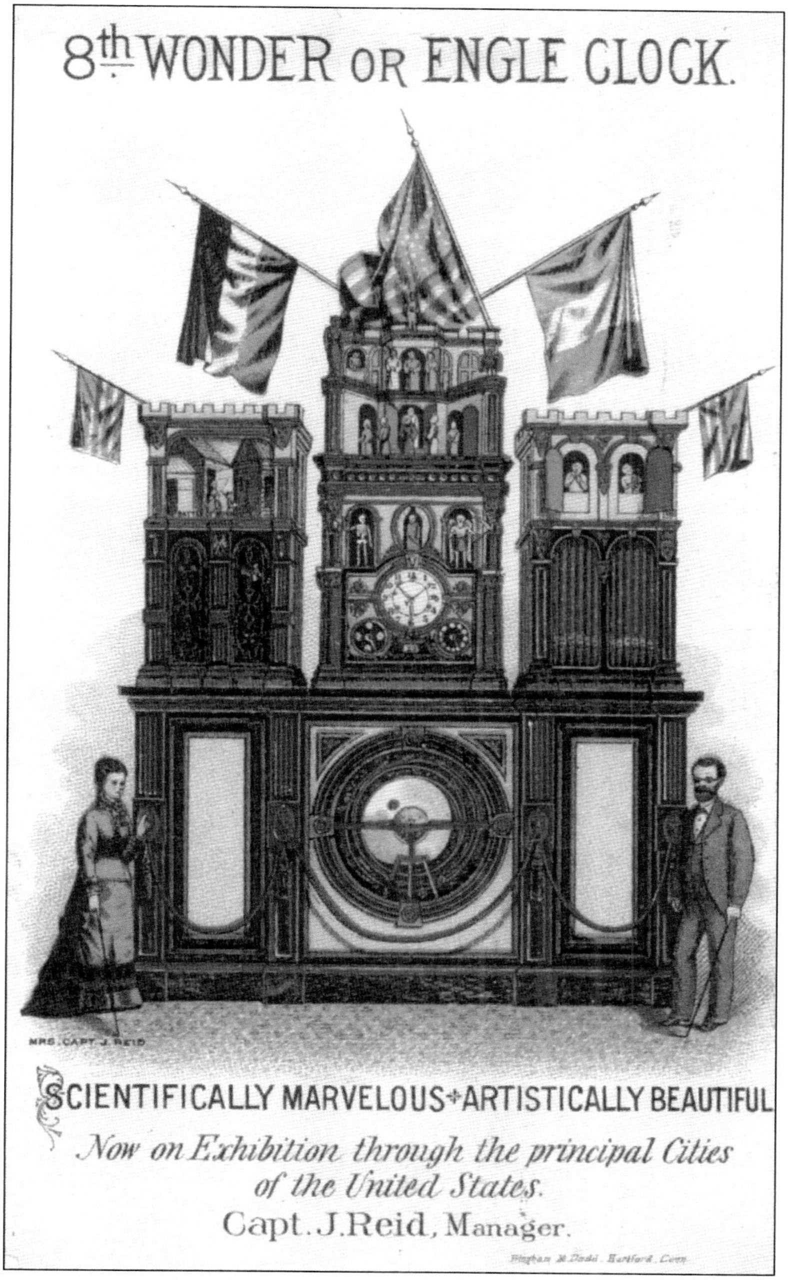


In 1887, it was not a musical act but rather a marvel of mechanical engineering that drew large crowds to the Grand Pavilion. For 10¢, visitors could view a traveling exhibit known as the Engle Clock. The clock, constructed by an amateur carver, was 11 feet high, eight feet wide, three feet deep, and weighed more than 1,000 pounds; it also had a mind-boggling array of moving parts. Depending on what time a visitor viewed the clock, he or she might see carved figures of Father Time and his companions, Youth and Middle Age; a platoon of Continental Army soldiers marching to the Battle of Monmouth (accompanied by patriotic music); or a procession of Jesus and his 12 apostles. (Author's collection.)

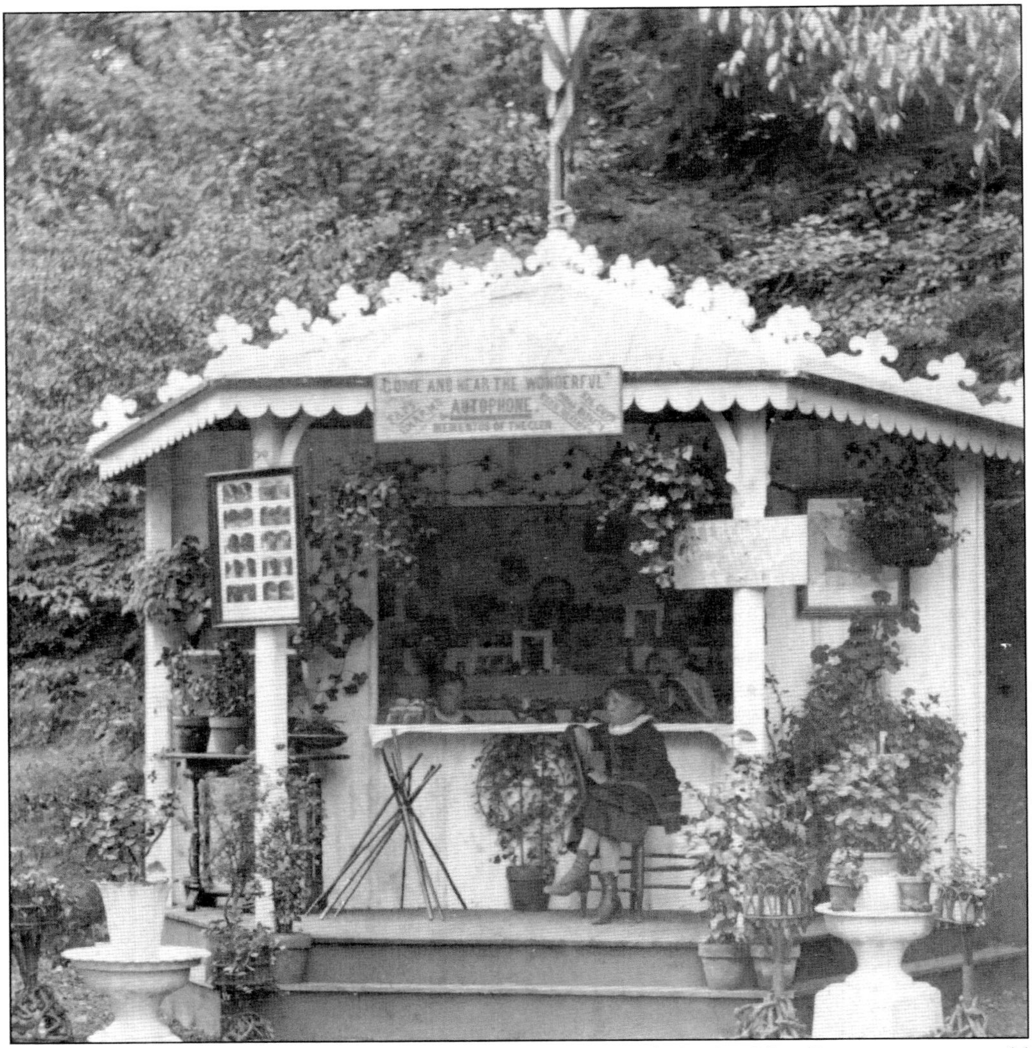


Like many parks, the High Bridge Glens had a souvenir stand. At the Glen Bazaar, visitors could buy mementos, including stereo views (note the framed set of Glens views on the left front post), or rent walking sticks or croquet sets. A sign near the roof advertises the availability of narrated tours of the Glens utilizing the Edison Autophone, an early phonographic device. The stand also sold fans, charms, and other remembrances. (John and Janet Waldsmith collection.)

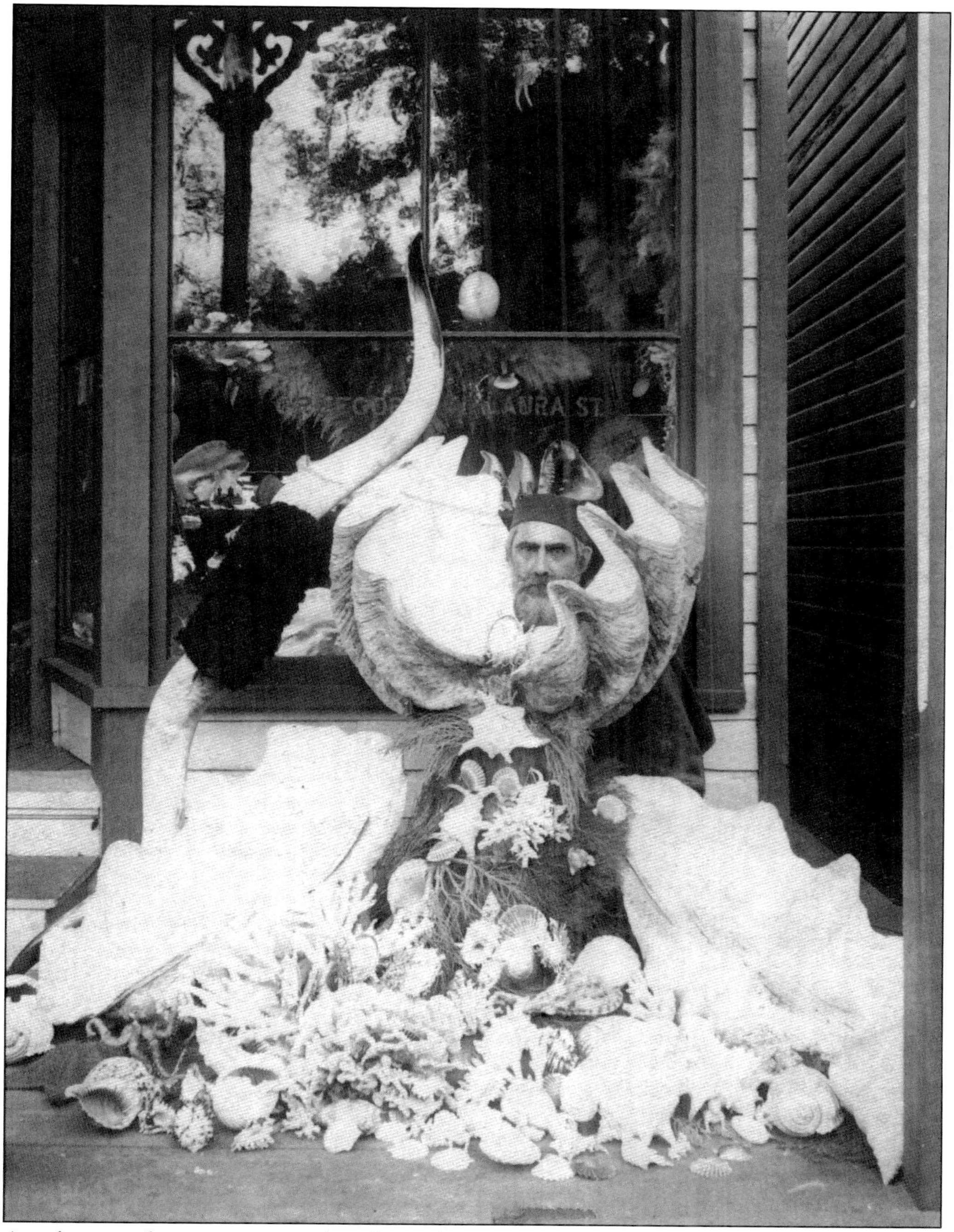


Another popular souvenir stand at the park was the seashell store owned by Isaiah Greegor. Greegor, an amateur naturalist, traveled to Florida each winter to collect shells and other curiosities, which his family fashioned into souvenirs and jewelry for sale at the Glens, Silver Lake Park, and Brady Lake Park, in Kent, Ohio, as well as at his store in Jacksonville, Florida. In this photograph, Greegor poses with several striking specimens in front of his Jacksonville store. (Paul Callomon/Academy of Natural Sciences, Philadelphia.)

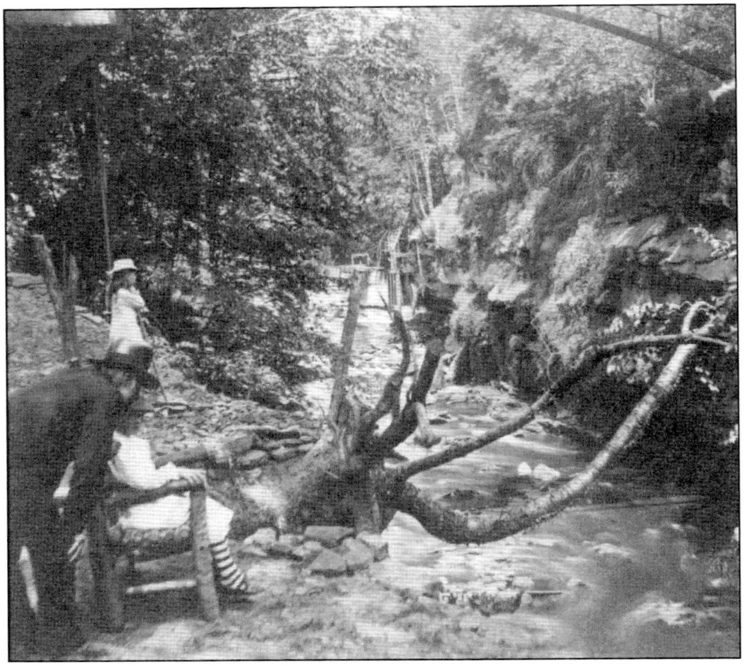

Just south of the pavilion and souvenir stand, a young girl sits by one of the park's scenic overlooks, surrounded by curiously shaped vegetation. Picturesque spots like this were extremely popular with local artists, who brought sketch pads and canvases to record the beauty of the Glens. (John and Janet Waldsmith collection.)

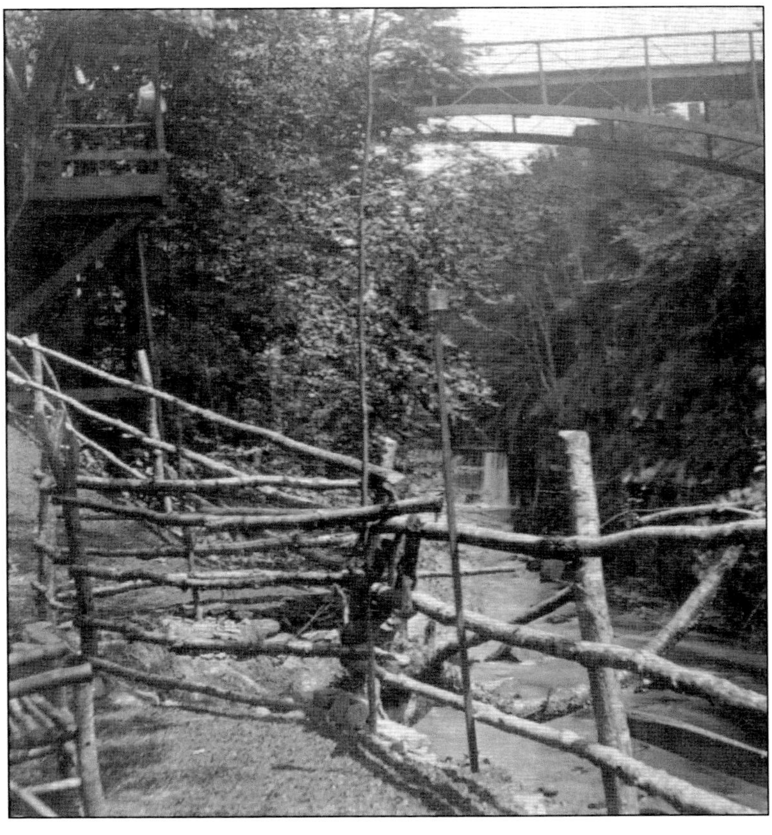

To keep visitors from tumbling 70 to 80 feet down into the river, the park's owners later placed stick fences along the edges of the trails. Note the metal pole with the glass top in the center; this is one of several kerosene torches used to illuminate the park's trails at night. (Author's collection.)

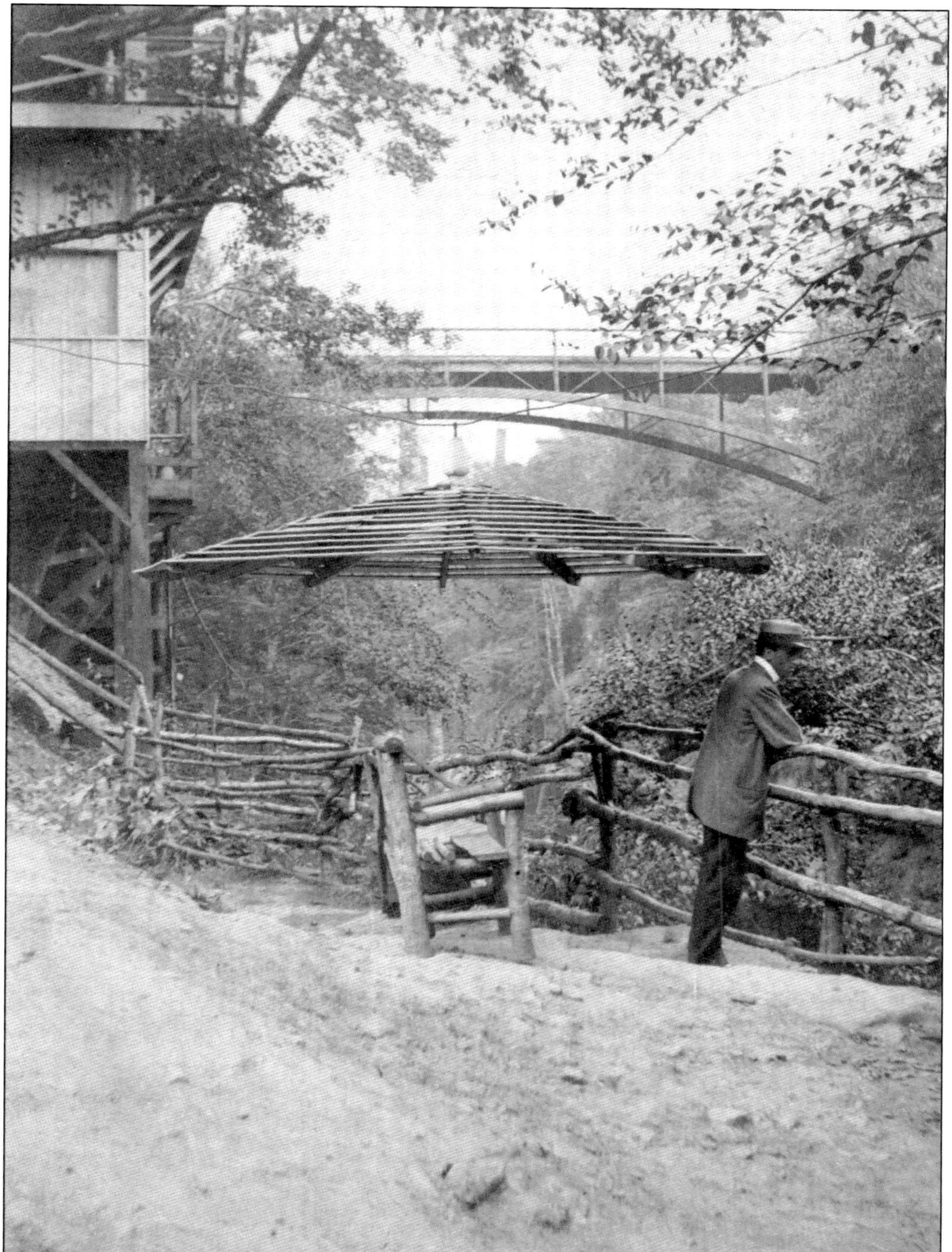

The owners also placed wooden seats by the overlooks and strung canopies on overhead wires to shield visitors from the hot rays of the sun. Here, a man stops to admire the scenery. On special occasions, the park's owners would light evening bonfires on the river, casting eerily beautiful lights and shadows on the park's trails and caves. (John and Janet Waldsmith collection.)

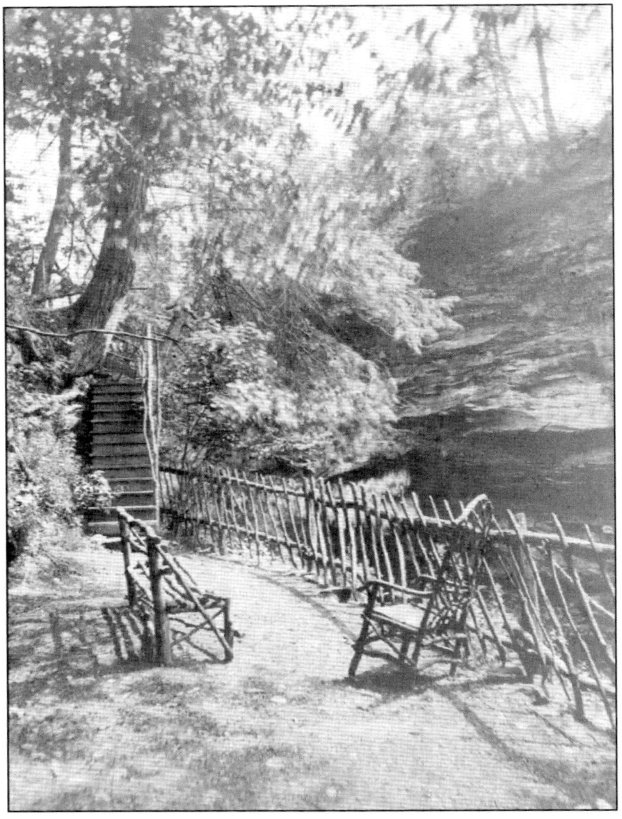

A short distance south of the pavilion, visitors could walk down a set of steps and arrive at a broad ledge named Lovers' Retreat. Seats were placed in this tree-shaded glade so that couples could escape from the bustling crowds and enjoy a more tranquil setting. (John and Janet Waldsmith collection.)

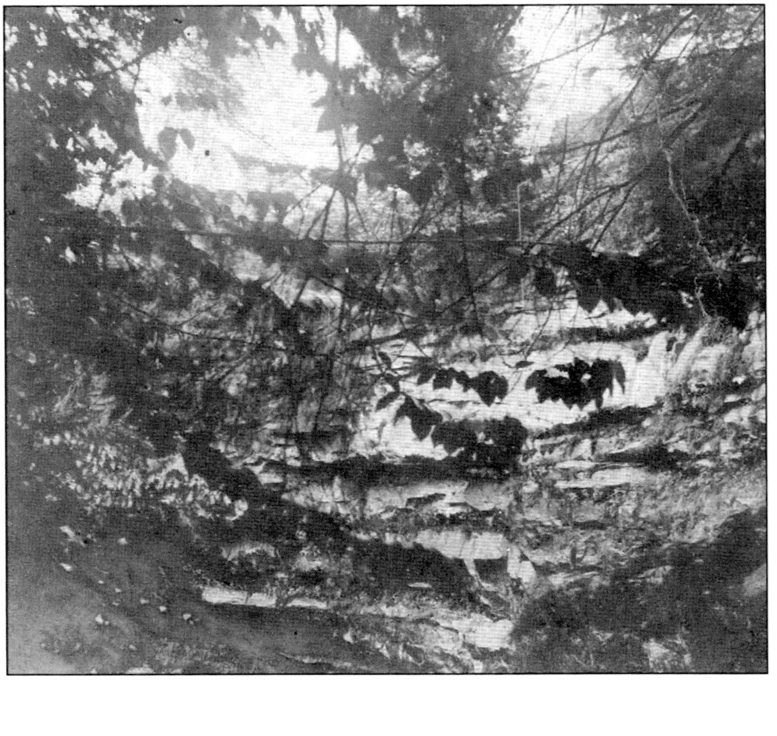

The photographer labeled this leafy view, "Across from Lovers' Retreat." The Glens and nearby Gorge featured charming scenery, including oak, black gum, tulip, and yellow birch trees and trailing arbutus. (Author's collection.)

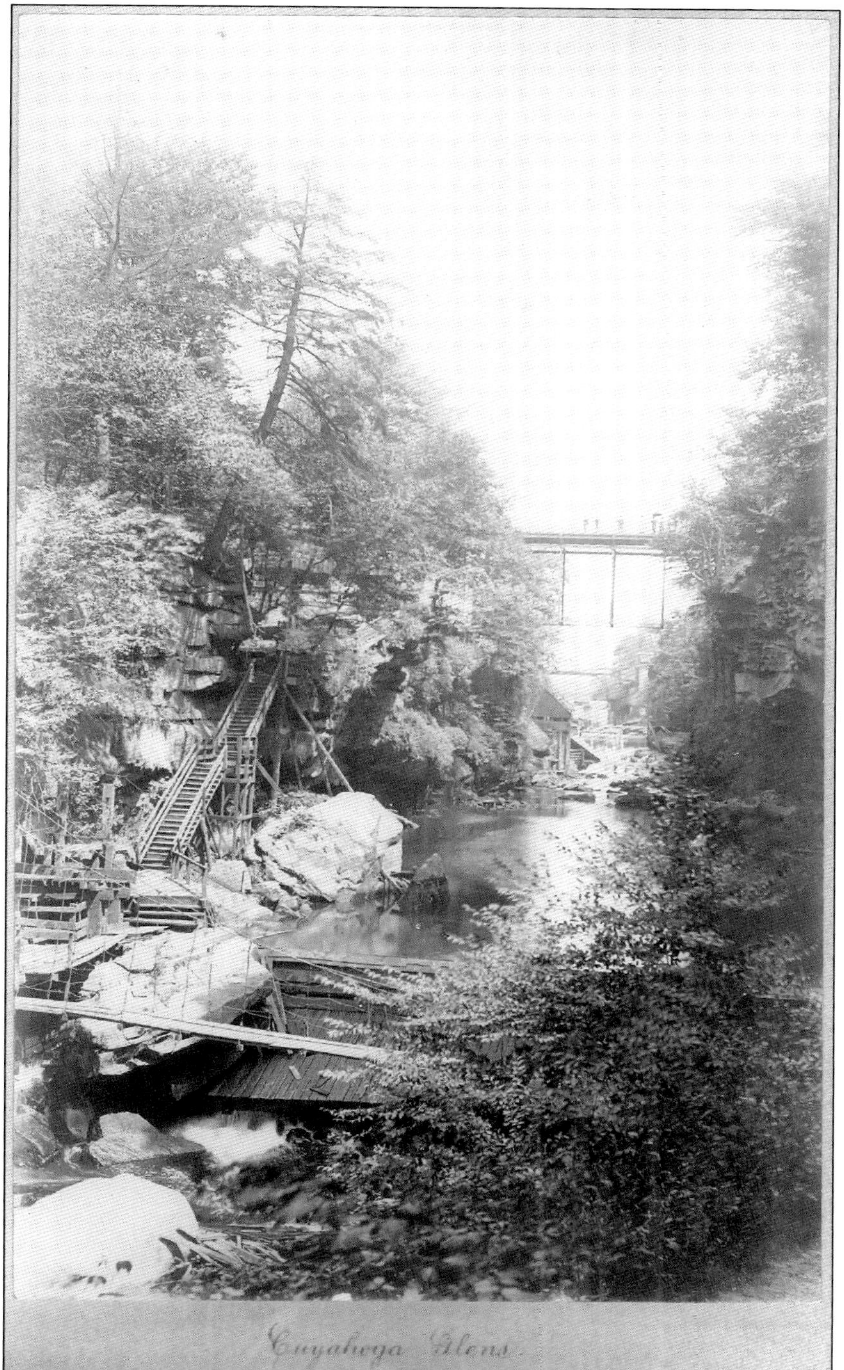


To reach the caves and other features located close to the river, visitors descended a large set of steps known as the Grand Staircase (at left). At the base of the steps was a large boulder, which, according to the owners, weighed more than 100 tons. It was known as Observation Rock. (David Neuhardt collection.)

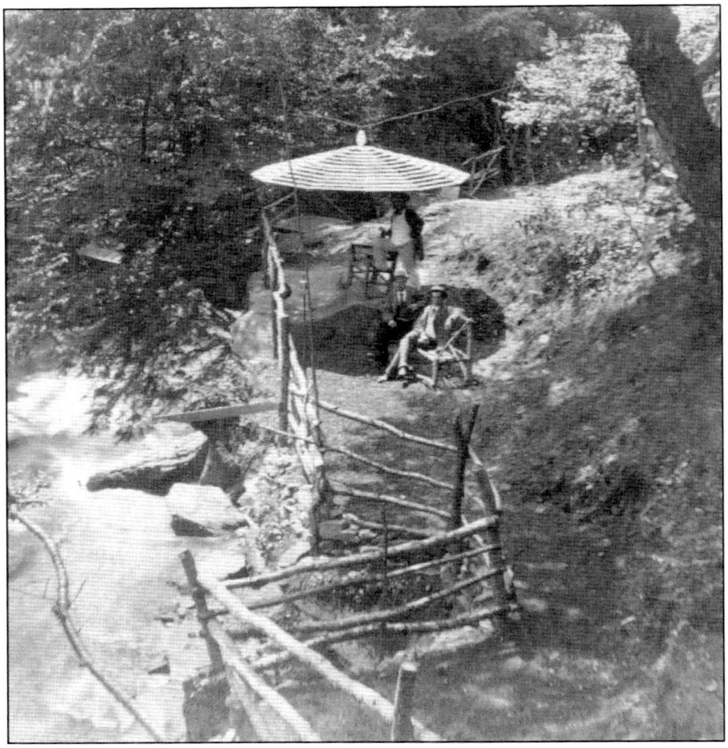

More scenic overlooks and shaded picnic areas were located farther south along the top of the Glens. Here, several jaunty gentlemen pose for the photographer. For visitors craving more excitement, the park offered various attractions, including a shooting gallery managed by H. Benscoten. (Author's collection.)

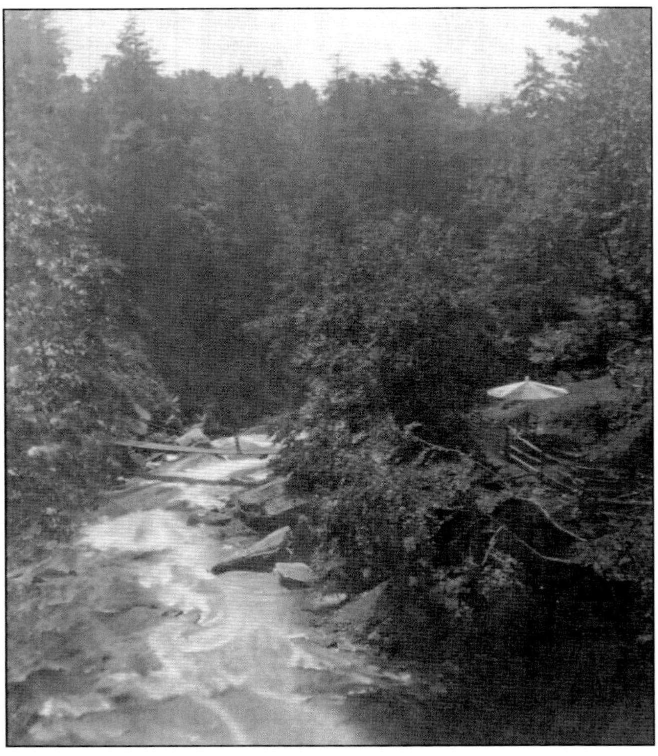

This distant view of the overlook area hints at another feature for which the High Bridge Glens and Caves park was named: its deep and mysterious caves (see dark area in the right foreground). The nearby Gorge, on the north bank of the Cuyahoga River, reportedly contained a "lost" cave, originally described by early Summit County historian Lucius Bierce. Later, various civic promoters discussed offering a prize to anyone who could find the location of Bierce's cave. (Author's collection.)

This rare image offers a closer view of Observation Rock and one of the park's smaller caves, known as Doves' Retreat. Advertisements for the park describe the cave as being located "immediately under Fern Cave," the largest cave at the park. (Eric Thompson collection.)

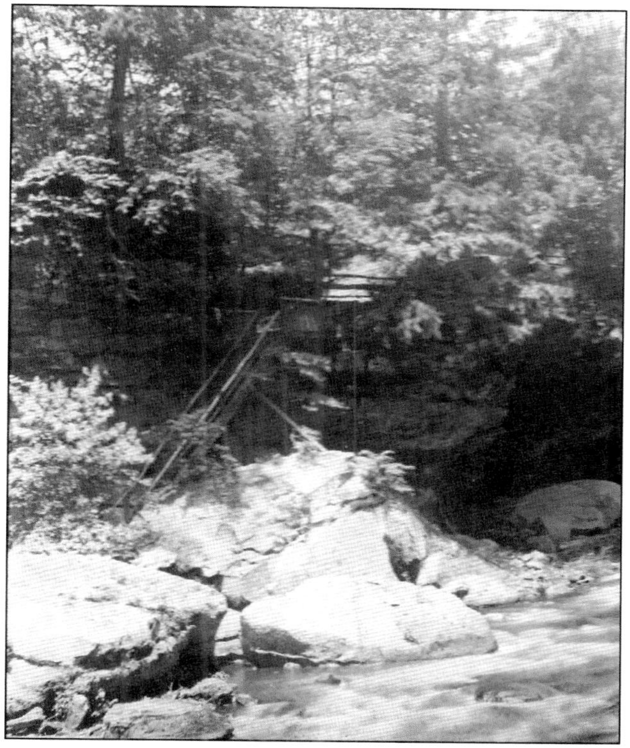

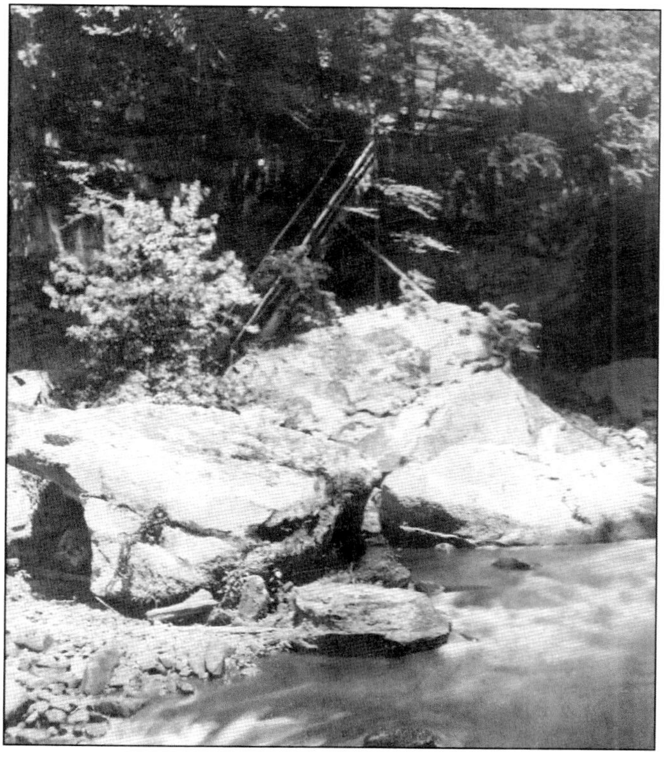

According to park brochures, Doves' Retreat, seen here with Observation Rock, was a large cavern with an overhanging rock roof 25 feet above ground level. As the name implies, doves, pigeons, and other birds flocked to this cool, shady cave. This particular scene was a favorite of artists and photographers. (Eric Thompson collection.)

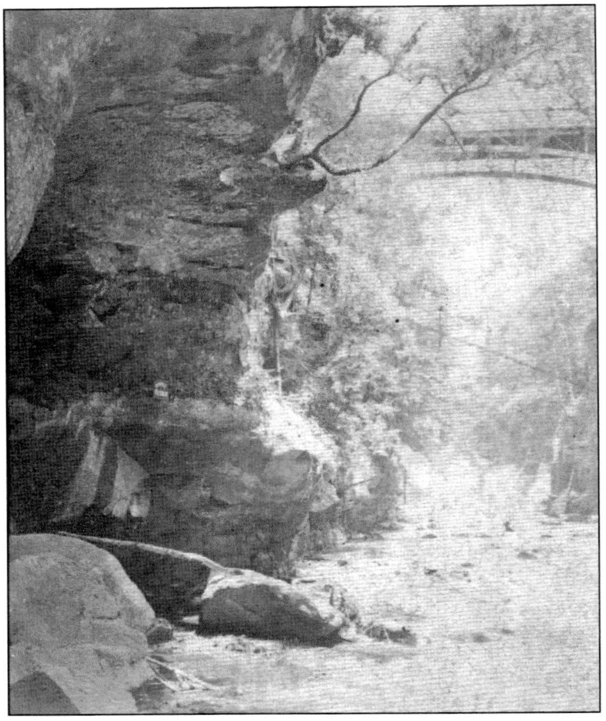

The views looking north toward the High Bridge from Doves' Retreat (note the wooden sign) were breathtaking; however, visitors choosing to walk along the river had to watch their steps. In 1891, prominent Akron judge J.S. Carpenter fell at the Glens, striking his head on a large boulder; he died several hours later. (Author's collection.)

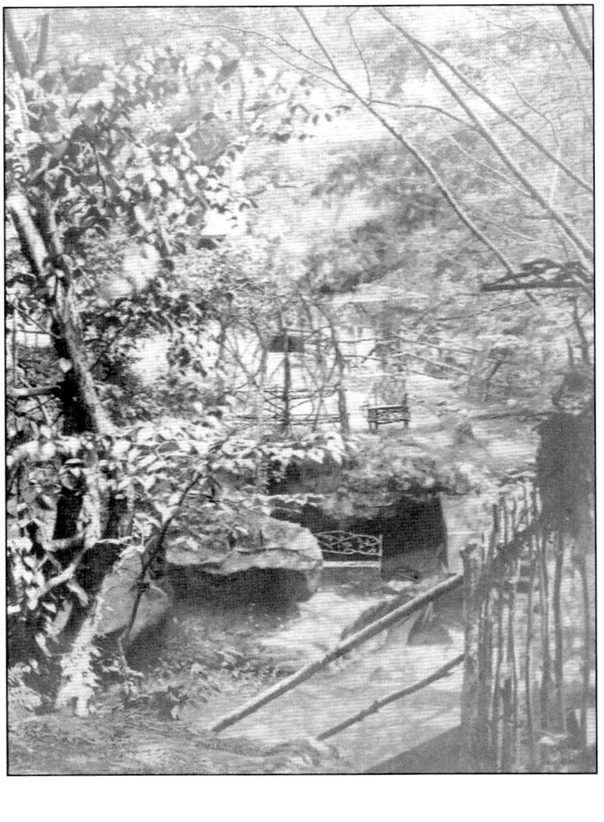

The largest of the park's caves was known as Fern Cave. It was located on the west side of the park, close to Doves' Retreat. This photograph shows several scenic seats and arbors on the overlook above the cave. (Author's collection.)

According to park brochures, Fern Cave was 35 feet deep and 54 feet wide and had a concave roof 10 feet overhead. Newspaper accounts indicate there were charred marks on the top of the cave's interior, as if Native Americans had possibly built fires in the cave for warmth or cooking, but it was never verified before being submerged when the dams were constructed. (Eric Thompson collection.)

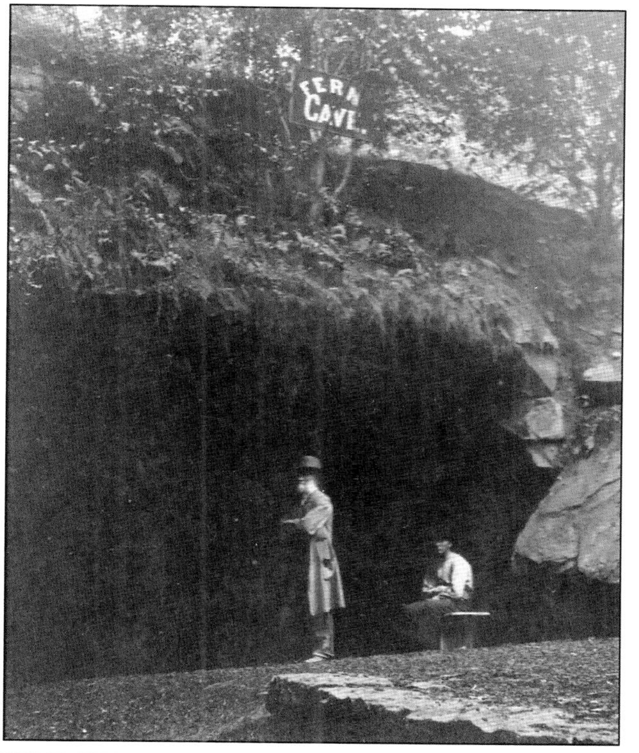


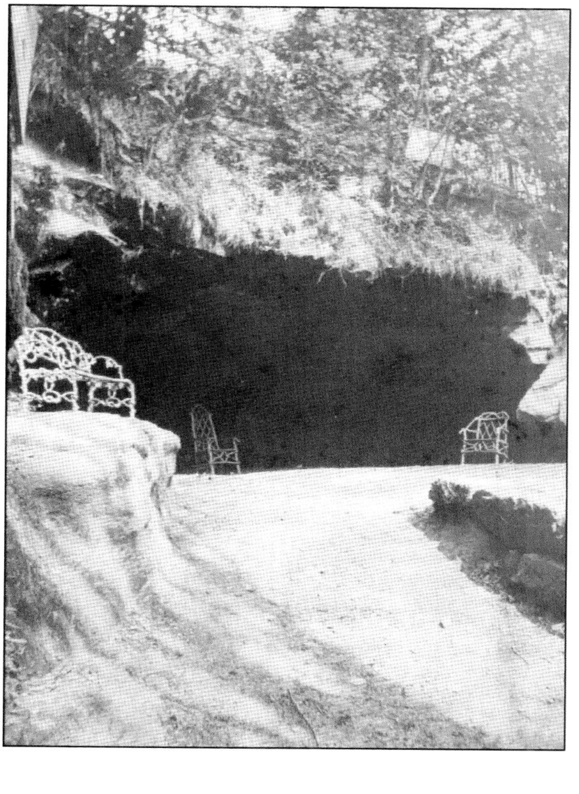

The owners placed rustic seats and benches in Fern Cave so visitors could escape from the midday sun and enjoy picnic lunches in a cooler setting. Note the wooden sign above the cave indicating its name. (Author's collection.)

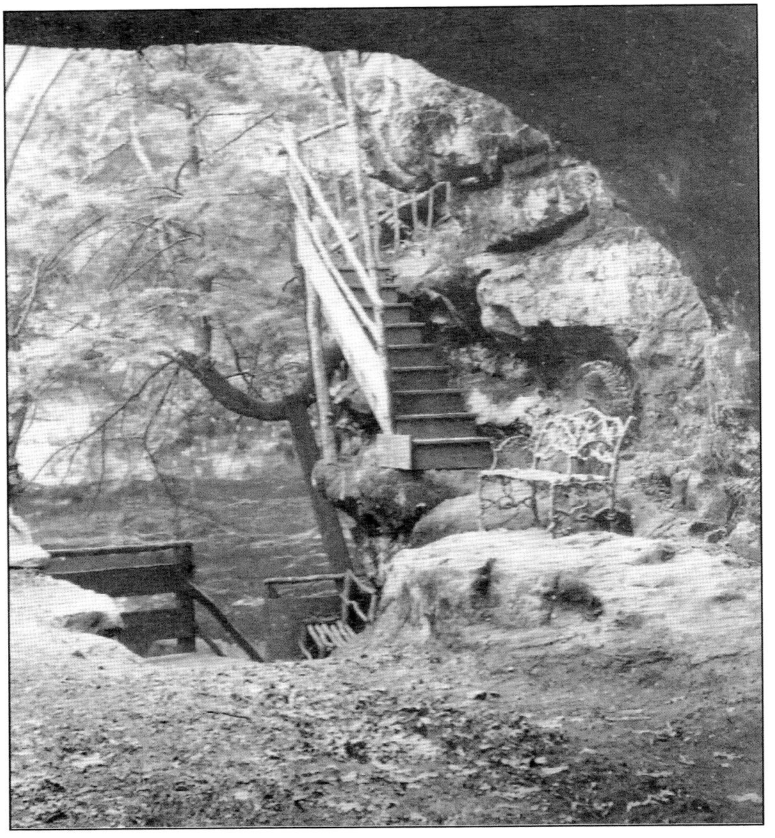

This rare photograph was taken from inside Fern Cave looking out from it. To the right are a bench and a set of stairs. In the background, visitors could see the rushing waters of the Cuyahoga River. (Author's collection.)

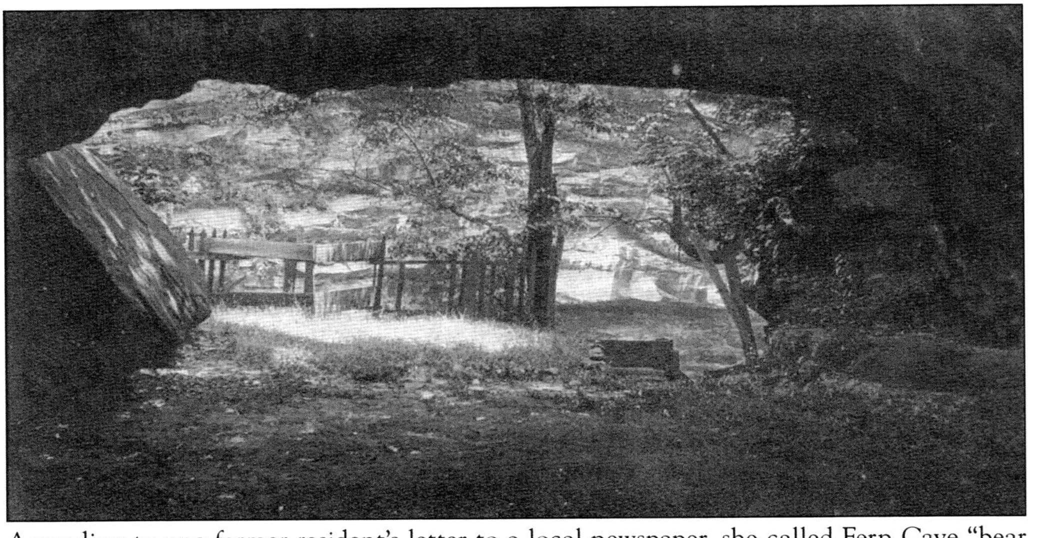

According to one former resident's letter to a local newspaper, she called Fern Cave "bear cave" because she thought its shape resembled a bruin. Another popular tale reported in early newspapers stated that picnickers enjoyed hiding small jugs containing pennies in the nooks of trees and in the caves and then trying to find them on subsequent visits to the Glens or Gorge. (Author's collection.)

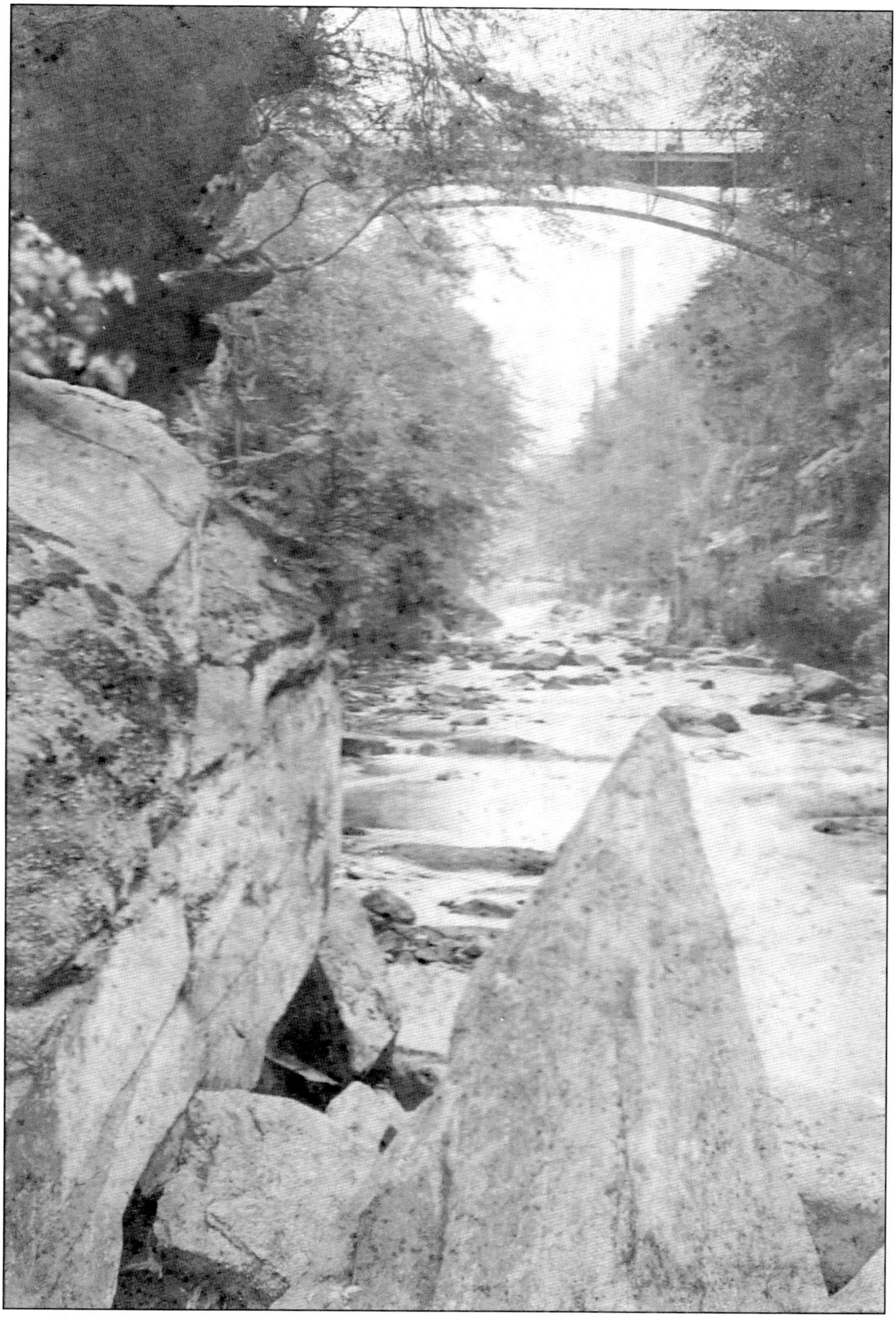

As was the case with Doves' Retreat, people looking upstream from Fern Cave could enjoy stunning scenery. One interesting but dubious tale told by Glens tour guides was that the park had the only true white mulberry bush in the state of Ohio. (Author's collection.)

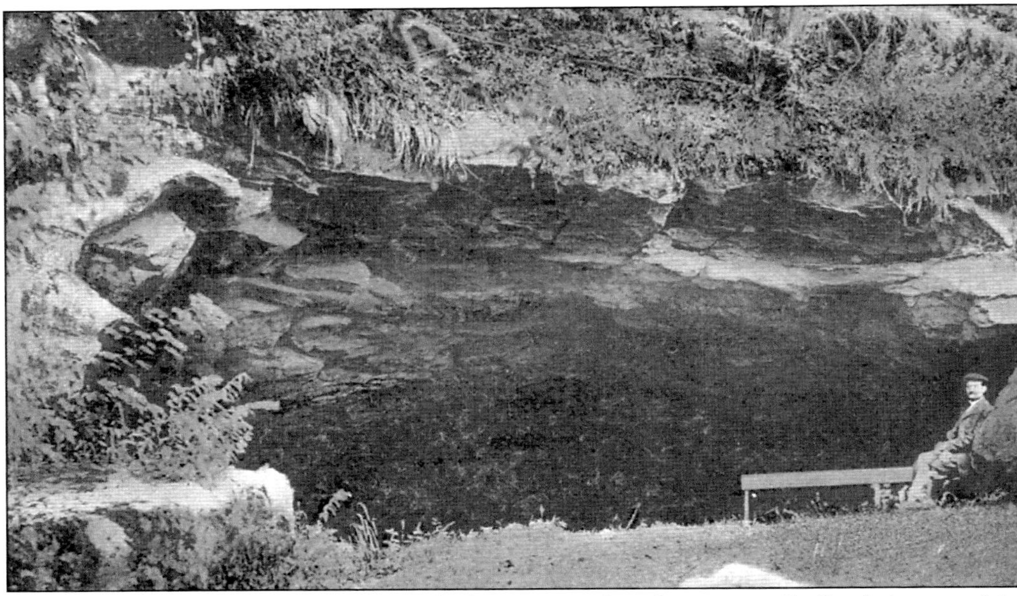

In the early 1900s, before construction of a downstream dam that eventually flooded many of the park's caves, hikers enjoyed the Glens' unique geological formations and caverns. Some residents recall playing hide and seek in the former Glens. (Author's collection.)

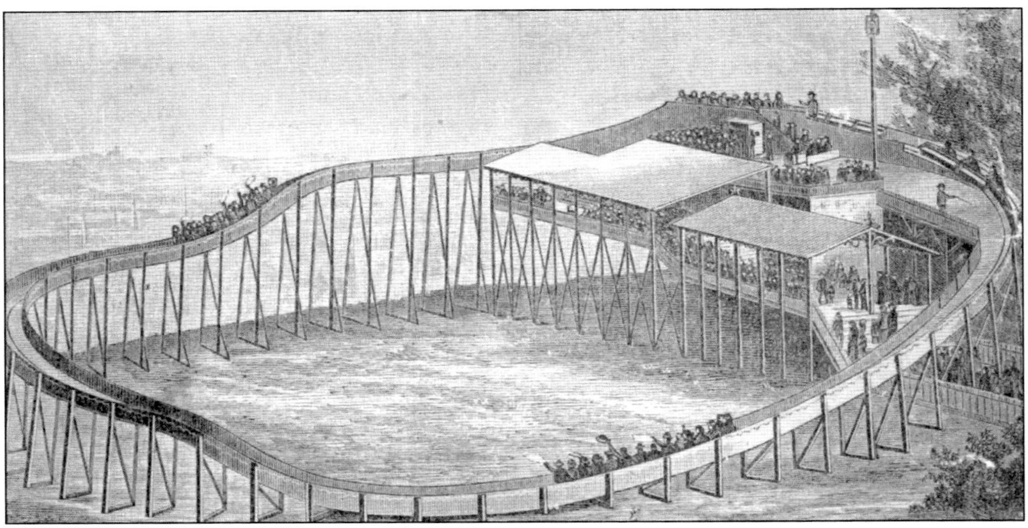

One of the park's most intriguing features was its roller coaster, which was built in 1884. Although no photographs have been found of the Glens coaster, Victorian-era newspapers indicate it was a circular gravity railway like the one depicted on this advertising card. According to patent owners, the ride lasted 10 seconds; thrill-seekers paid a nickel for a spin around the track. The Glens coaster was located south of the Grand Pavilion at the top of the Glens. (Author's collection.)

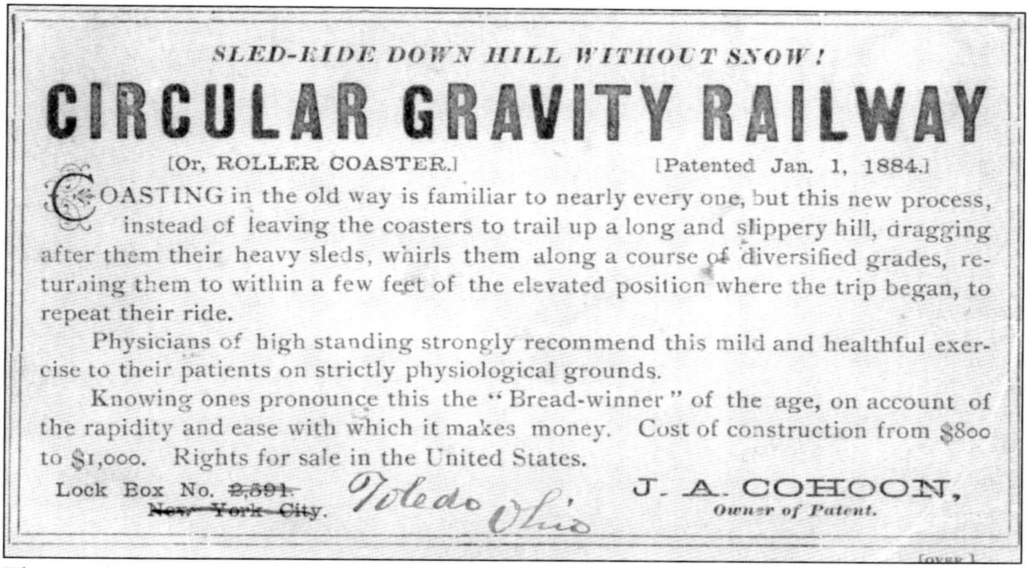

SLED-RIDE DOWN HILL WITHOUT SNOW!

CIRCULAR GRAVITY RAILWAY

[Or, ROLLER COASTER.] [Patented Jan. 1, 1884.]

COASTING in the old way is familiar to nearly every one, but this new process, instead of leaving the coasters to trail up a long and slippery hill, dragging after them their heavy sleds, whirls them along a course of diversified grades, returning them to within a few feet of the elevated position where the trip began, to repeat their ride.

Physicians of high standing strongly recommend this mild and healthful exercise to their patients on strictly physiological grounds.

Knowing ones pronounce this the "Bread-winner" of the age, on account of the rapidity and ease with which it makes money. Cost of construction from $800 to $1,000. Rights for sale in the United States.

Lock Box No. ~~2,591~~ ~~New York City~~. Toledo Ohio

J. A. COHOON,
*Owner of Patent.*

[OVER.]

The circular gravity railway was patented by Toledo inventor Alanson C. Wood and J.A. Cohoon. According to this trade card, doctors promoted roller-coaster riding as an aid to good health. The inventors promoted it as a moneymaker. Local newspapers estimated that the owners of the Glens coaster made more than $700 in one of its first days of operation. (Author's collection.)

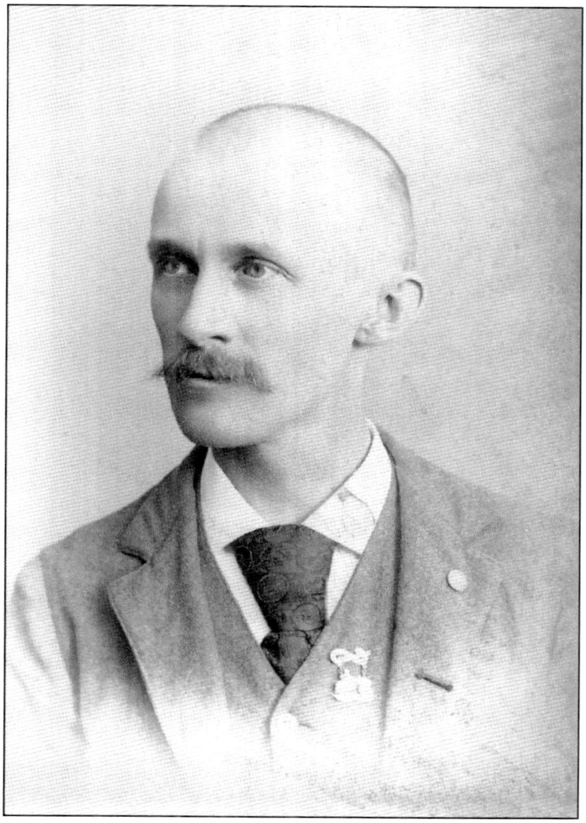

Local resident D.C. Freer helped operate the Glens coaster. On one occasion, when riders reported that the coaster seemed to stick or slow down on a portion of the track, Freer and several other park employees took a ride on the coaster to locate the source of the problem. Unfortunately, the coaster car came up off the tracks and flew through the air, taking its passengers with it, and landed on the ground with a resounding thud. No one suffered any long-term injuries, and the coaster was soon fixed and back in operation. Freer later served as a firefighter. (Cuyahoga Falls Historical Society.)

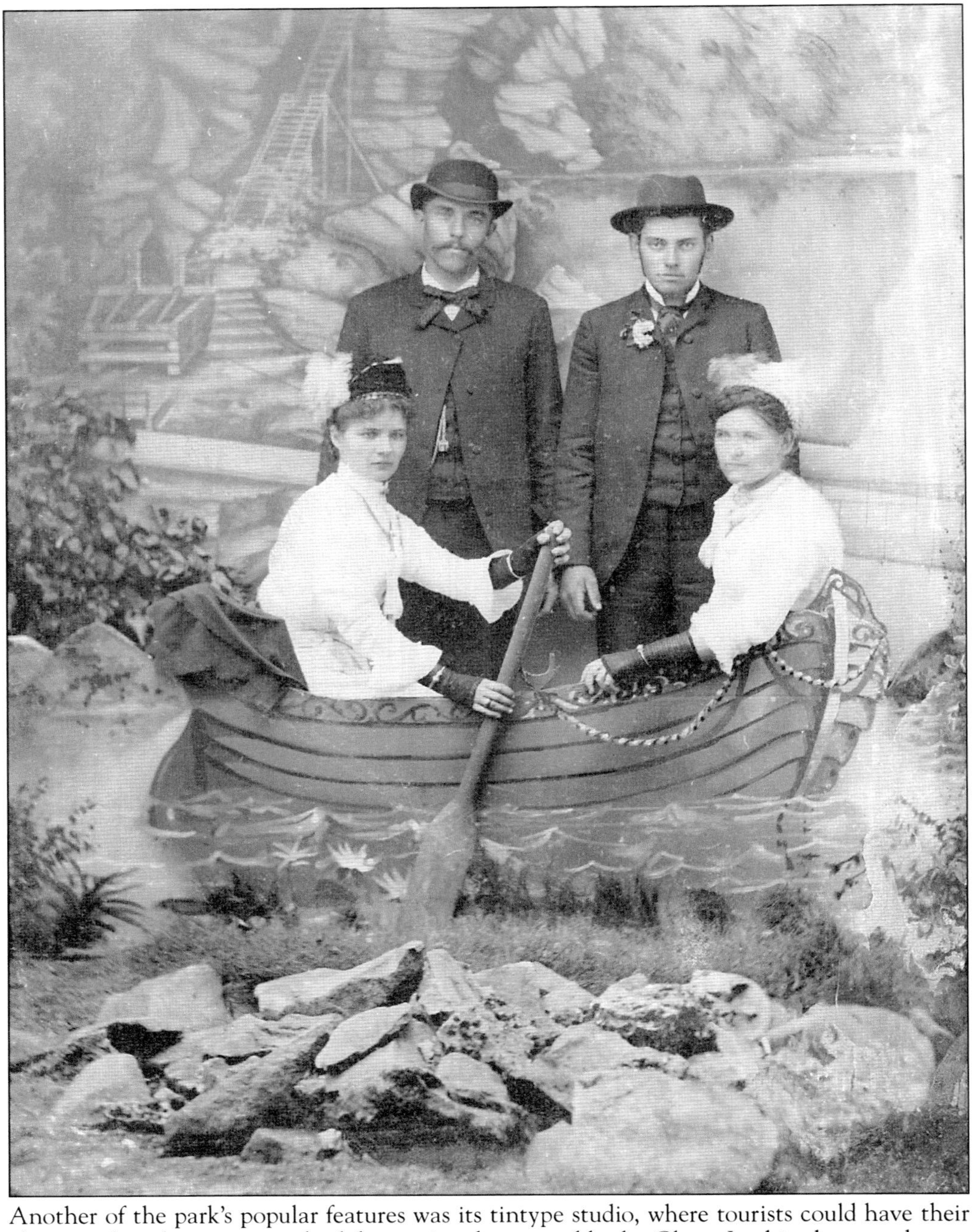

Another of the park's popular features was its tintype studio, where tourists could have their photographs taken against a backdrop painted to resemble the Glens. In this photograph, two couples pose in a mock rowboat with the Grand Staircase and the suspension bridge in the background. (Author's collection.)

# *Three*

# Crossing the Glens

## Bridges and Ferry Boats

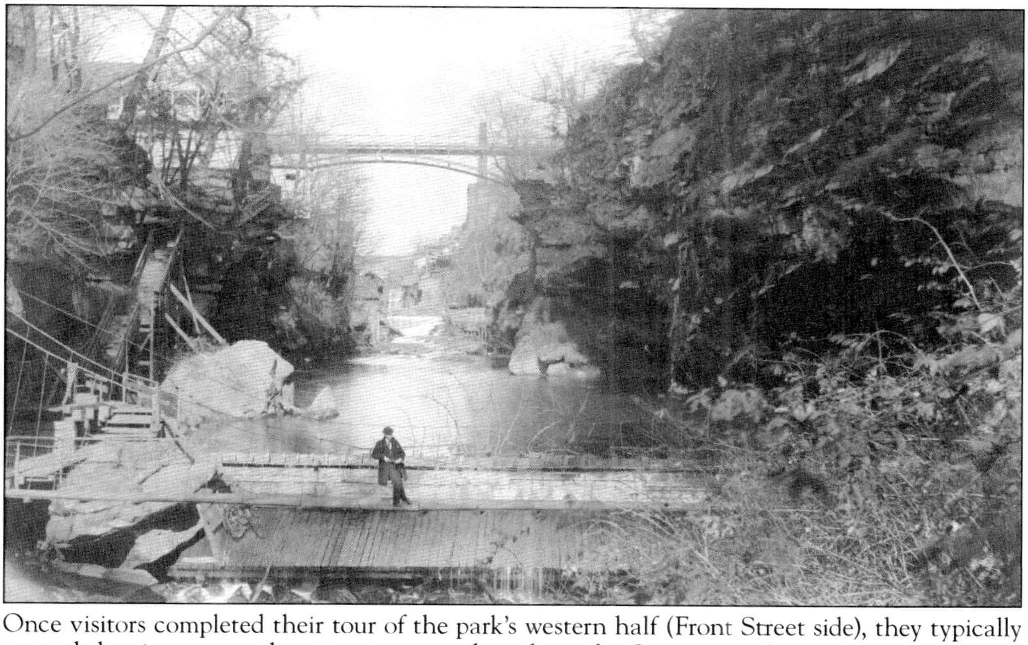

Once visitors completed their tour of the park's western half (Front Street side), they typically crossed the river to see the attractions on the other side. One option for reaching the eastern half of the park was a walk across the suspension, or swinging, footbridge. The bridge, built below the rapids and above the high water mark of the Cuyahoga River, was strung on heavy iron cable and had a six-foot-wide wooden plank floor. Heavy ropes were added to the side of the bridge so visitors could steady themselves to avoid falling into the river. (Cuyahoga Falls Library.)

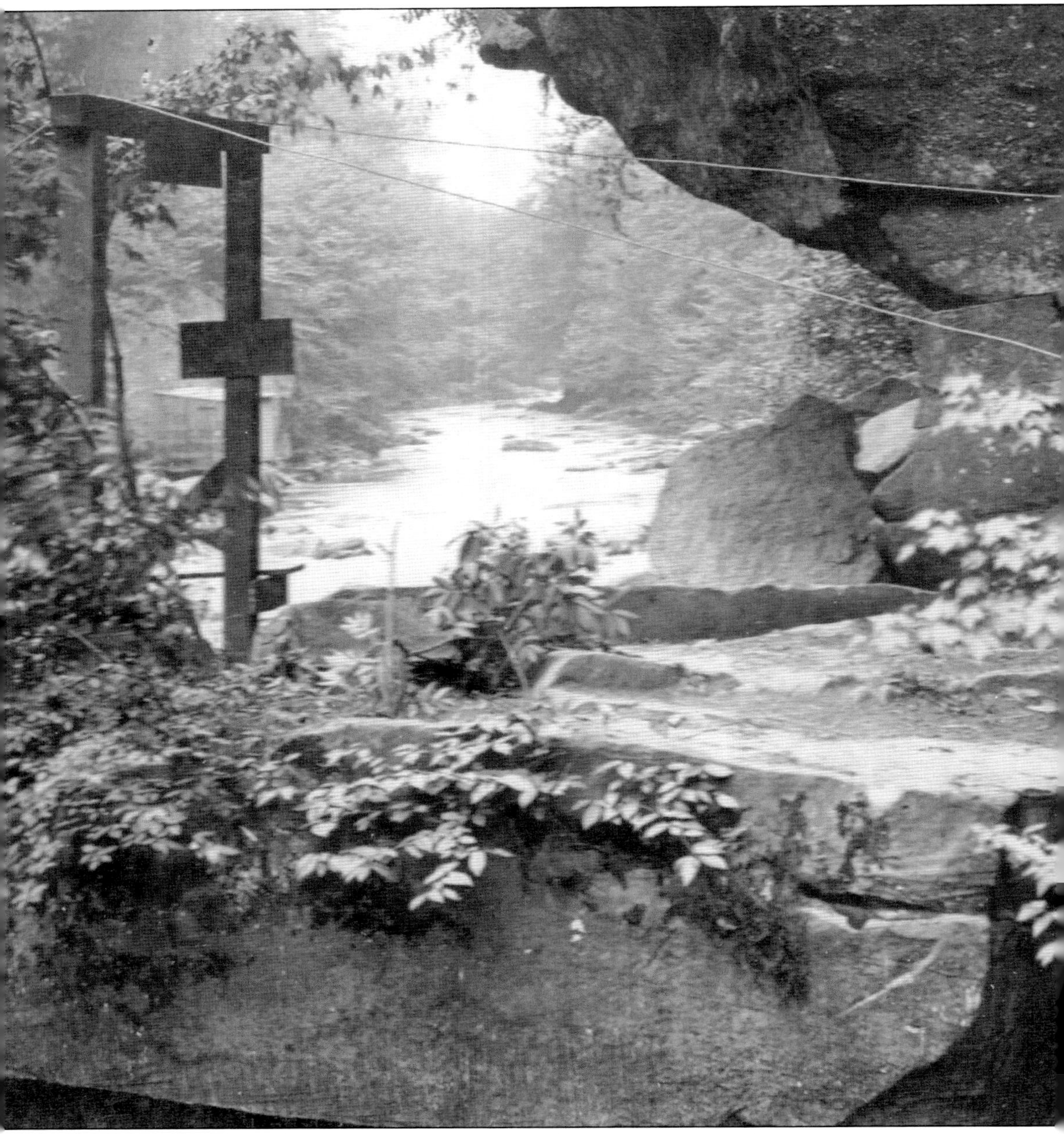

Although park brochures indicated that tourists faced no danger walking on the suspension bridge, signs posted on both ends urged people to "go slow" when crossing. Just beyond the bridge, on the left side of the photograph, is a small wooden bathhouse at the river's edge. A sign on the building advertises the availability of bathing costumes, now known as swimsuits. (Author's collection.)

For many couples, having their picture taken on the suspension bridge was the ultimate "photo opportunity." In fact, this was one of the most frequently photographed features of the park. In other views not seen in this book, a few brave souls posed on rocks in the middle of the river. (Author's collection.)

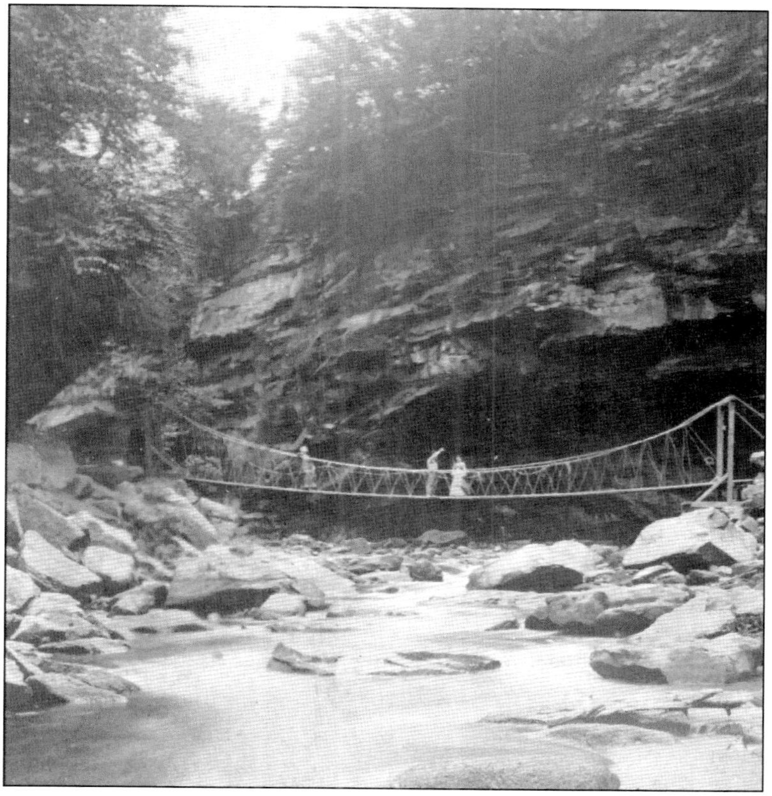

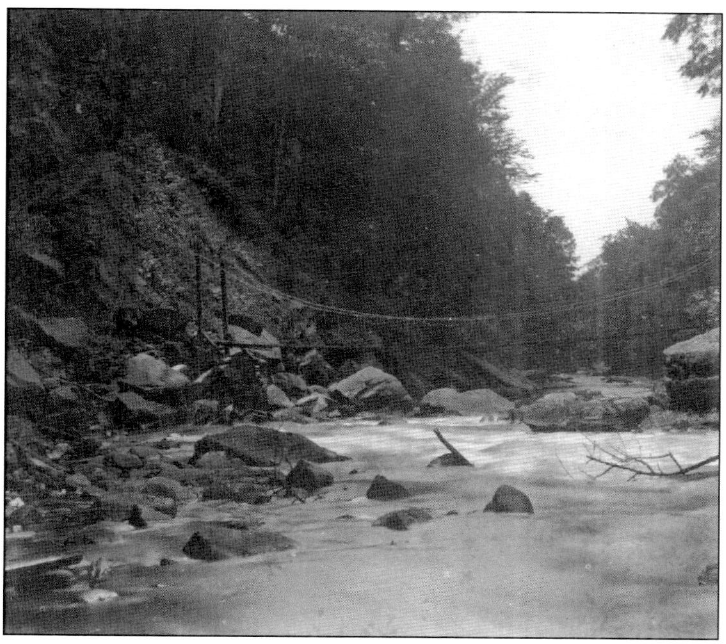

While the park's owners may have maintained that the suspension bridge was steady as a rock, residents who visited the Glens as teenagers had a very different impression. One woman recalled that when she and her friends reached the halfway point on the bridge, teenage boys would suddenly appear and—in an attempt to scare the girls—jump up and down on their end of the bridge, causing the floor of the bridge to move up and down and sway from side to side. (Author's collection.)

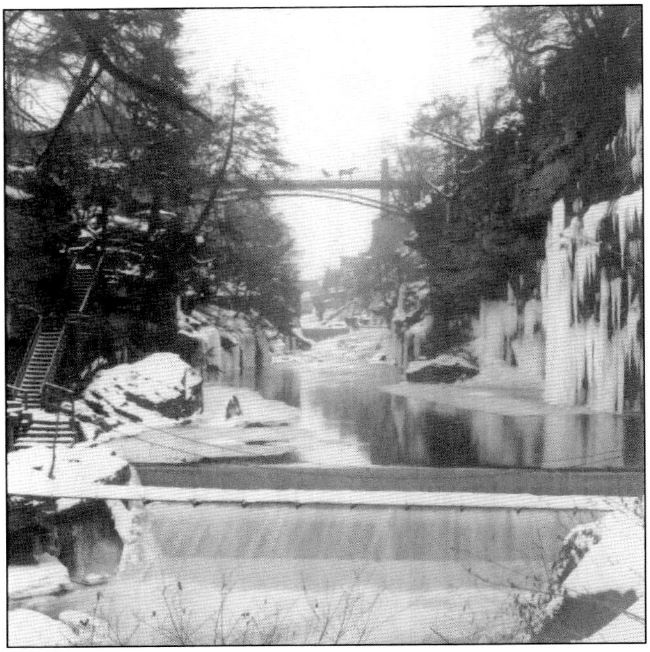

According to the park's owners, the bridge was extremely safe to cross. In fact, it was held in place with heavy iron rods embedded in huge boulders on both ends; however, it was not indestructible. During a flood in 1881, the bridge was washed out and had to be rebuilt by a Cleveland shipbuilder. The bridge was especially lovely in winter. Note the horse and buggy on the High Bridge in the background. (Cuyahoga Falls Historical Society.)

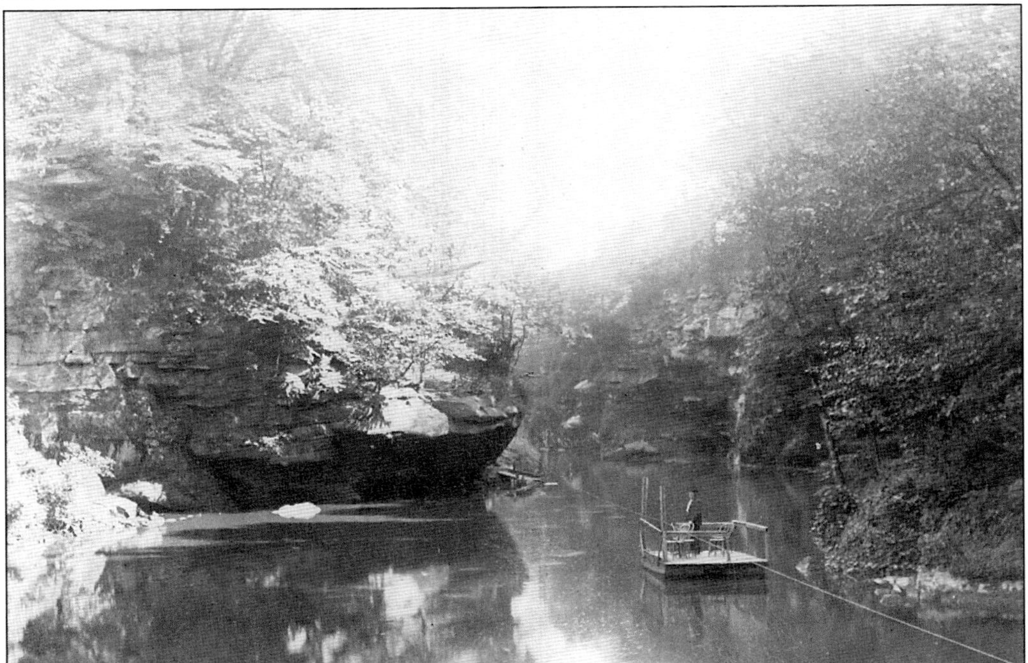

Visitors who did not want to walk across the bobbing suspension bridge had another option for enjoying the beautiful river views: a leisurely ride on Fenton's Ferry. According to a *Falls News* article, Luther Fenton got the inspiration to create the ferry ride after a flood destroyed a nearby dam. Using the existing metal supports from the dam, he strung a cable from just below Observation Rock to a point further south on the river and transported passengers on a wooden raft by pulling hand-over-hand on a towrope. (Cuyahoga Falls Historical Society.)

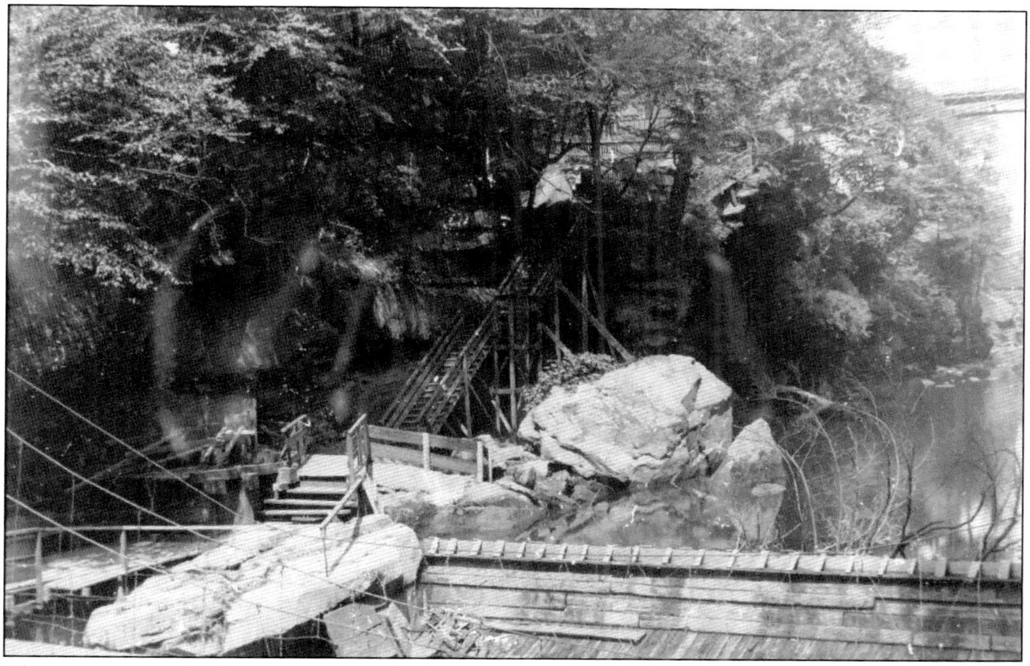

The entrance to the ferry ride was at the bottom of the Grand Staircase just beyond the suspension bridge. An early newspaper estimated that Luther Fenton transported thousands of visitors during his career. At one point, he also managed the Glen House hotel. (Cuyahoga Falls Library.)

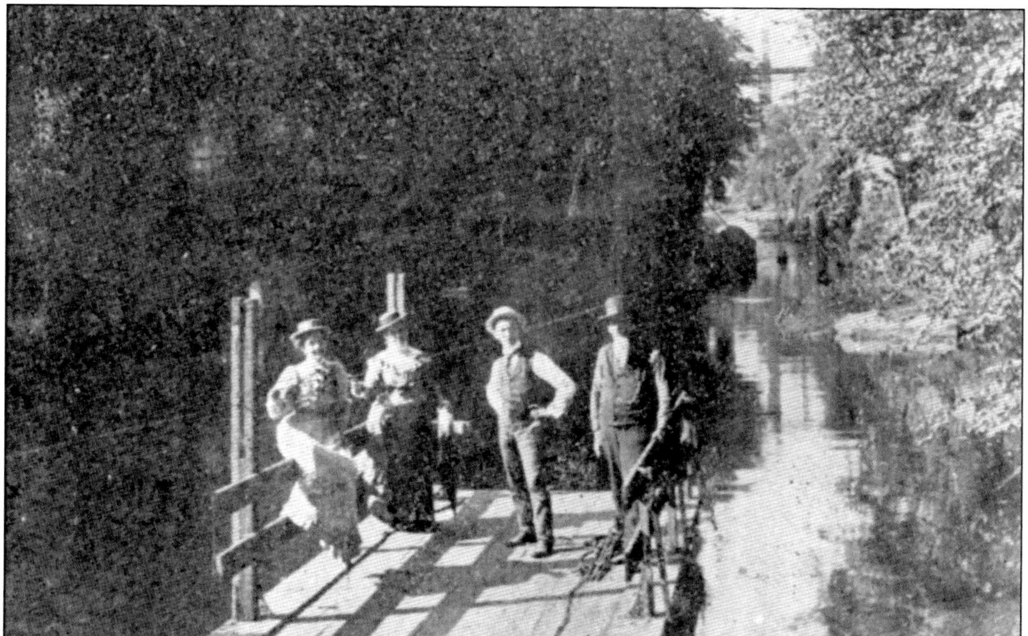

For many Glens visitors, a ride on Fenton's Ferry was a thrilling experience. Those seeking additional thrills could visit the roller-skating rink located across from the Glens. The Glen Rink featured exhibitions by champion skaters, as well as local races. (Pete Mellinger collection.)

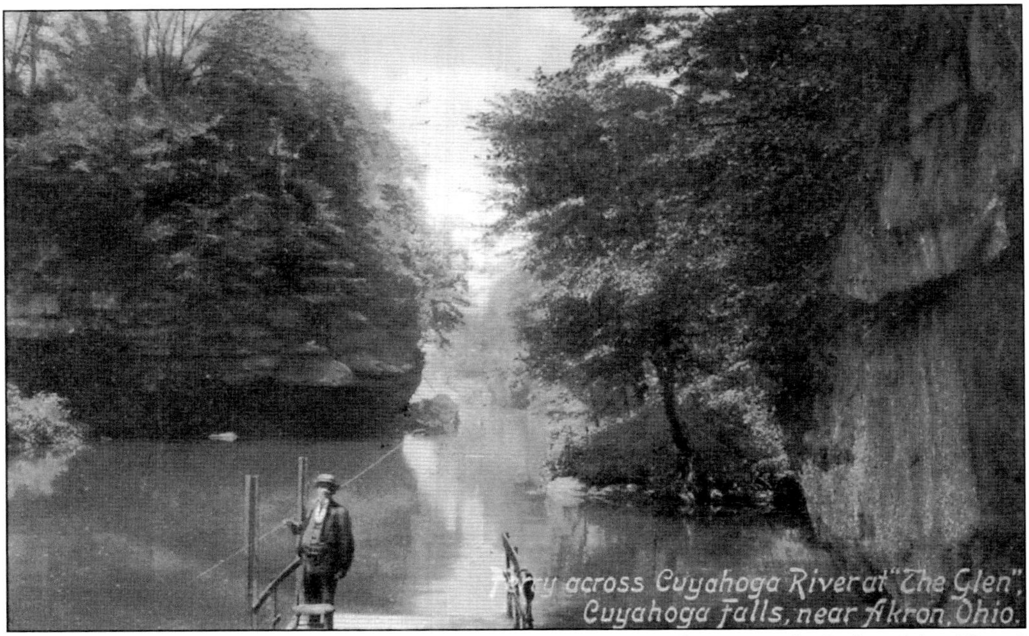


During the 16 years that he operated the ferry, Luther Fenton was known as the "pilot of the Glens." He was remembered as being a gracious host who delighted passengers with detailed descriptions of the scenery in the Glens. Fenton operated the ride well into his 80s. (Author's collection.)

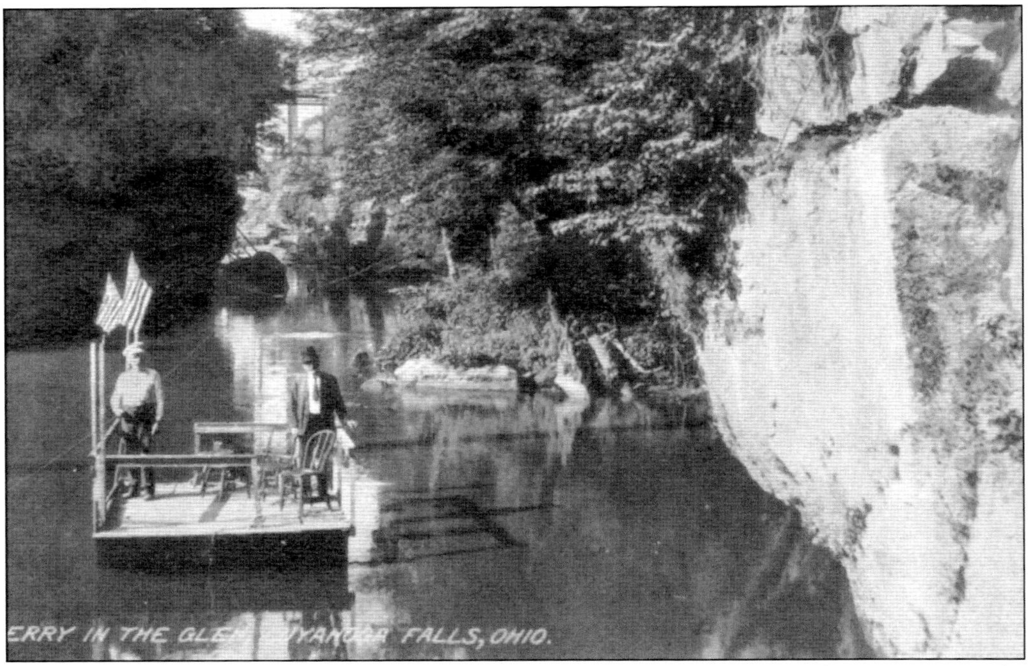


Most of Fenton's trips were uneventful; however, according to an *Akron Daily Democrat* article, on one ill-fated day Fenton's raft was overloaded, and all the passengers ended up in the river. Fortunately, the raft was close to shore and no one was injured, although several passengers reportedly lost their watches. (Author's collection.)

# *Four*

# Touring the Glens

## The East Side of the Park

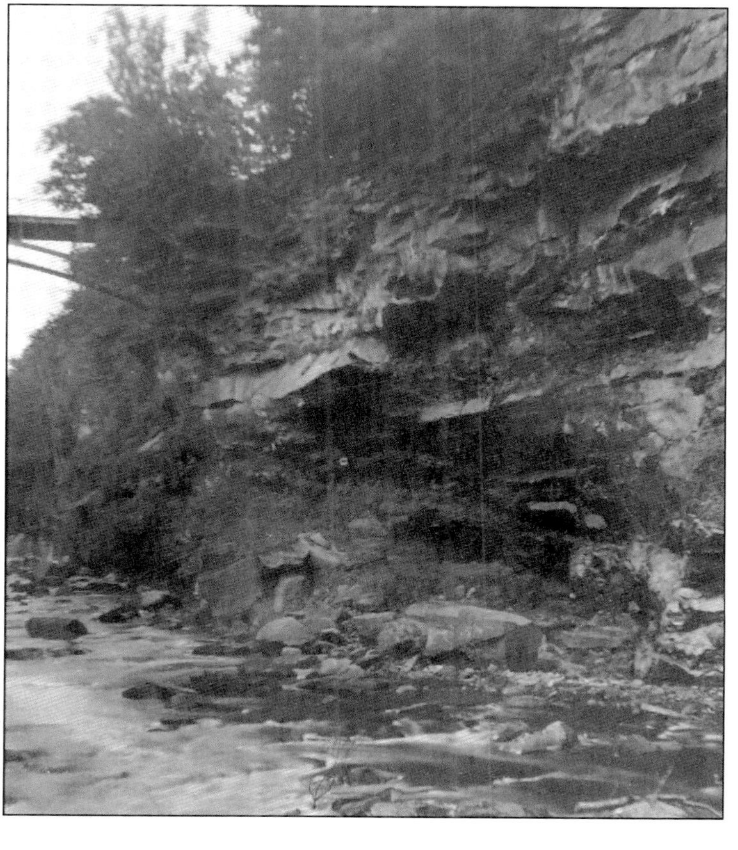

Upon crossing the suspension bridge, one of the first features visible to visitors on the eastern side of the park was the beautiful Weeping Cliffs. This large rock face was so named because of the many small cracks and fissures in the rock that allowed water to seep through and stream down the cliff face. In the summer sun, the water glistened like diamonds, giving the appearance that the cliffs were weeping. (Eric Thompson collection.)

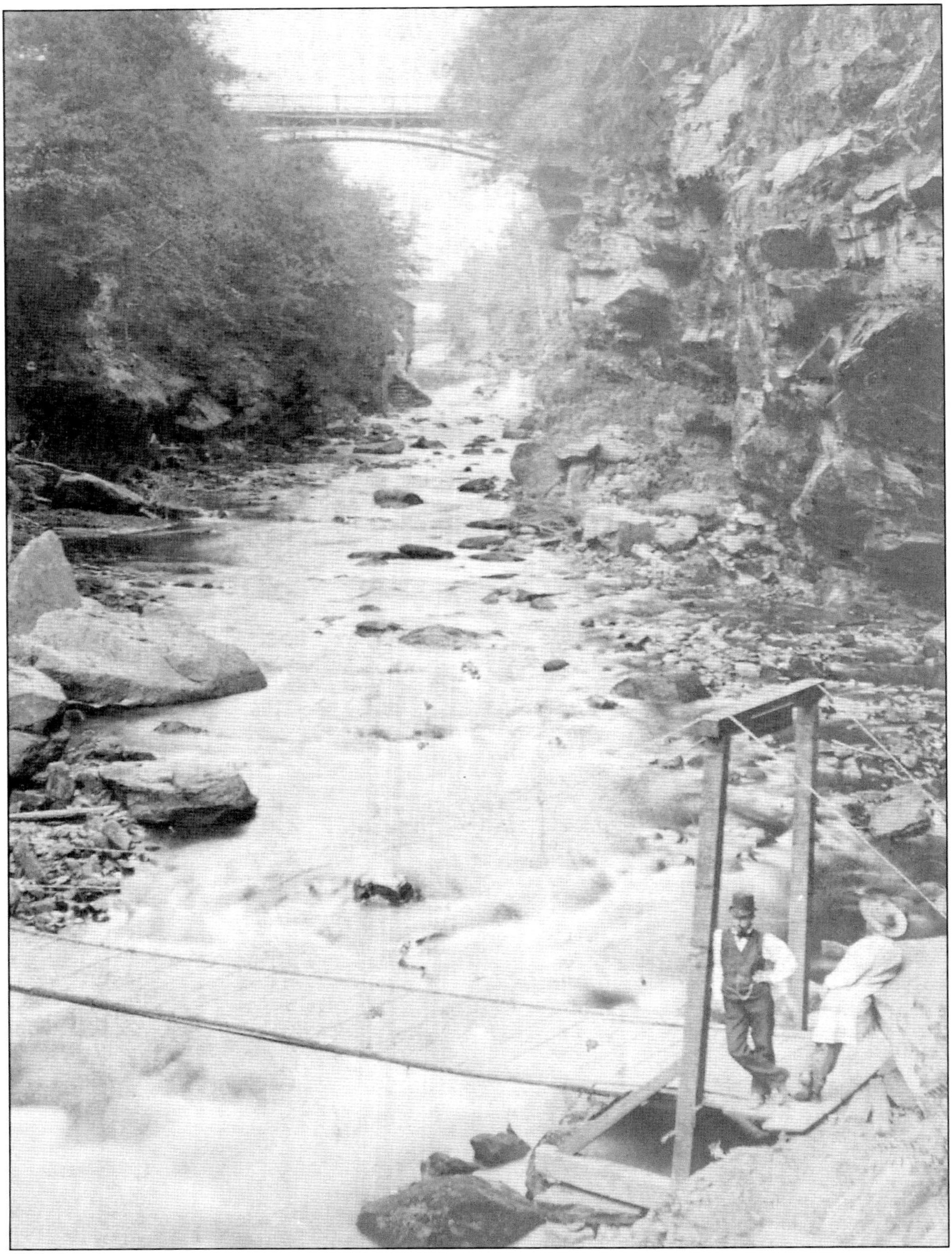

Having safely made his way across the suspension bridge, a Victorian tourist pauses for the photographer on the park's eastern side. At the time this photograph was taken, the level of the Cuyahoga River was quite low. (John and Janet Waldsmith collection.)

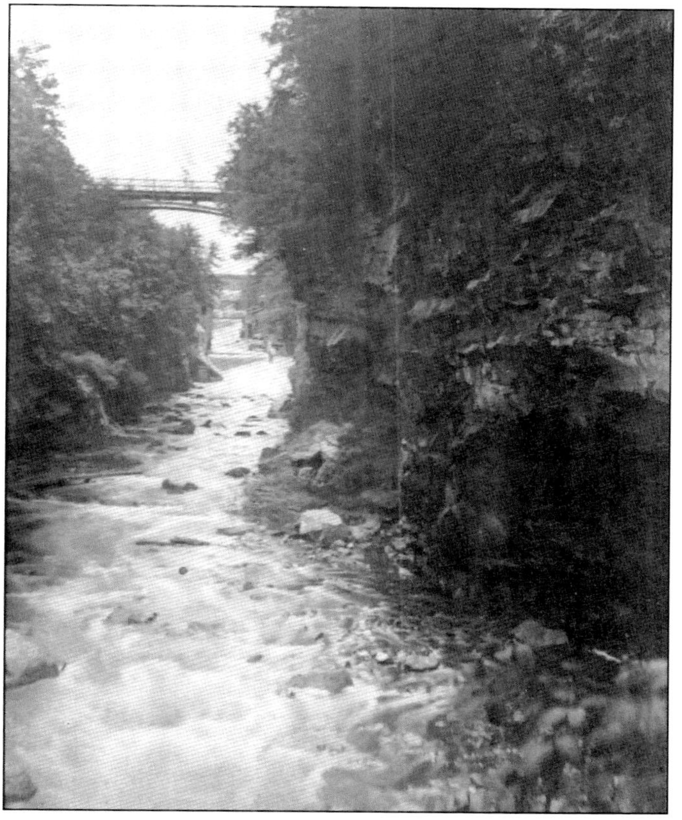

This image shows the views visitors enjoyed when looking north toward the High Bridge from Weeping Cliffs. While the park was known for its great beauty, it also had its share of tragic accidents. One night, in 1893, a young couple driving their horse and carriage across the High Bridge fell through an open area of the bridge floor that was being reconstructed. Both people lost their lives. Miraculously, the horse landed unharmed on a rock ledge. (Eric Thompson collection.)

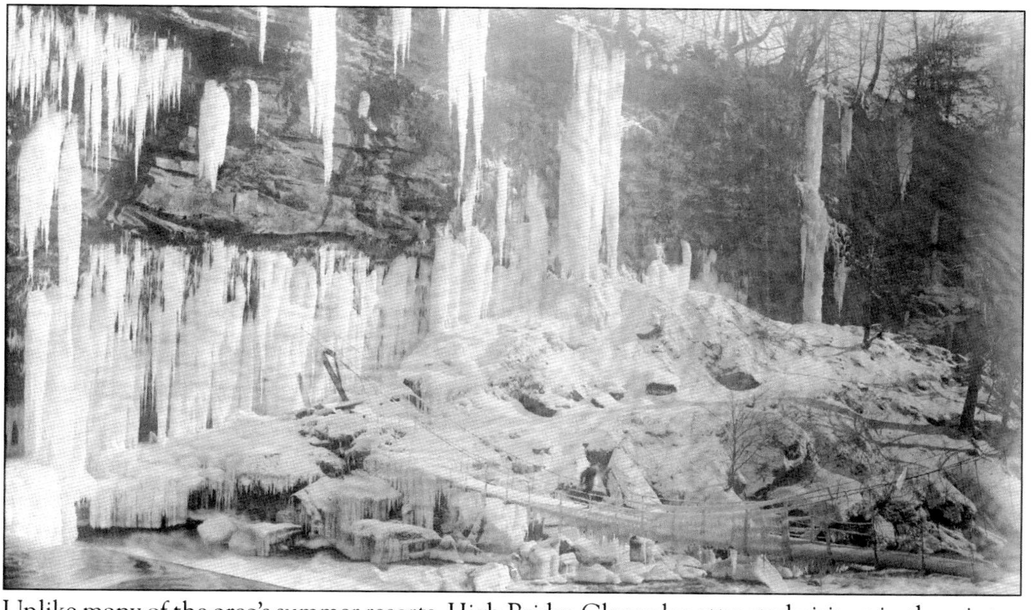

Unlike many of the area's summer resorts, High Bridge Glens also attracted visitors in the winter. During colder weather, the Weeping Cliffs froze, creating a veritable icicle palace with icicles ranging in color from white to light blue. (Cuyahoga Falls Historical Society.)

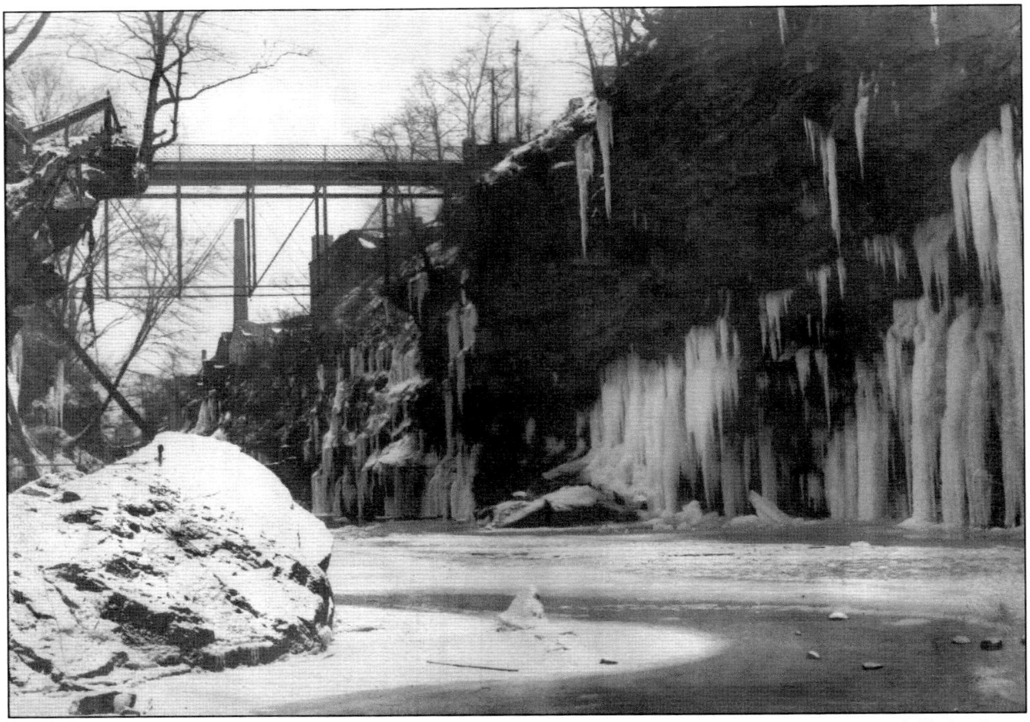

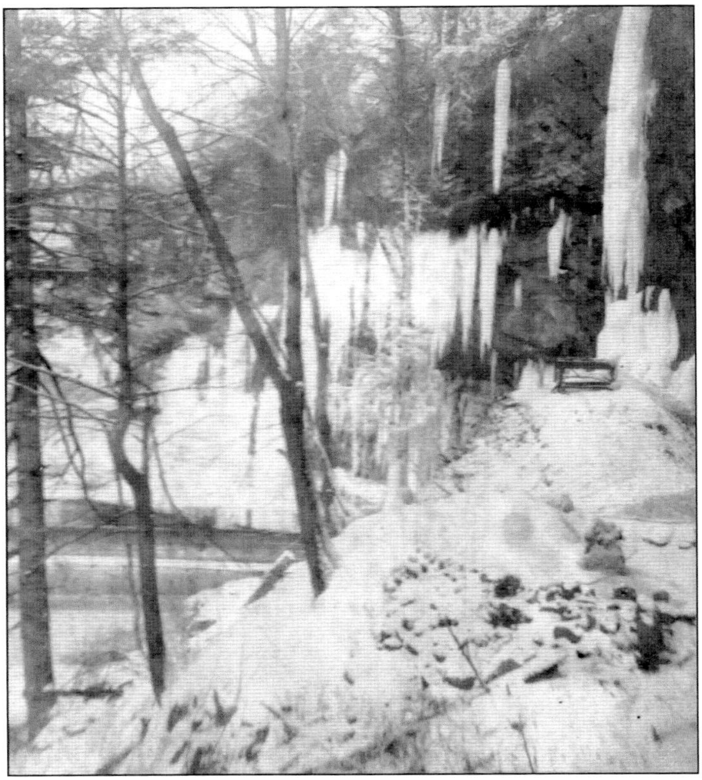

The Weeping Cliffs had some of the most impressive icicle displays in the area. In fact, the Weeping Cliffs still draw visitors to the Glens to this day. (Cuyahoga Falls Library.)

In addition to being a tourist attraction, the icicle displays at Weeping Cliffs garnered the attention of local and national photographers, including James Wark of Kent, Ohio, and Gates of Chicago. (Author's collection.)

This wintry view was taken from an area known as Mirror Lake looking north toward the High Bridge. On at least one occasion, a visitor fell through the ice on the river and had to be rescued. (Author's collection.)

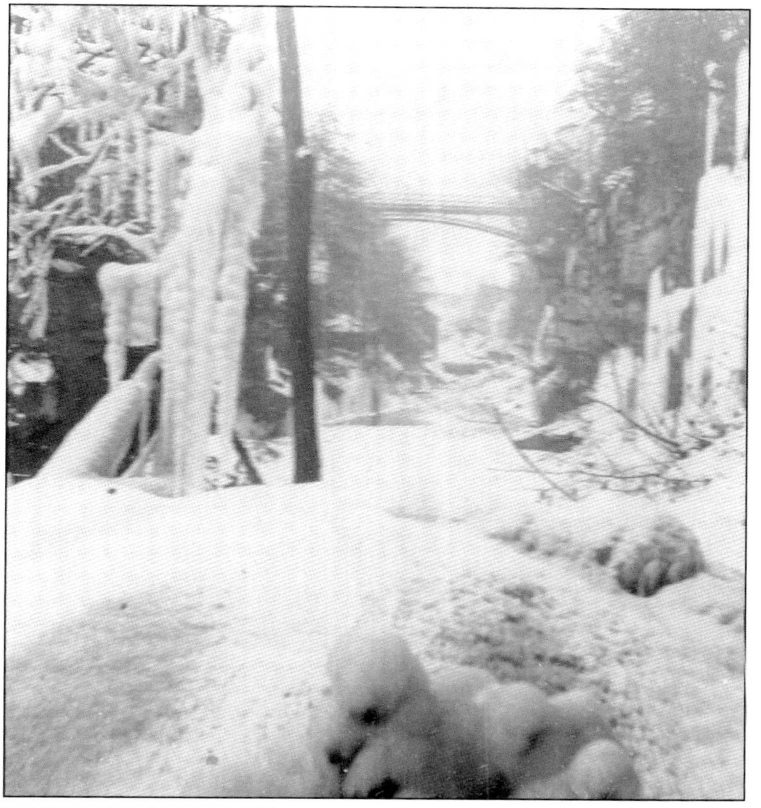

A look toward the Front Street half of the Glens reveals that the Weeping Cliffs did not have a monopoly on massive ice displays; this early image shows the area near the pavilion draped in icicles. Over the years, the owner of the Glens expanded the pavilions, adding a long dining hall. (Cuyahoga Falls Library.)

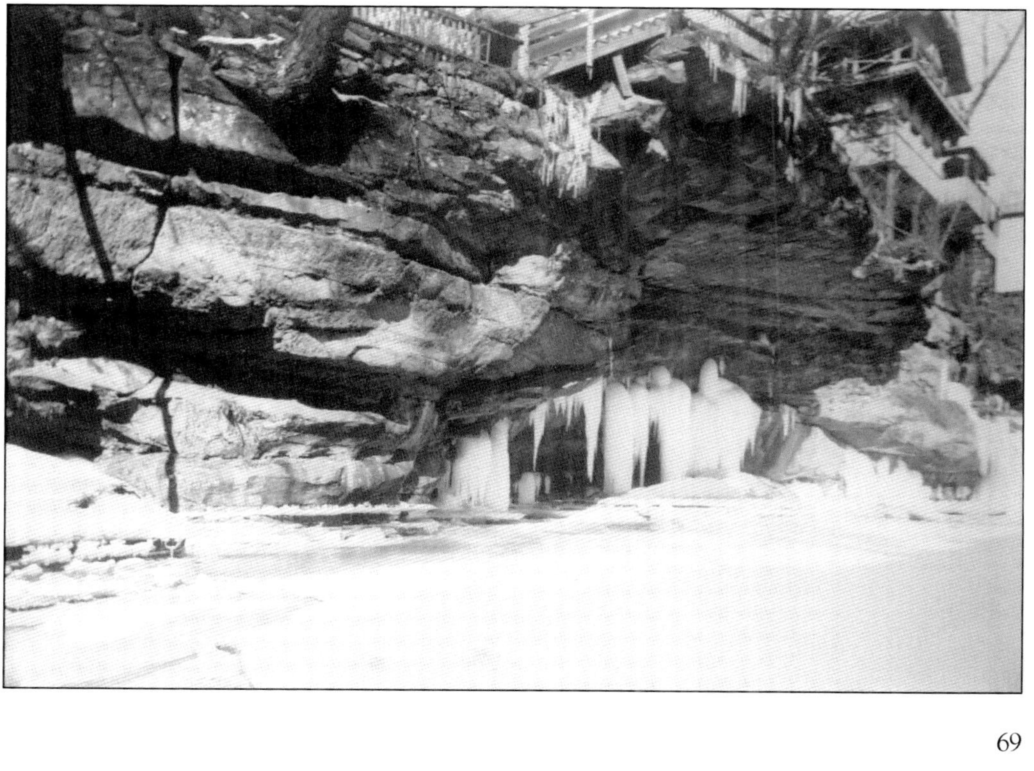

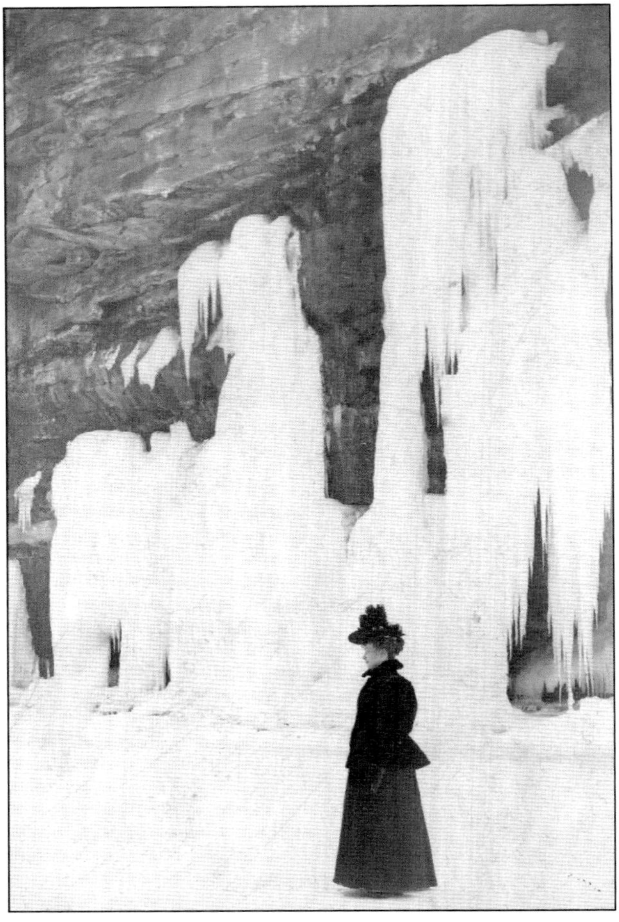

Cleveland photographer James F. Ryder and others came to the Glens to record winter views. Here, a woman stands near Weeping Cliffs. (Cuyahoga Falls Historical Society.)

This man chose to have his photograph taken on the iced-over suspension bridge; note how nattily attired he is. Though the park was a popular stop in winter, it did not draw the same volume as at the height of the summer, when up to 60 trainloads of passengers arrived daily. (Cuyahoga Falls Historical Society.)

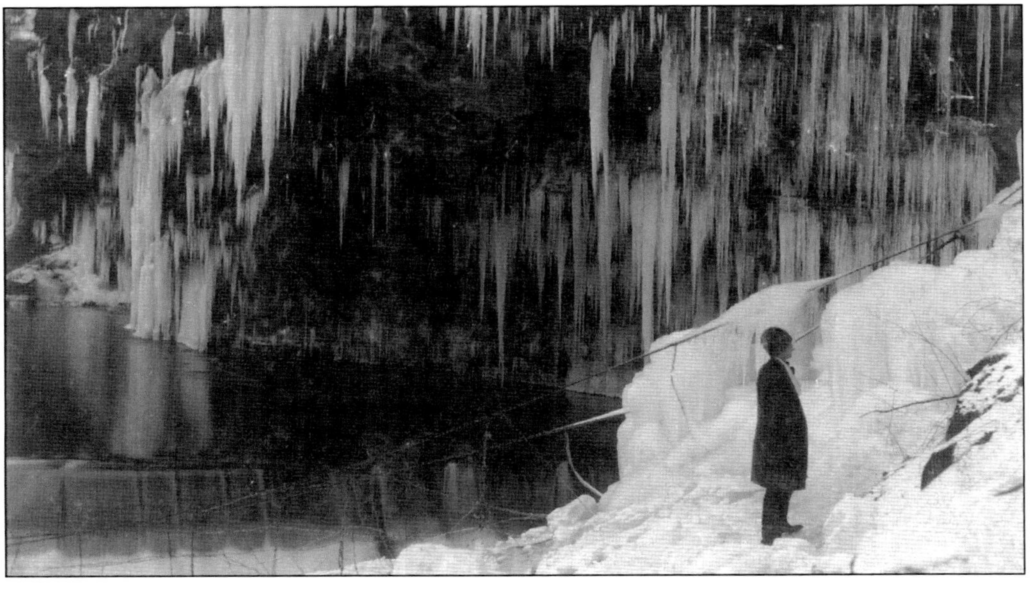

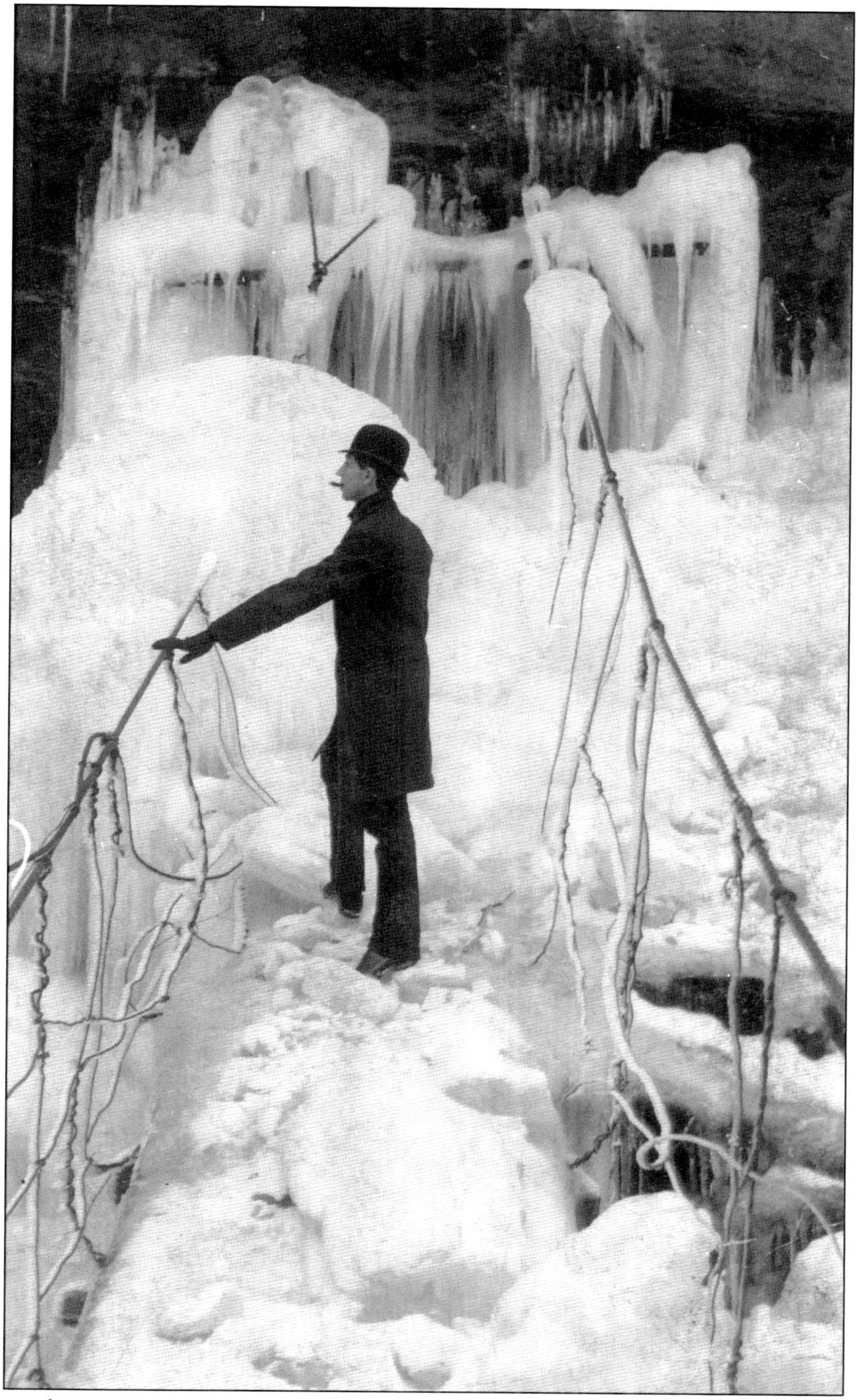

If crossing the suspension bridge seemed difficult in summer, it was doubly tricky when it was caked in ice, as shown in this rare winter scene. The harsh weather conditions rapidly aged the bridge, necessitating ongoing maintenance and repairs. (Cuyahoga Falls Historical Society.)

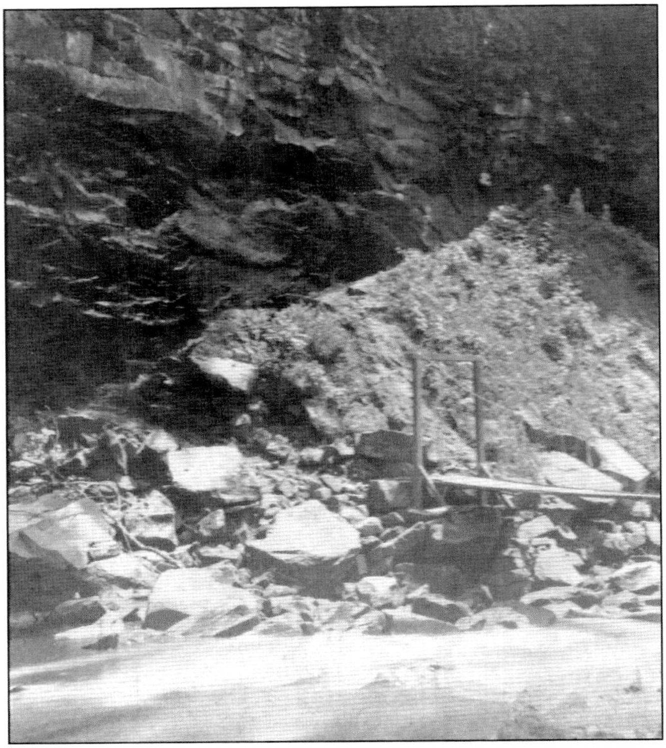

In the summer season, after stopping to admire Weeping Cliffs, visitors could walk along a one-mile camelback trail called the Grand Promenade. The path was bounded by tall cliffs on one side and by shady trees on the other. (Eric Thompson collection.)

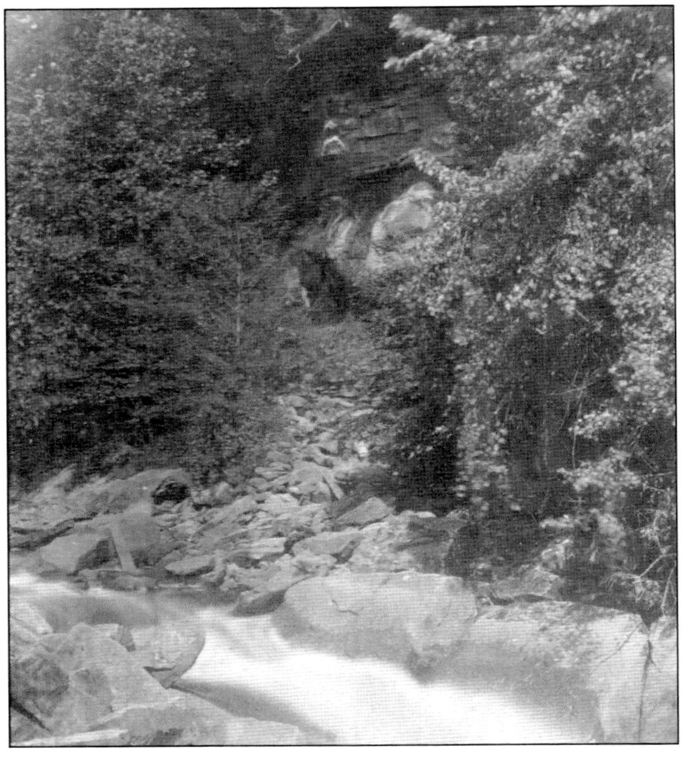

The trail of the Grand Promenade followed the remains of a former water race known as the Chuckery. In 1837, Dr. Eliakim Crosby of Akron had a plan to divert water from the Cuyahoga River, just south of the High Bridge at the Glens, into a race or channel. The water would then be channeled southward and used to power a new community in Akron to be known as Summit City. Construction of the race began around 1840 or 1841 and was completed in 1844. After several leaks developed, the Chuckery was abandoned. (Eric Thompson collection.)

This view, taken from the western half of the Glens looking east, shows the remains of the Chuckery from a distance. The Chuckery got its name after someone inquired about the population of Dr. Eliakim Crosby's Summit City, and since the Chuckery did not fulfill its ambitions, the reply was reportedly "one man and 9,999 woodchucks." (Eric Thompson collection.)

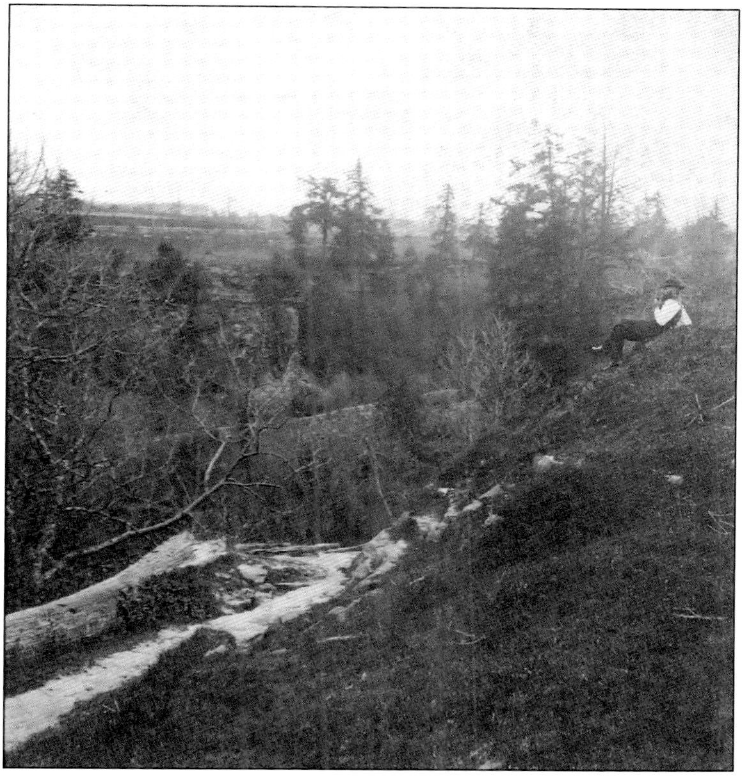

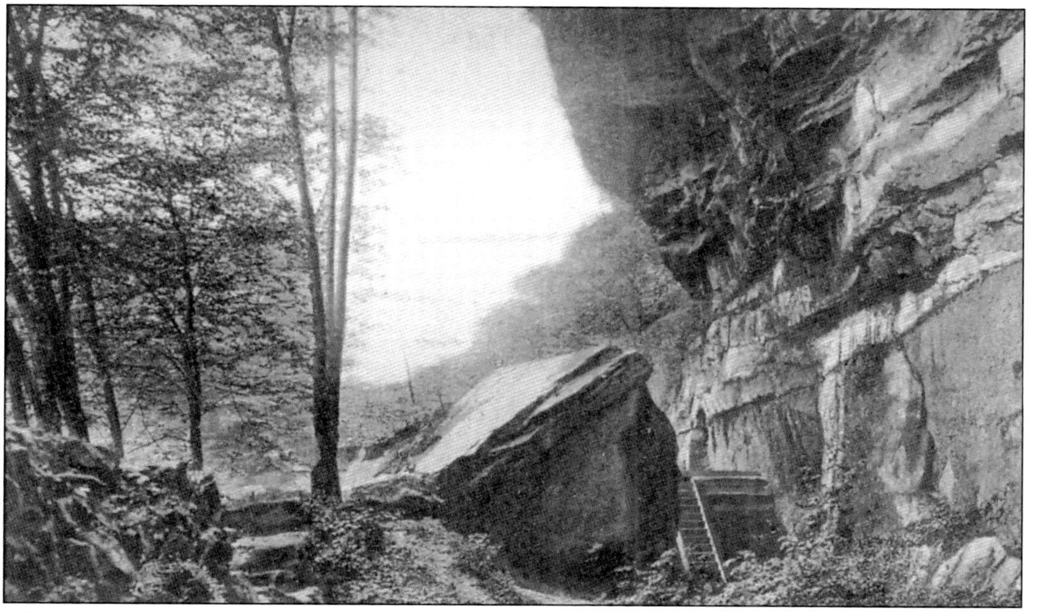

Although the Chuckery did not work out as planned, Victorians were still in admiration of the tremendous vision and engineering it took to create the water race. According to early newspaper accounts, visitors to the Glens could hike along the Chuckery and, for an additional fee, pass into the Gorge and enjoy its stunning scenery. (Author's collection.)

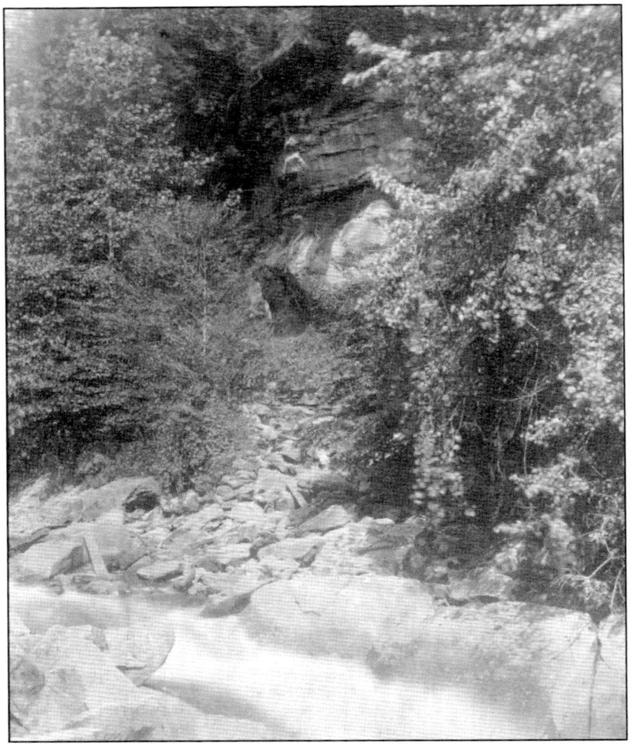

This 19th-century photograph depicts fast-moving water and a break in the Chuckery. According to local historians, the Chuckery Race was approximately 30 feet wide and eight feet deep. (Eric Thompson collection.)

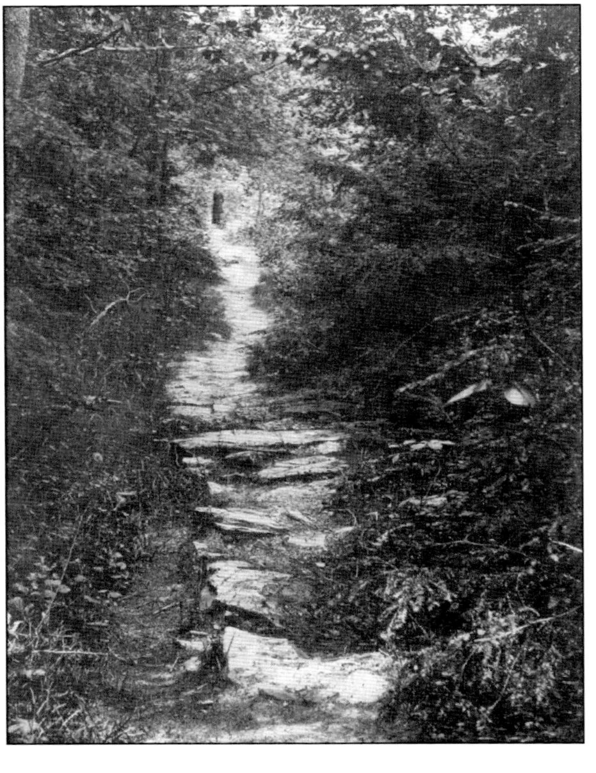

In this image, the stones from the old water race are visible on the path. One side of the Chuckery race was built with sandstone blocks cut by hand. Today, the remains of the Chuckery are listed in the National Register of Historic Places. (Cuyahoga Falls Historical Society.)

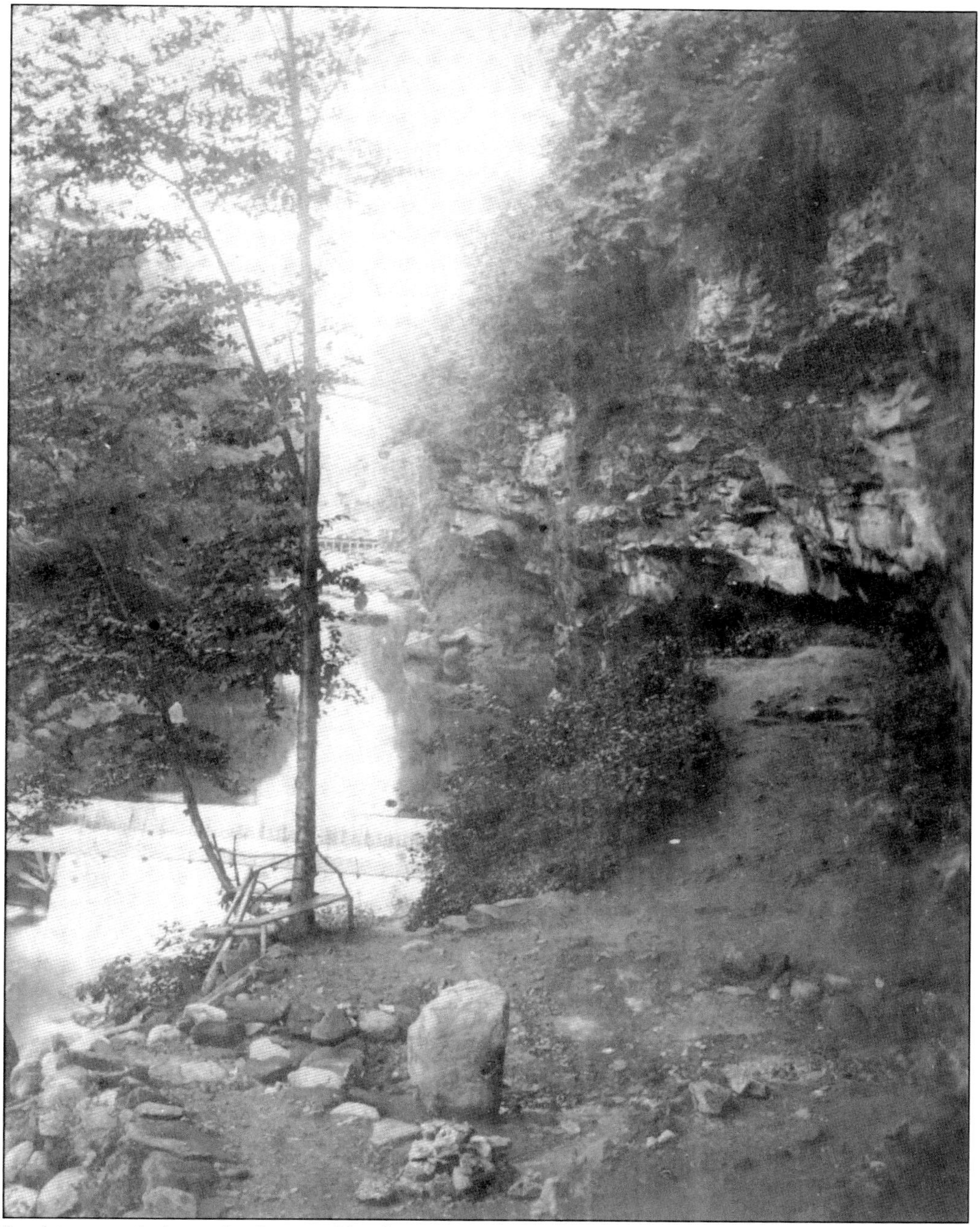

Looking north from the former Chuckery, visitors saw beautiful scenery. In the late 1800s, one local resident proposed creating a "trotting path" along that route so couples could drive along the Glens via horse and carriage; the plan never became a reality. (Author's collection.)

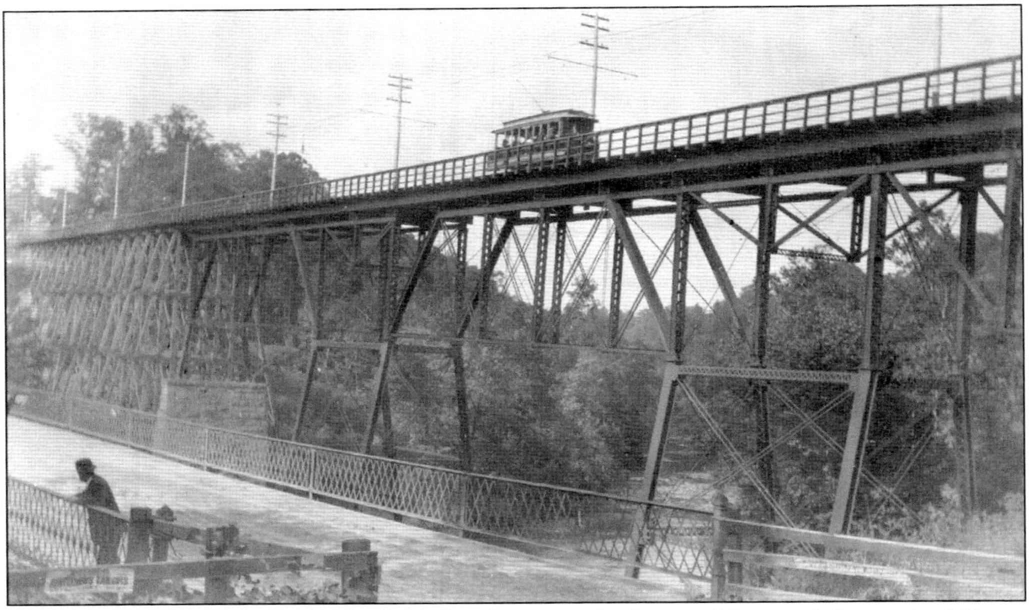

The area that currently marks the boundary between the former Glens and the original Gorge park once contained two bridges. The taller bridge carried streetcar traffic, while the shorter one was used for pedestrians or horse-and-buggy traffic. (Cuyahoga Falls Historical Society.)

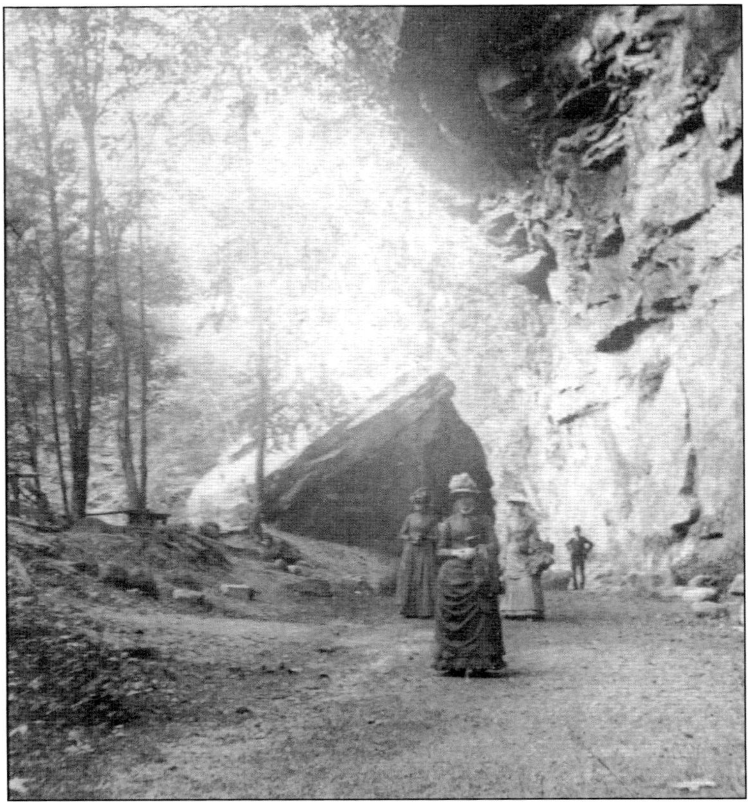

This area was known by a variety of names, including Cathedral Pass (presumably due to its proximity to the Cathedral Cliffs). The large, triangular-shaped formation in the background was called Anchor Rock. Local historians wrote that the rock was given this name because it was used to "anchor" one part of the dam at the Chuckery. (Cuyahoga Falls Library.)

Boards lined the path by Cathedral Pass. No specific details about this area have been found, but modern historians speculate that the boards were either remains of a structure at the path or Chuckery, or that they were perhaps placed there to keep the hems of women's dresses from dragging through the mud as they hiked in the Glens. (John and Janet Waldsmith collection.)

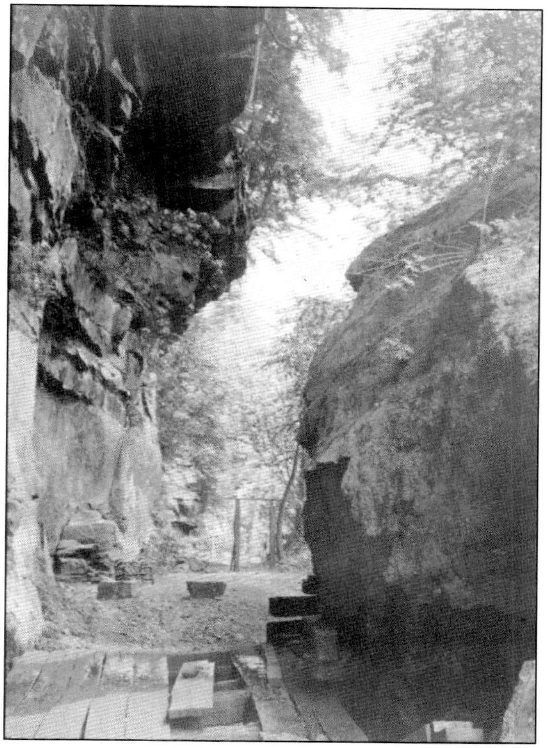

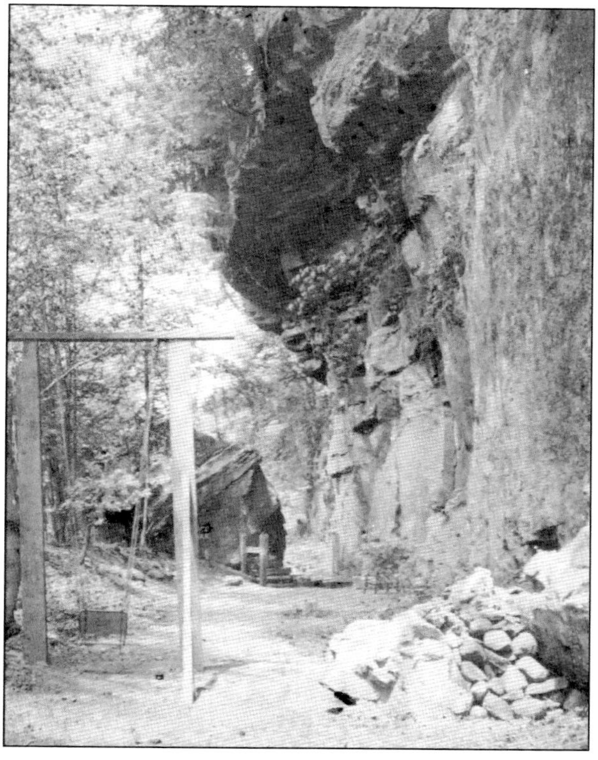

In addition to benches and rustic seating, the park's owners placed swings near Cathedral Pass. While these swings are quite sedate, later owners added a ride known as the "Mikado Swing" to the park. Swing seats were hung from a central metal pole; as riders spun around the pole, they were carried higher and higher into the air. (Author's collection.)

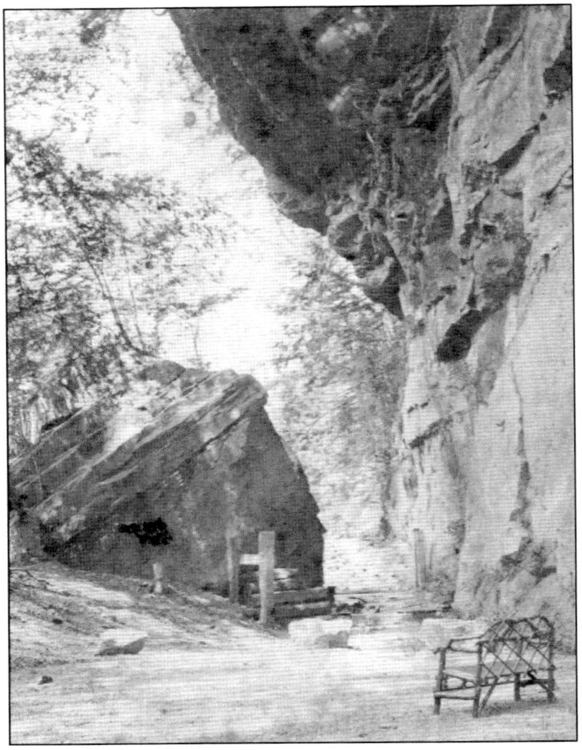

Ornamental chairs were also placed at this popular picnic spot. Where the owners had to place man-made articles throughout the park, they endeavored to make those items blend in with the park's natural features. (Author's collection.)

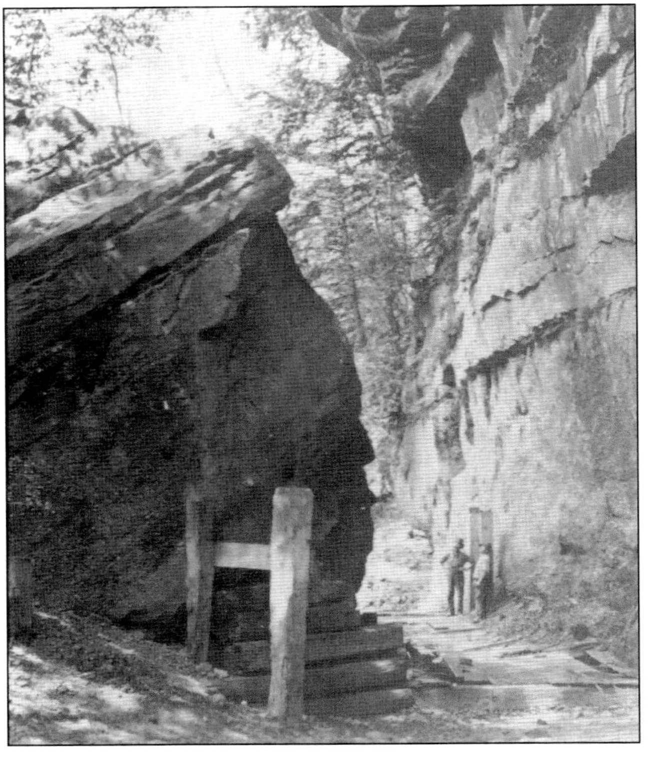

Thanks to stunning scenes such as these, newspaper reporters who visited the Glens thought the park was more picturesque than Watkins Glen (in New York), the Franconia Glen (in New Hampshire), or other naturally gorgeous spots across the United States. Newspapers quickly dubbed the Glens "the Niagara of Ohio" and the "Switzerland of Ohio." (Author's collection.)

Cathedral Pass was a lovely spot for visitors to have photographs taken. It was also a very scenic hiking spot. According to information painted on the left side of the rock, there was a special path designated as a "Ladies Walk." (Author's collection.)

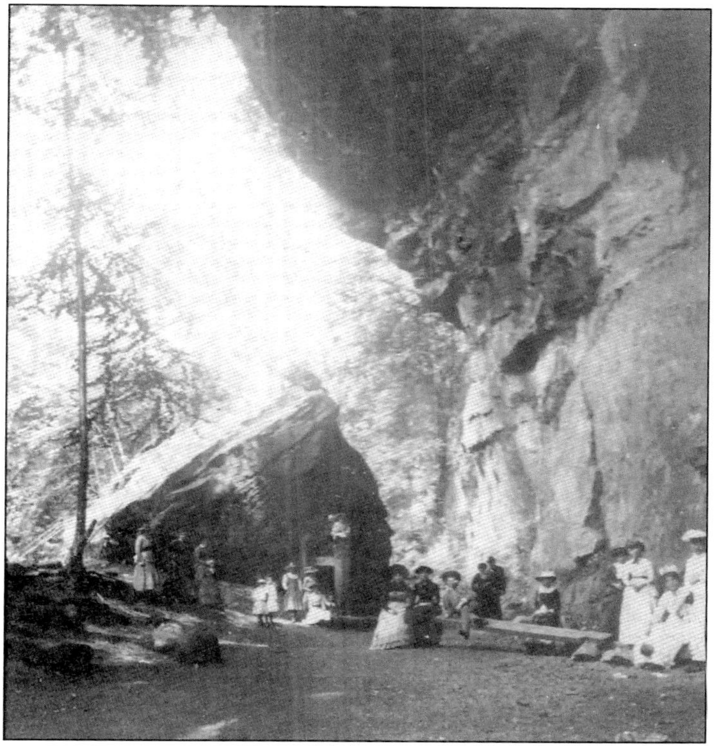

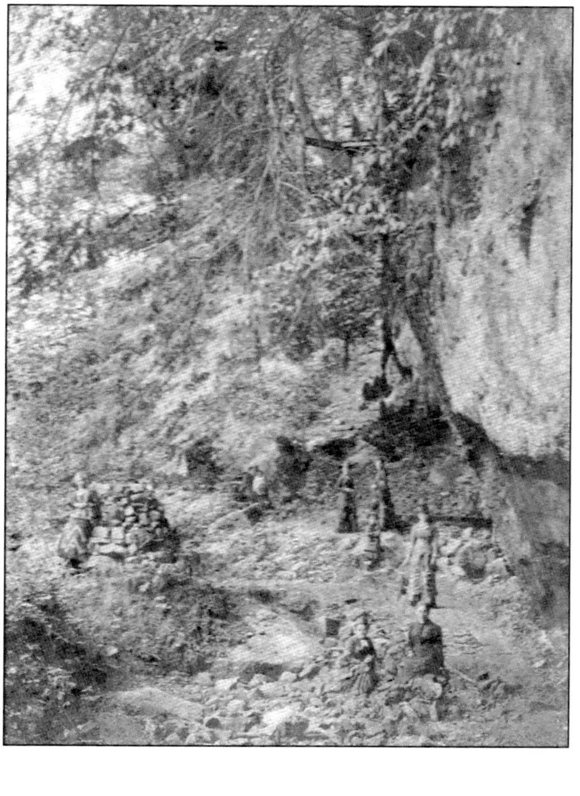

The towering sandstone provided a dramatic backdrop for this photograph, which shows women at Cathedral Cliffs. Modern-day visitors to the former Glens occasionally have trouble maintaining their footing on the trails and frequently marvel at how Victorian women managed to avoid tripping on the rocks and roots along the paths while wearing high-button shoes. (Author's collection.)

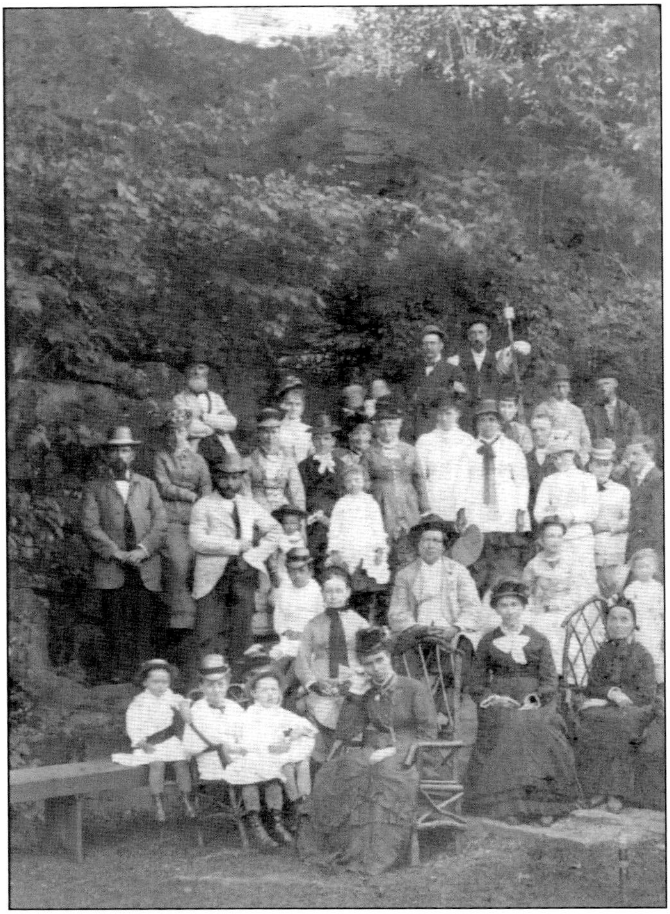

A picnic group poses for a photograph at an area believed to be near Cathedral Pass. In the park's early years, before alcohol was allowed, the Glens was considered an ideal spot to hold a Sunday school excursion or school trip. (Cuyahoga Falls Library.)

Anchor Rock was another popular place to pose for pictures. Although the Cuyahoga River has since covered many features at the former Glens park, Anchor Rock is still visible today. (Cuyahoga Falls Historical Society.)

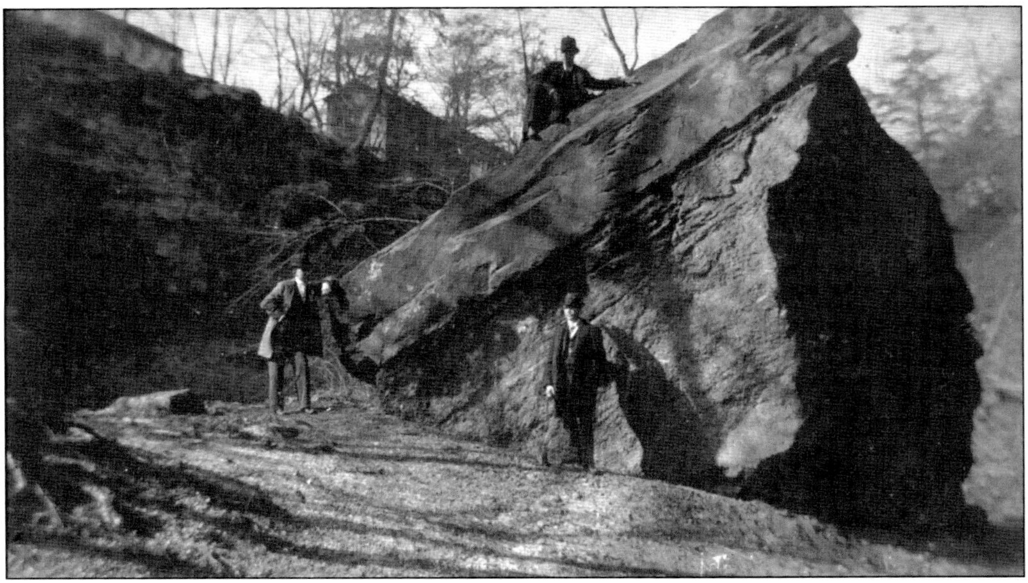

This is another view of Cathedral Cliffs. The Glens, especially beautiful when the plants and trees begin to bud in spring, are also quite lovely in the fall, when the leaves turn all shades of gold, red, and brown. (John and Janet Waldsmith collection.)

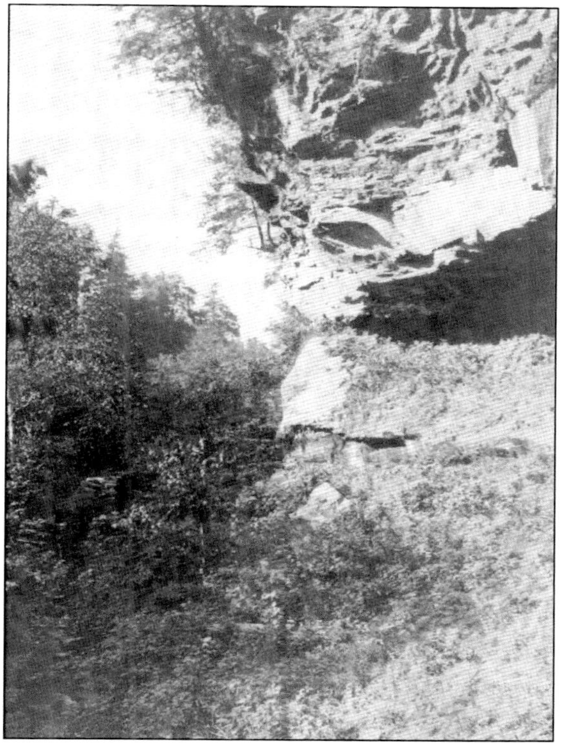

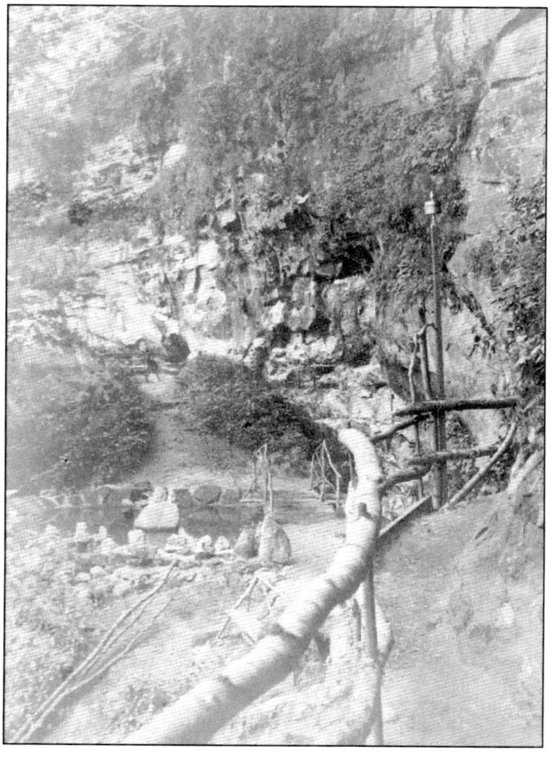

From this overlook, visitors could see a small body of water ringed by small, pointed rocks. This area was known as Mirror Lake and Crown Point. The names were in recognition of the reflective qualities of the lake and because the rocks that circled the lake resembled points on a crown. Also visible are a rustic bridge over the little lake and a kerosene lantern (visible at right) by the stick fence along the overlook. (John and Janet Waldsmith collection.)

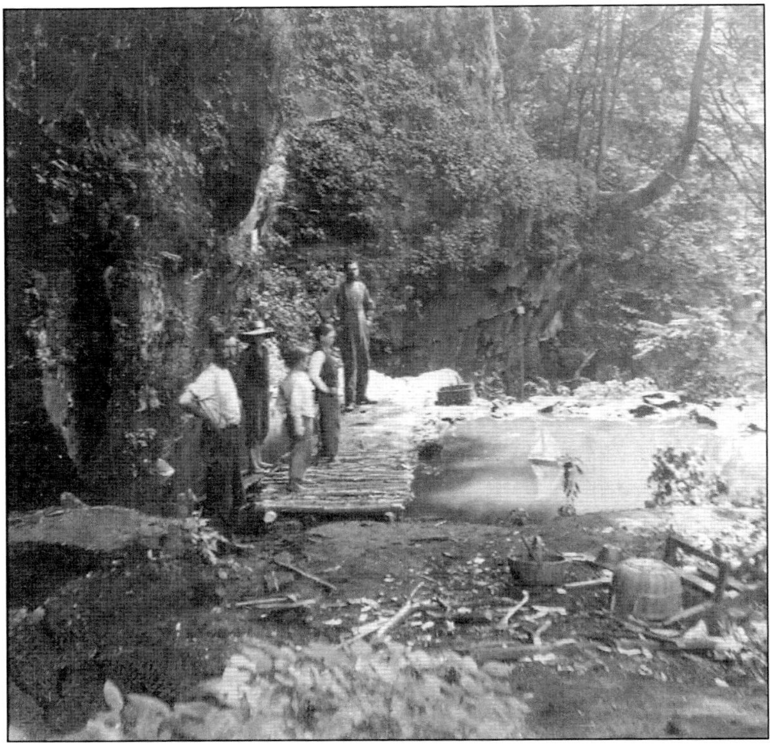

The park's owners had Mirror Lake and Crown Point specifically constructed for young children. Note the toy boat on the lake, as well as the picnic baskets in the foreground. (Author's collection.)

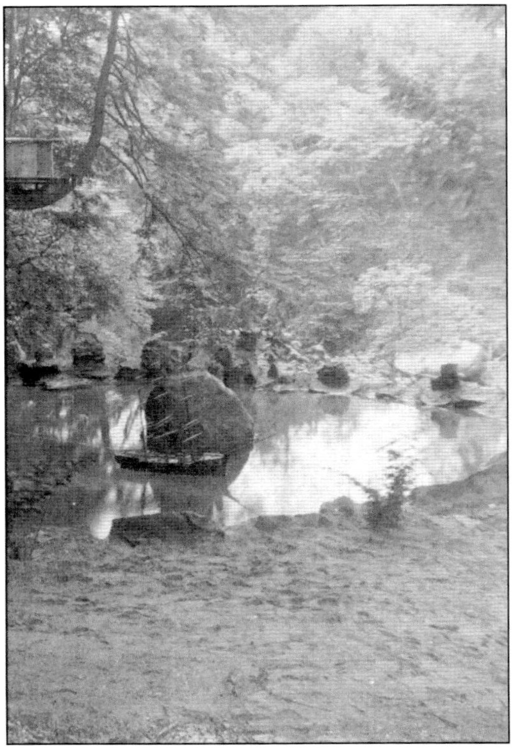

Floating toy boats was a well-loved pastime for children at Mirror Lake. According to reporters, in the early years of the Glens visitors and their children could enjoy a trip to the park without being bothered by ne'er-do-wells; however, in one rare incident, a man snatched a paper fan out of the hands of a young girl and refused to return it. (John and Janet Waldsmith collection.)

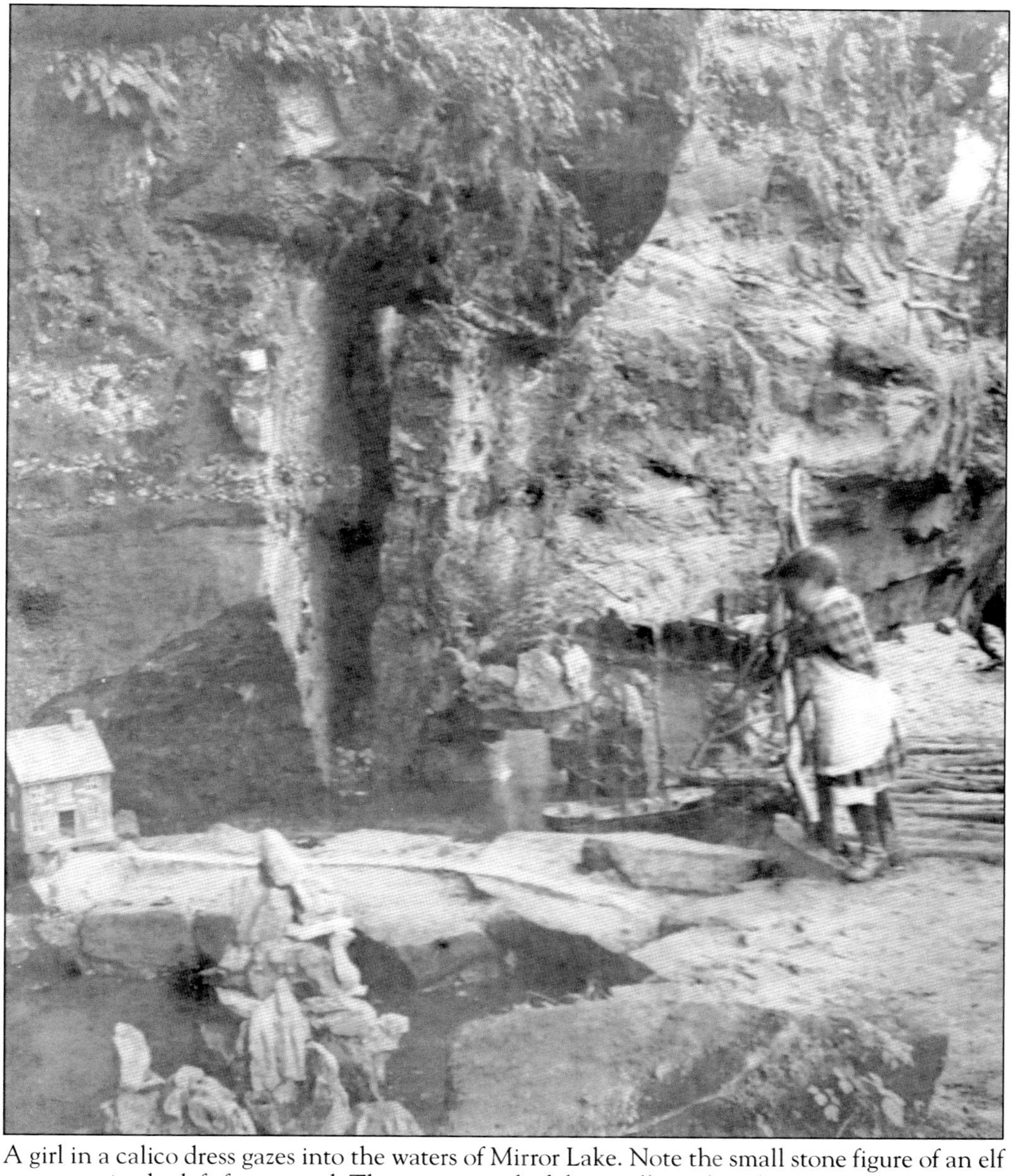

A girl in a calico dress gazes into the waters of Mirror Lake. Note the small stone figure of an elf or gnome in the left foreground. This was typical of the small touches the owners added to the park specifically for children. (John and Janet Waldsmith collection.)

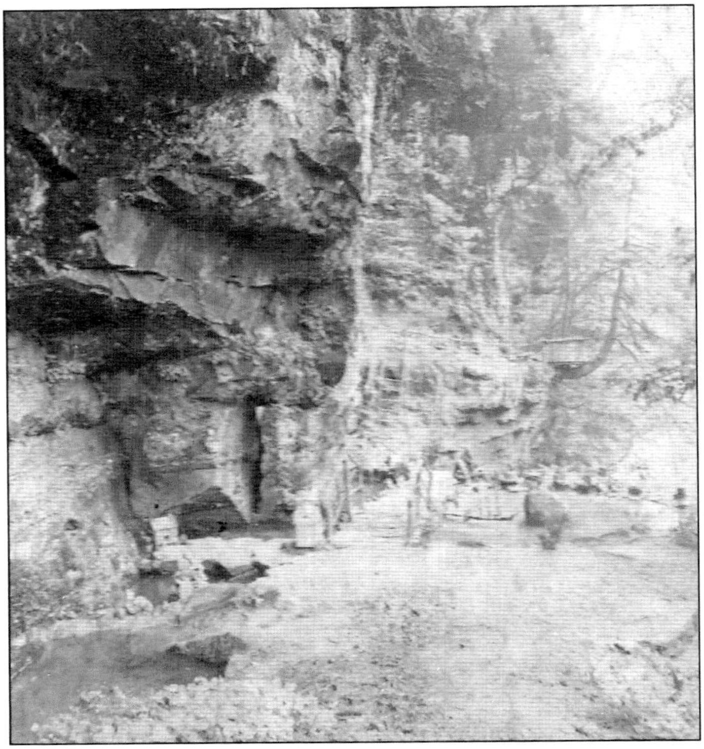

A small bridge provided safe passage from Mirror Lake to an observation platform in the trees. Artists particularly enjoyed painting this vista by moonlight. (Author's collection.)

Besides offering many amusements for children, the area near Mirror Lake offered thrilling vantage points for visitors of all ages. Note the crude stairs leading to a wooden viewing platform tucked into the curve of a tree. (Cuyahoga Falls Library.)

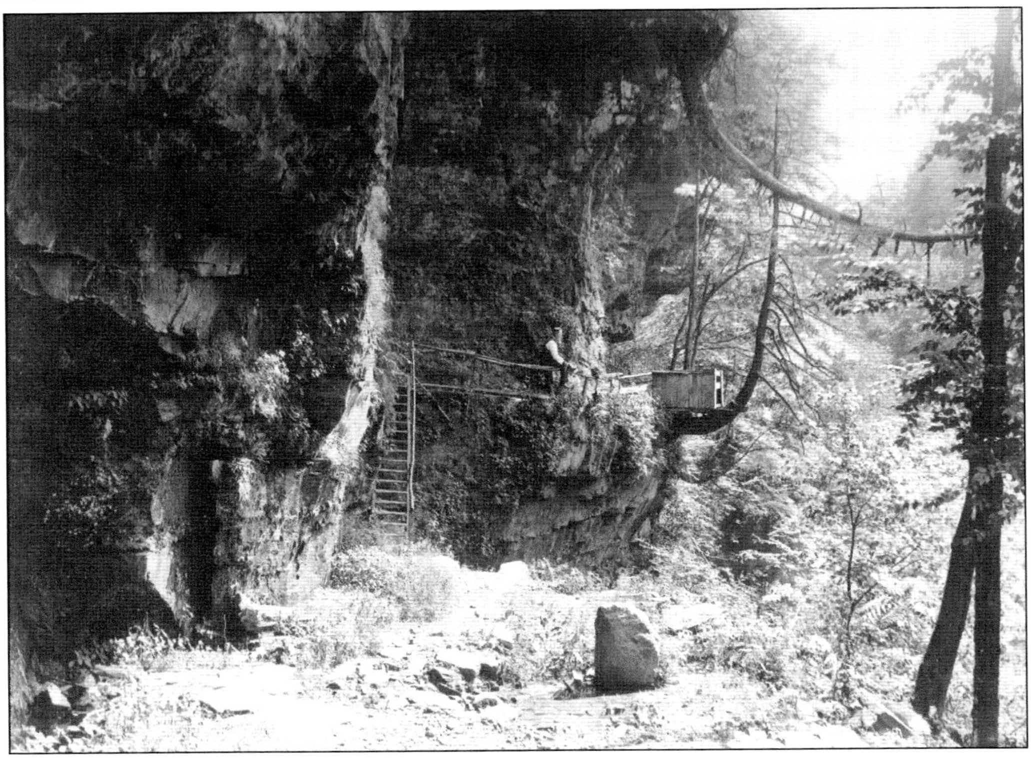

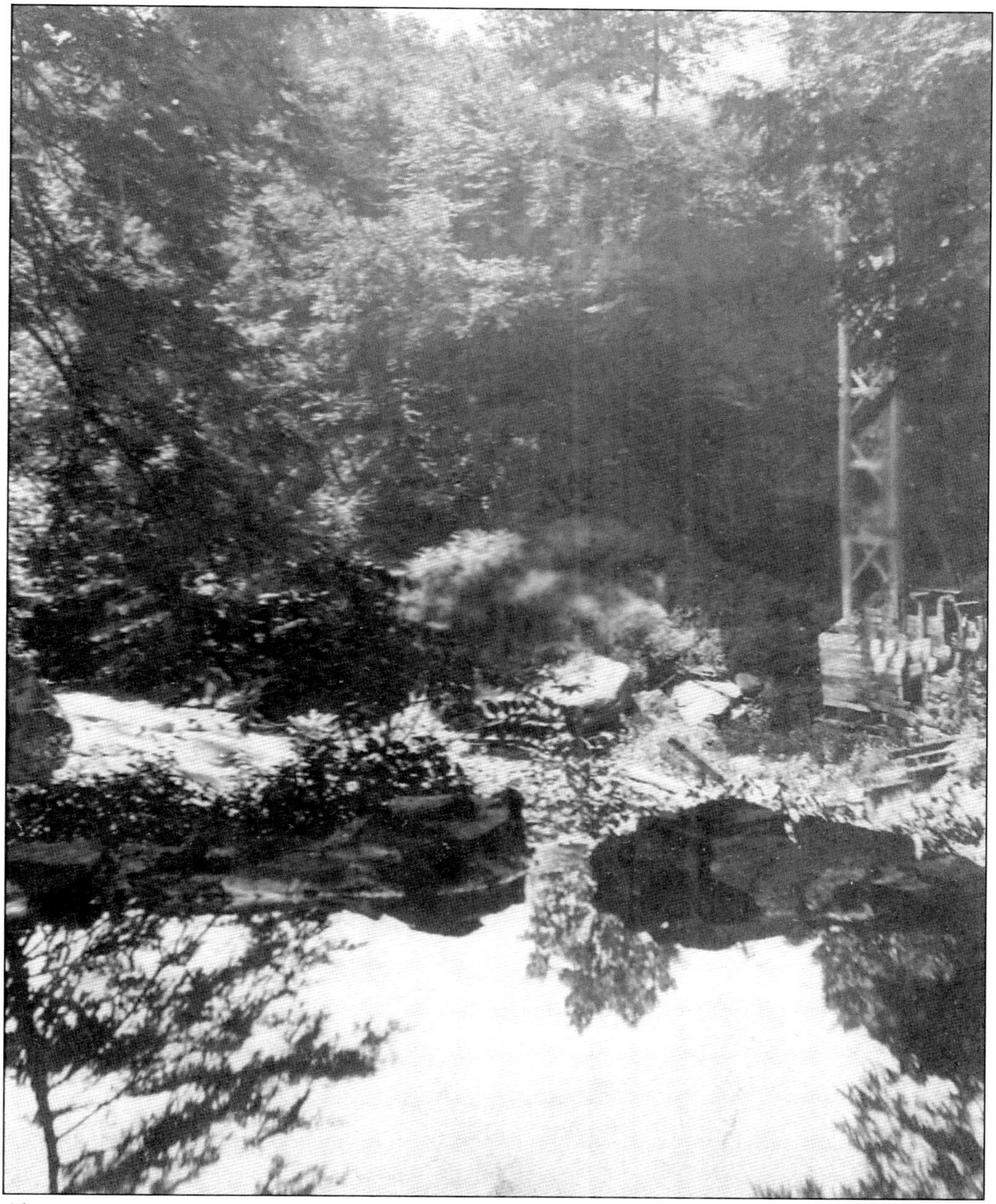

Close to Mirror Lake was a feature identified by the photographer of this image, H.L. Shumway of Cuyahoga Falls, only as "Ruins of Husk." Contemporary historians have speculated whether the husk was a portion of some early manufacturing operation predating the park. Others have described it as a sort of elevator or observation tower. To date, no definitive answer has been found. (Eric Thompson collection.)

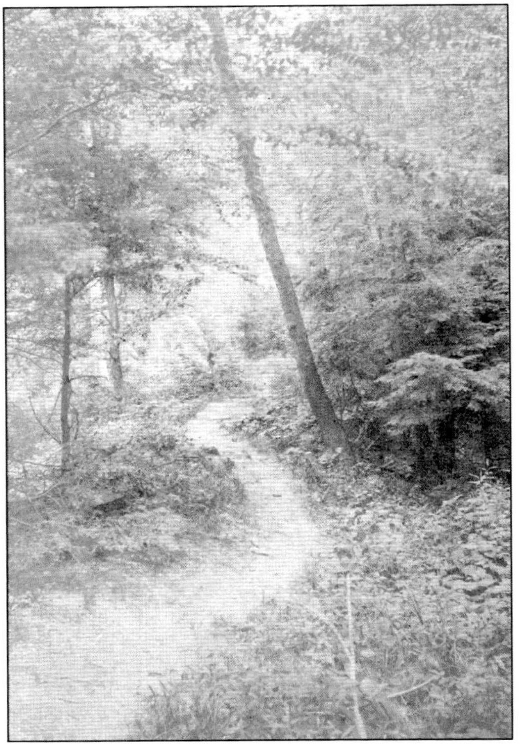

Like many summer resorts, the Glens had winding paths and Lovers' Lanes where sweethearts could be alone. According to early newspaper accounts, while the young men who visited the Glens enjoyed the natural scenery, they also admired the park's many female visitors, including "the face and form divine." (John and Janet Waldsmith collection.)

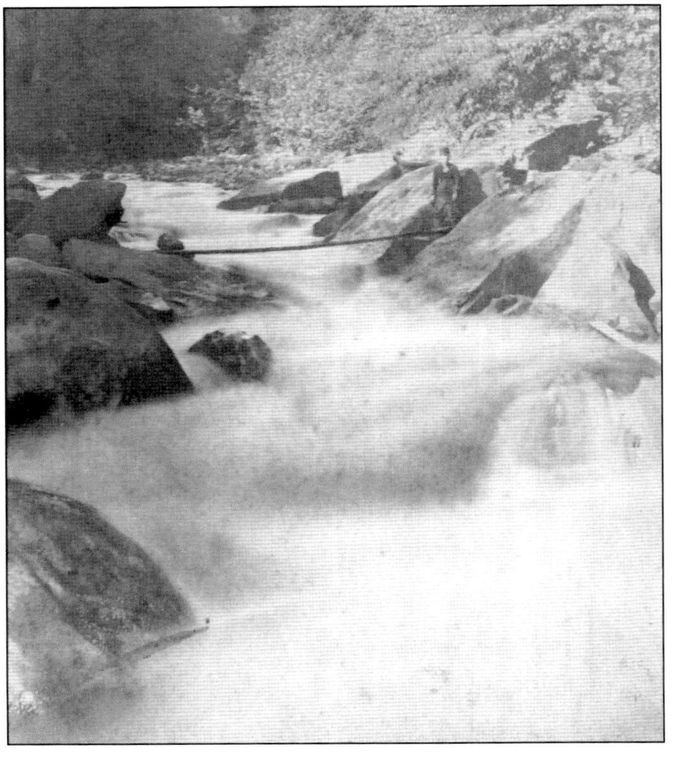

The raw waterpower of the Cuyahoga River thrilled Victorian visitors. Here, a woman poses by the fast-moving water. Other visitors were photographed sitting on the rock and reading a book while the mighty Cuyahoga made its way downstream. (John and Janet Waldsmith collection.)

*Five*

# Enhancing the Glens

## Other Thrilling Features

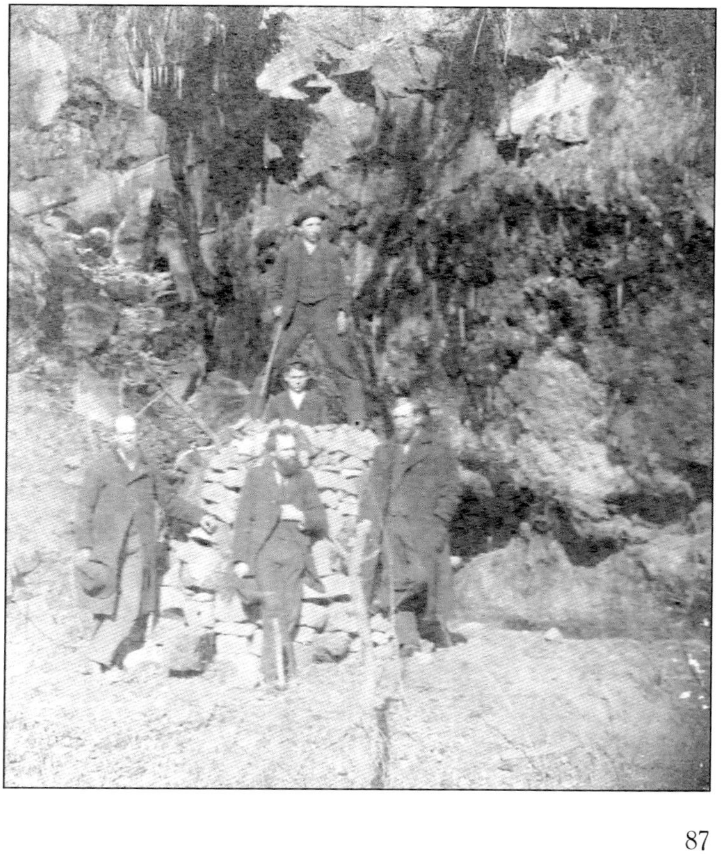

Although park brochures and Victorian-era newspaper articles provide valuable clues about where various features were located at the Glens, the location of certain features captured by photographers is not as clear. While many of the views in this chapter are part of the Glens, others appear to be more closely associated with the nearby Gorge. An unidentified photographer labeled this scene at the Glens as "Pompey's Pillar." (Author's collection.)

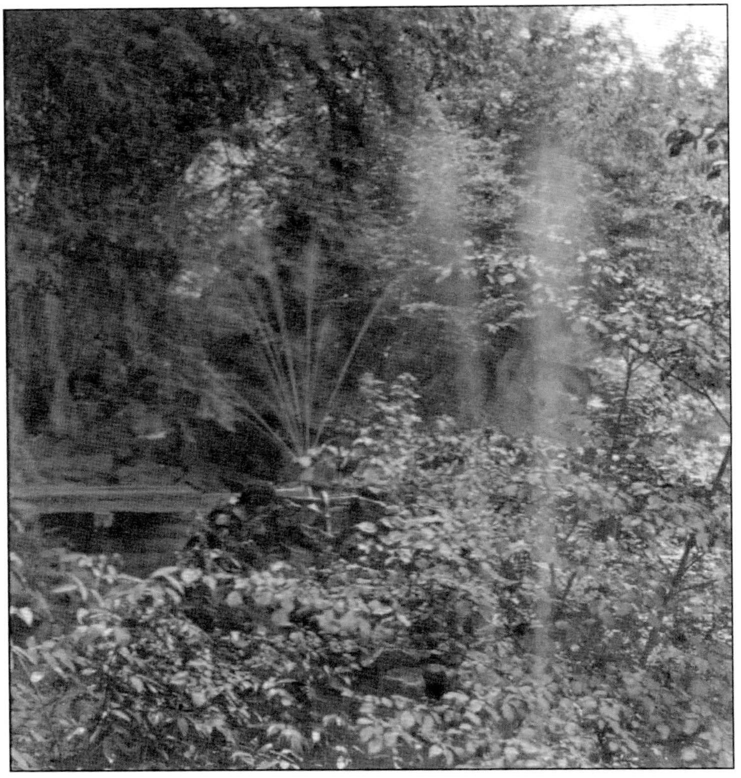

In 1879, the owners added a feature known as Needle Springs to the park. Needle Springs was described as a "pretty arch of water" jetting from the rocks in a cooling spray. Cooling waters were especially appreciated, as visitors wore full-length gowns or woolen suits to the park—even on the hottest summer days. (John and Janet Waldsmith collection.)

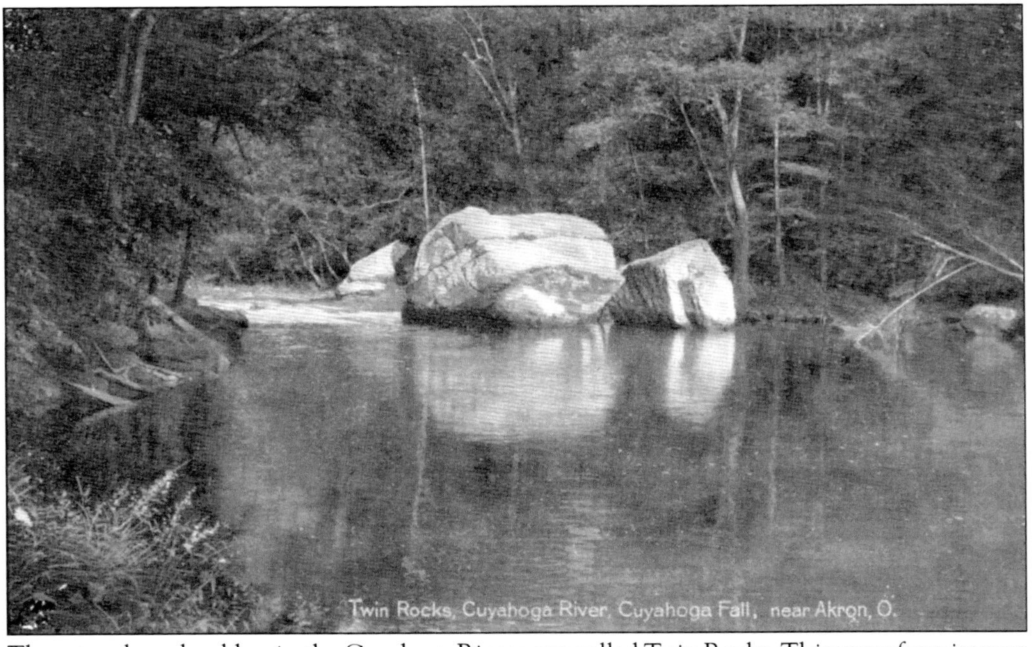


These two large boulders in the Cuyahoga River were called Twin Rocks. This was a favorite spot for children, who enjoyed sunning themselves on the rocks after a brisk dip in one of the area's popular swimming holes. (Author's collection.)

Other photographers labeled this scene "Artist's Study," because Victorian ladies drawing in their sketchbooks frequently recorded it. Mrs. T.F. Walsh, a prominent local resident, owned a large oil painting of the Glens. (John and Janet Waldsmith collection.)

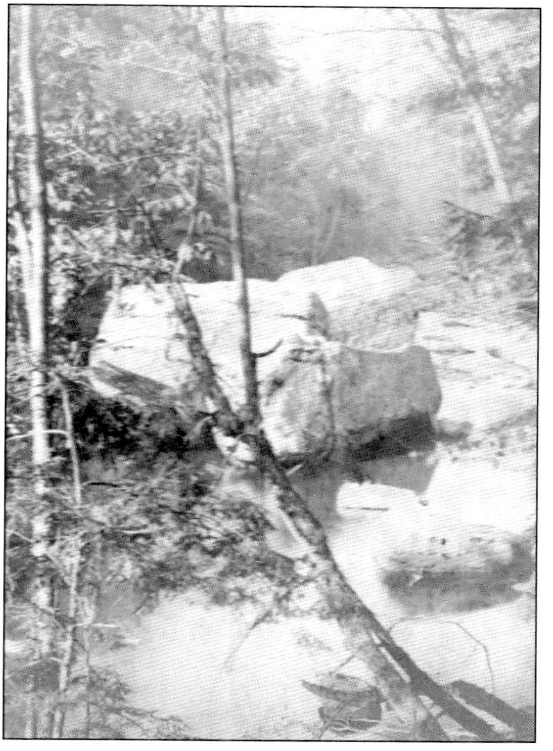

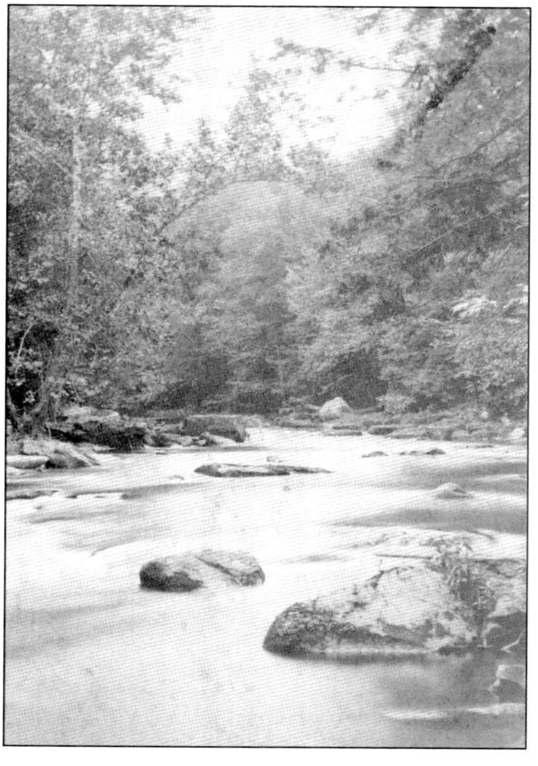

Further downstream from the Glens, the Cuyahoga River formed this charming scene. Although the photographer labeled this scene and subsequent views as being in the High Bridge Glens series of stereo views, some of the features appear to be located in the nearby Gorge park. (John and Janet Waldsmith collection.)

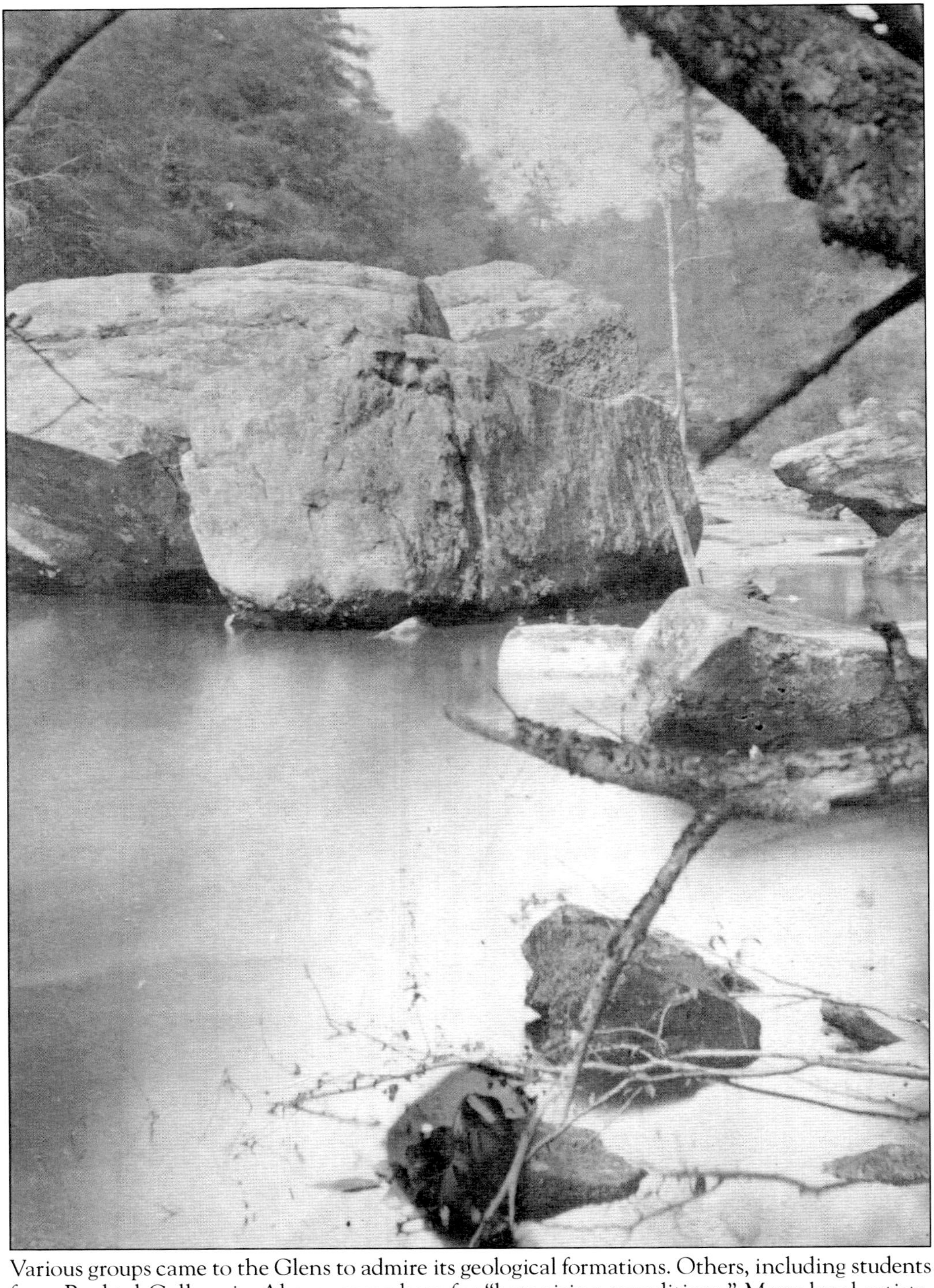

Various groups came to the Glens to admire its geological formations. Others, including students from Buchtel College in Akron, came here for "botanizing expeditions." Many local artists, including A.T. Van Lair of Buchtel College's art school, came to the Glens to sketch the scenery, including the Twin Rocks pictured here. (John and Janet Waldsmith collection.)

All along the paths in the Glens were seeps and springs where visitors could refresh themselves by splashing cool water on their faces. Buchtel College Cary Society members held an annual picnic at the Glens and enjoyed dangling their feet in the cool waters of the Cuyahoga. (Cuyahoga Falls Library.)

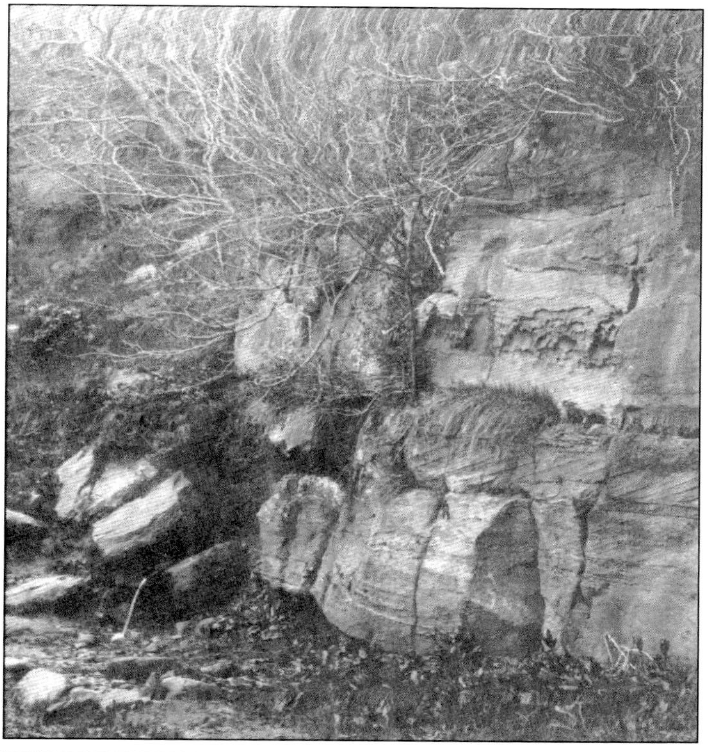

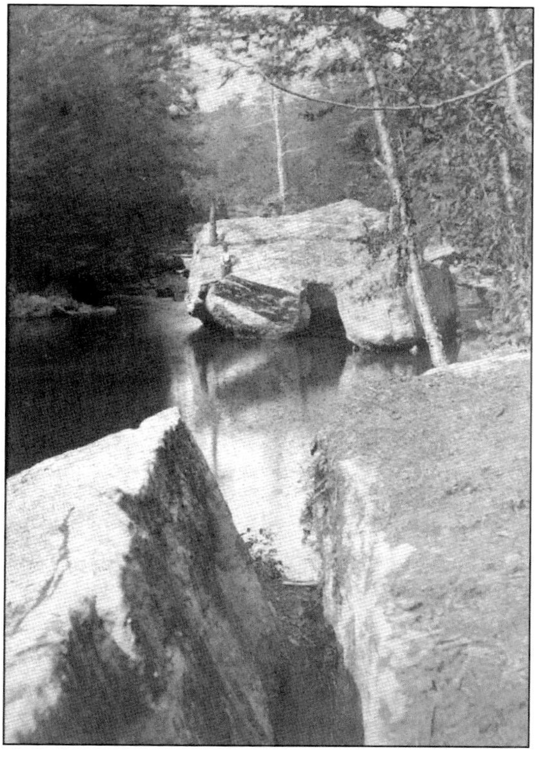

The photographer titled this view "Split Rocks" because of the rocks in the foreground. In the background are the Twin Rocks. These two large boulders gave swimmers yet another convenient place to sun themselves after splashing in the Cuyahoga River. (Cuyahoga Falls Library.)

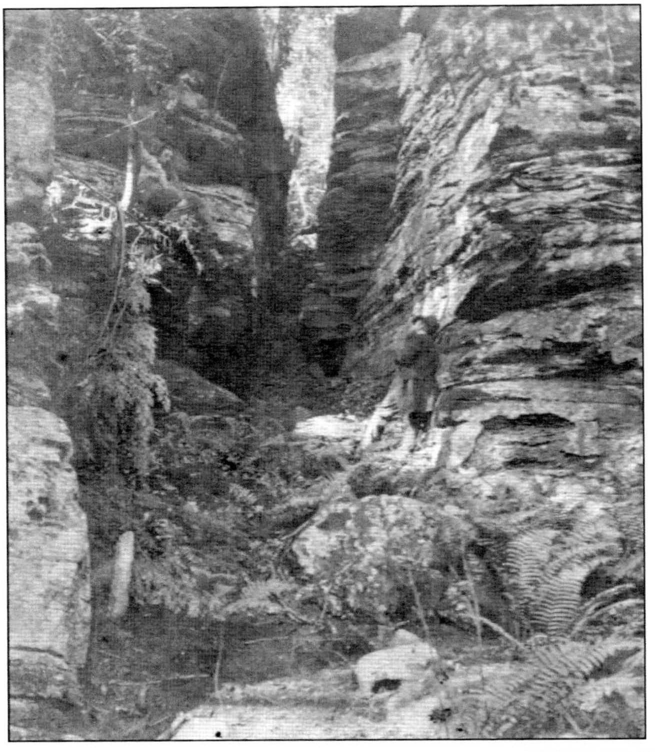

This scene, part of the High Bridge Glens series of stereo views by Gates, is named "Labyrinth." Although it is labeled "Glens," it may actually be part of the nearby Gorge. Note the man posing to the right of the split in the rocks amidst ferns and other vegetation. (Author's collection.)

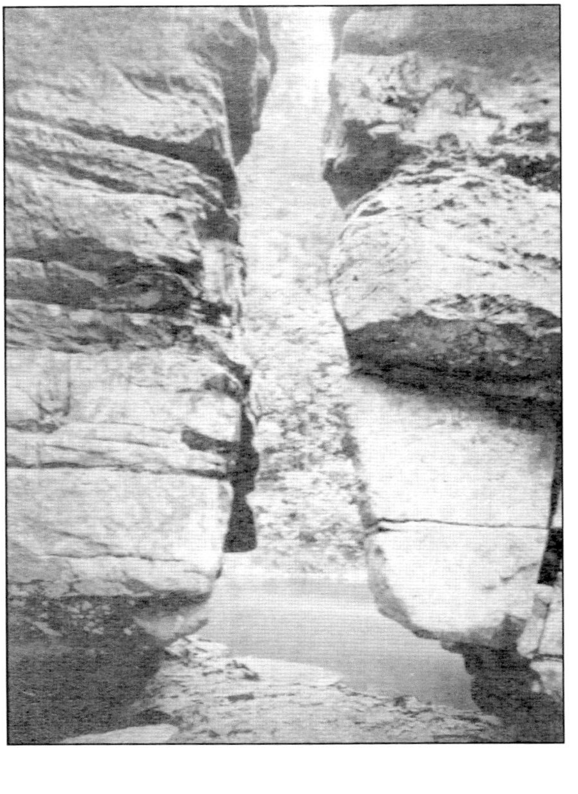

The trail that ran between these two rocks was known as Sentinel's Pass. An early visitor to the park wrote, "If a traveler were to visit all the famous spots within a radius of 1,000 miles, he could not find one more attractive by nature." (Author's collection.)

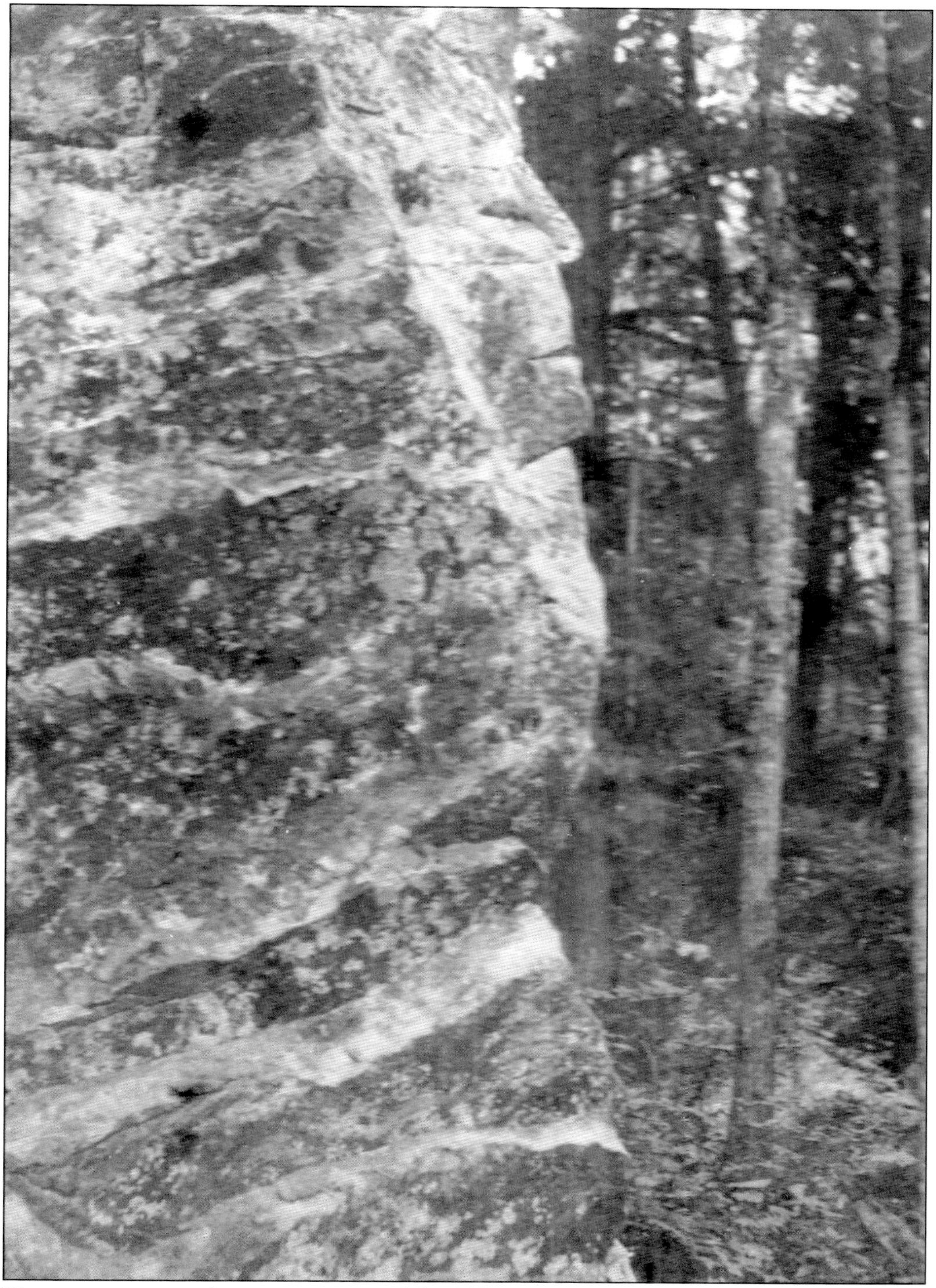

This intriguing stone formation was named the Old Guard of the Glens. Note how there appears to be a man's face in profile in the top third of the rock formation. No information has been found about whether the guard's face was man-made or a naturally occurring feature. (Author's collection.)

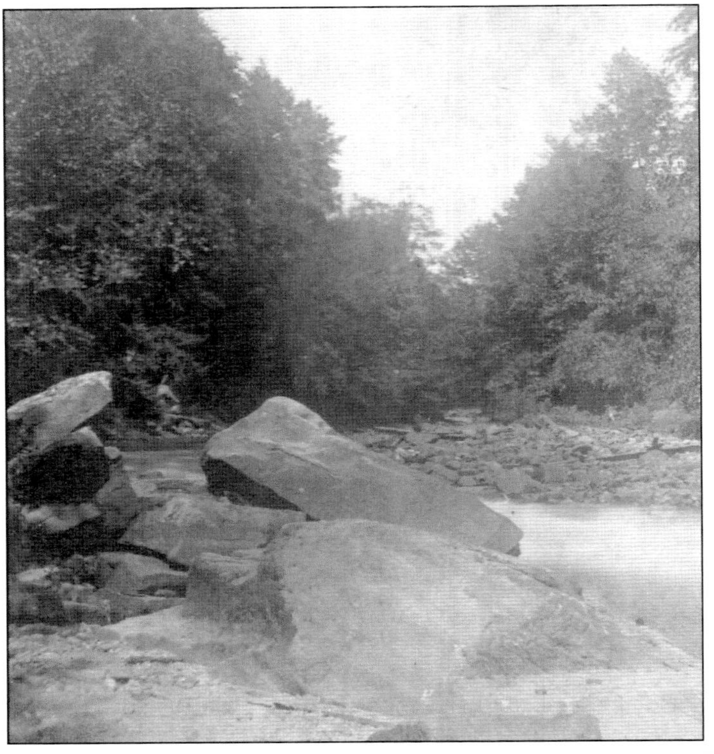

This photograph was taken along an area of the Cuyahoga River up from the "Old Starchery." (Eric Thompson collection.)

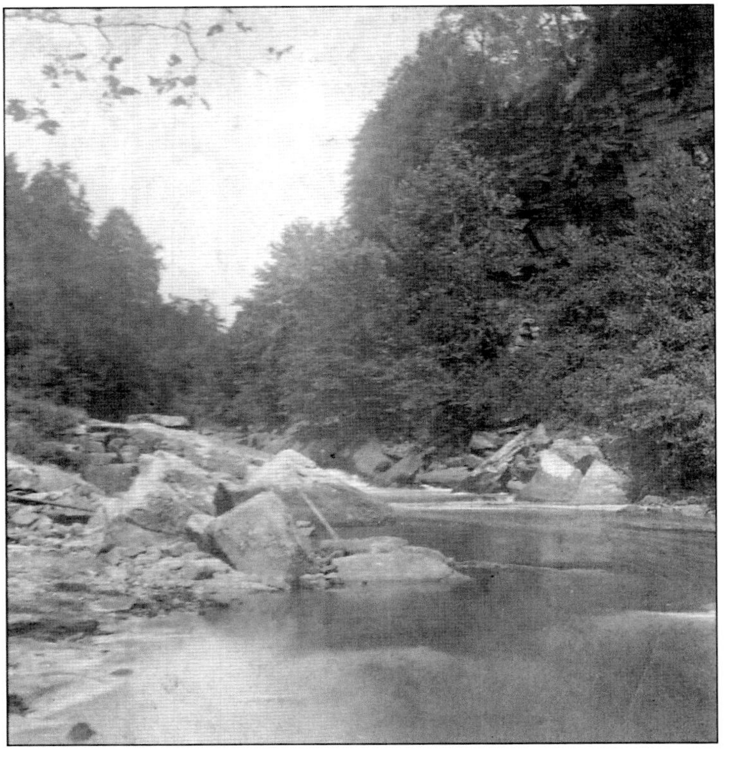

Contemporary historians are not certain about exactly what or where the "Starchery" was, but it may be an old starch factory that early resident Birdsey Booth reportedly operated along the Cuyahoga River in the Glens or Gorge. (Eric Thompson collection.)

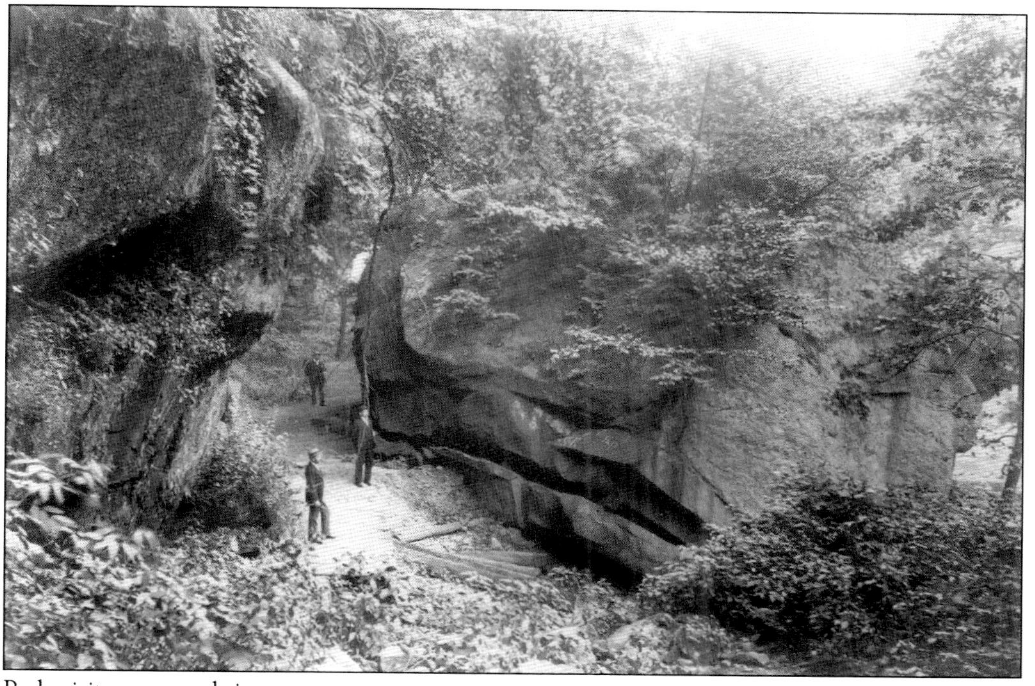

Park visitors seemed tiny compared to the mammoth cliffs and boulders at the High Bridge Glens. (Neuhardt collection.)

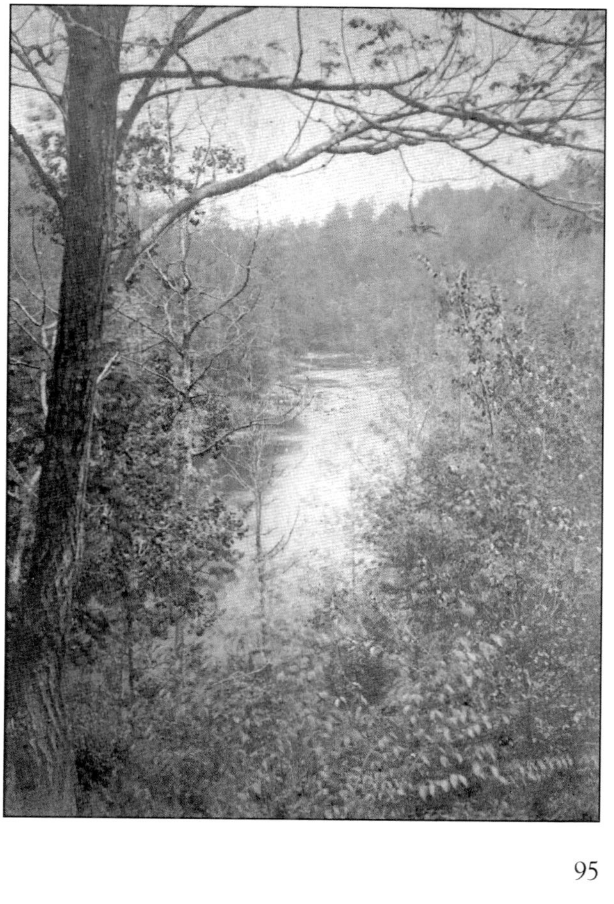

This distant view of the Cuyahoga River captures the grandeur of the scenery of the park. (Cuyahoga Falls Library.)

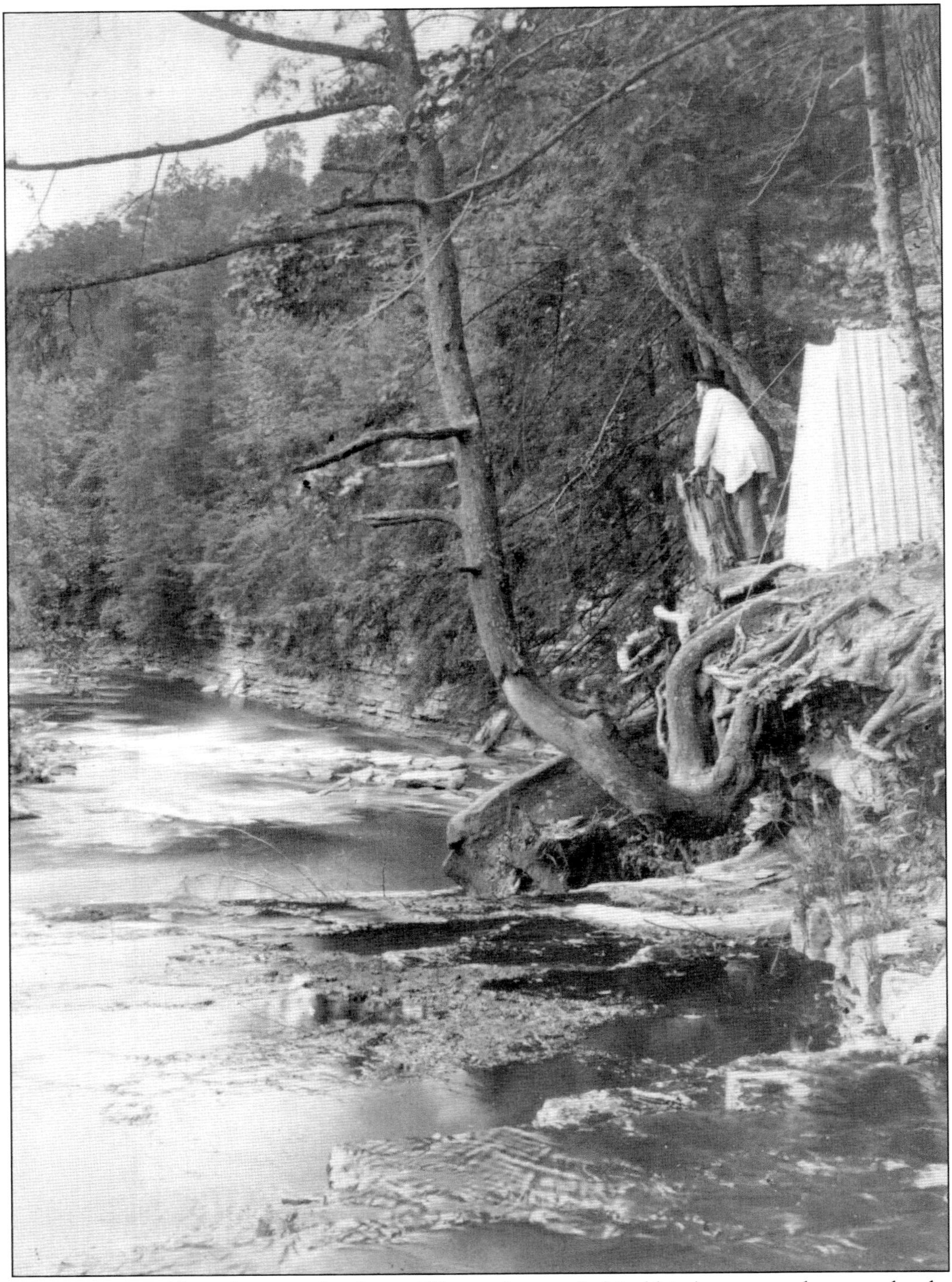

This man, possibly a photographer himself (note the tent behind him), gazes at the stony banks of the Cuyahoga River. In 1890, the Pittsburgh Amateur Photographers Association visited the Glens. Recalling the visit in a photography journal, one member wrote, "Sky, wood, rocks and streams never had a greater bombardment of cameras." (Author's collection.)

The photographer of this massive stone labeled it "Standing Rock." Other rock formations included imaginative names such as Sentinel Rocks, Boulder Pass, Hunter's Pass, and the Labyrinth. (Author's collection.)

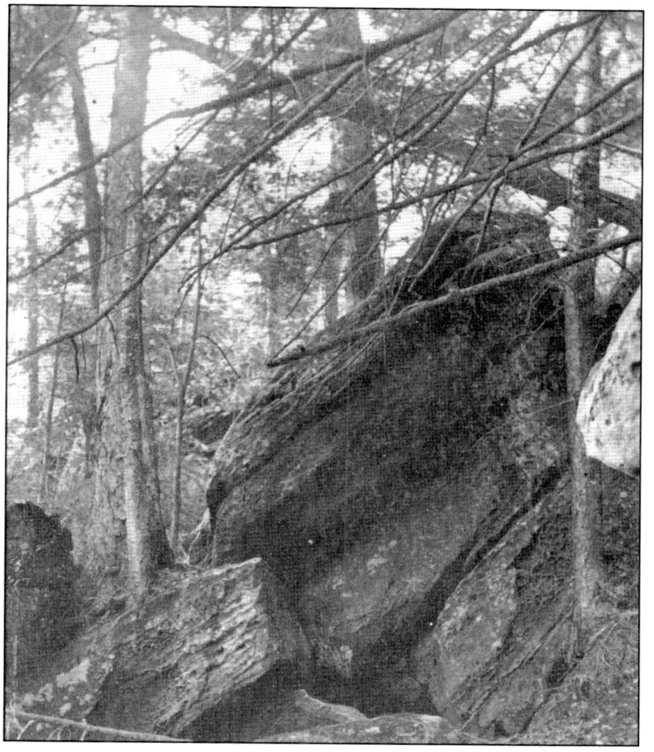

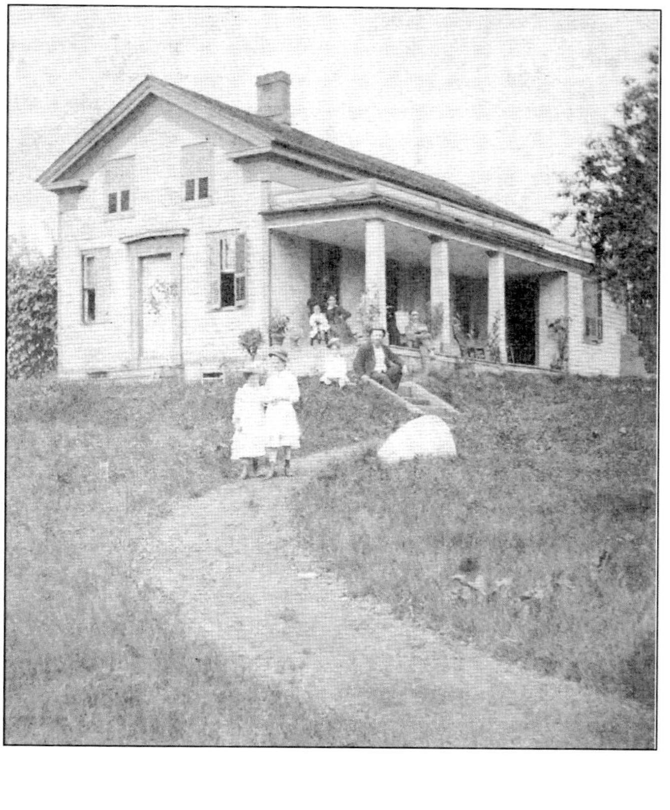

Within one year of opening the Glens, the owners found it necessary to provide additional lodging for the growing throng of park visitors. Loomis and his partners purchased a private home located across the street from the Glens. This home, located just south of the Glens between Front and Second Streets, became the Glen House hotel. (John and Janet Waldsmith collection.)

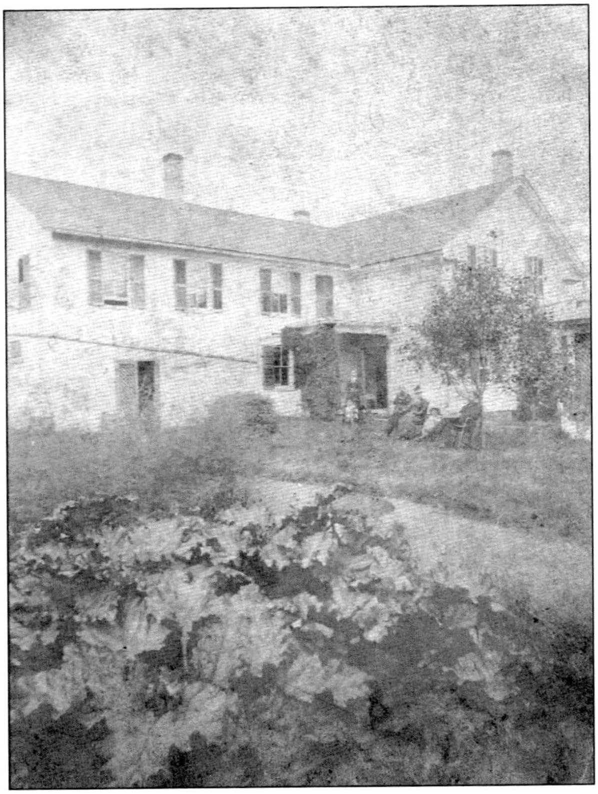

At one point, Luther Fenton, who also ran the Glens ferry, managed the Glen House. He not only enlarged the hotel, but he also made numerous improvements. Before moving to Cuyahoga Falls, Fenton lived in nearby Tallmadge and worked in the pottery business. (Author's collection.)

At the height of the season, the High Bridge Glens had up to 8,000 visitors per day. While some out-of-towners came for the day, others spent an entire week at Cuyahoga Falls visiting the Glens, Silver Lake Park, and other attractions. This meant good business for area hotels, including the Clifford Inn. (Pete Mellinger collection.)

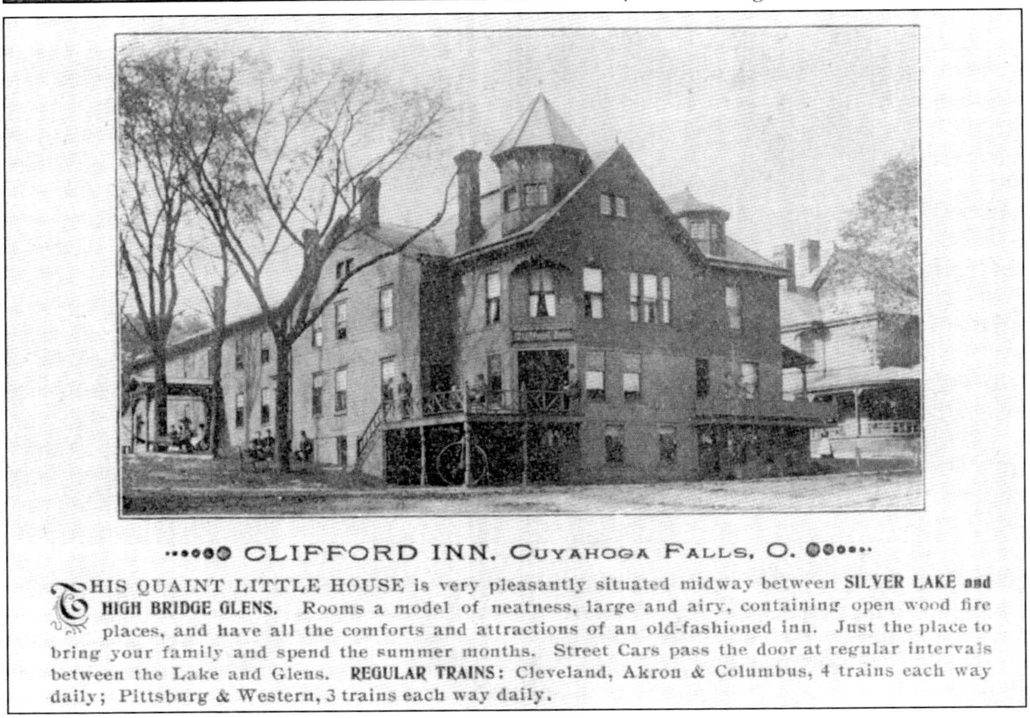

# *Six*

# The Fall of the Glens

## Changing Fortunes

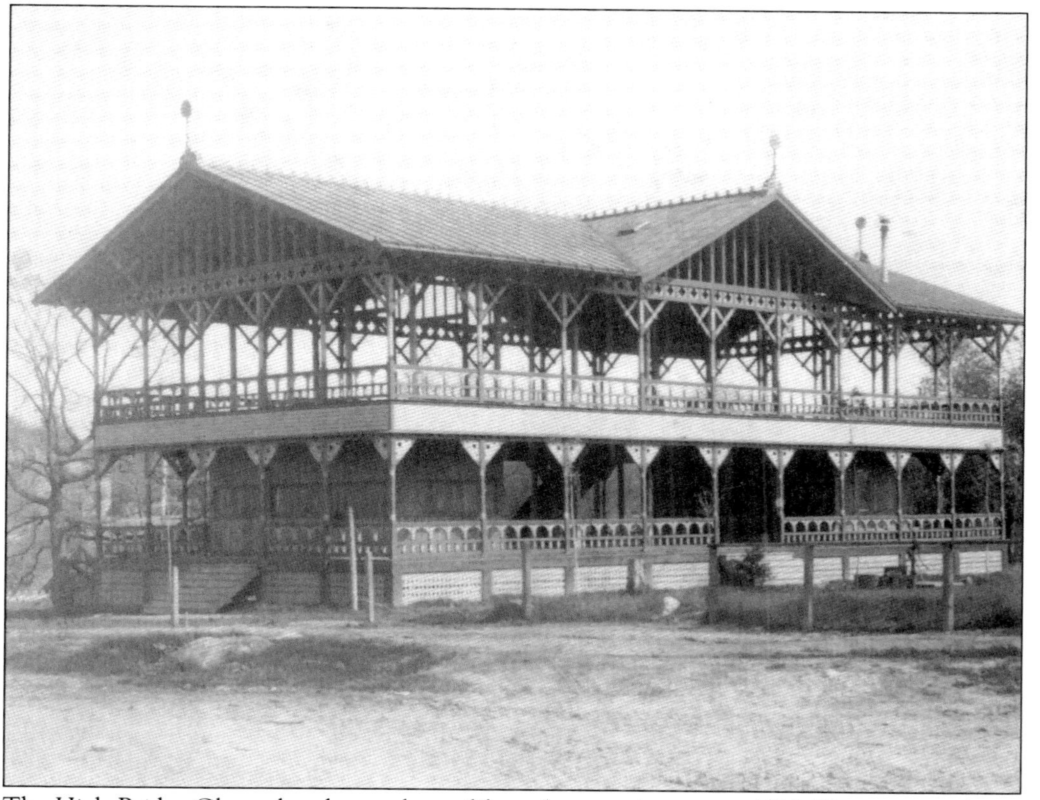

The High Bridge Glens closed as a place of formal entertainment in 1895. Historians indicate the Glens had declined in popularity due to "rowdyism" at the park. An auction was held to sell the park's dishes, tables, and other equipment, and soon after the majority of its buildings were demolished. Thomas F. Walsh bought the former Glens' Grand Pavilion and moved it to Randolph Park, a summer resort he created near Crystal Lake to compete with neighboring Silver Lake Park. The Glens pavilion enjoyed a new life as one of Randolph Park's major structures. (Cuyahoga Falls Library.)

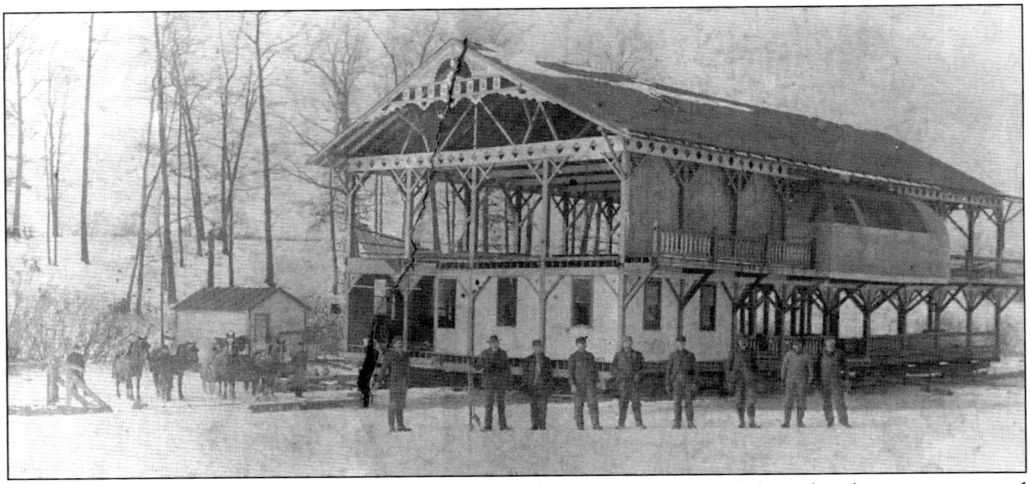

After Randolph Park closed, the owners of nearby Silver Lake Park bought the property and buildings at Randolph in 1903. In the winter of 1905, Silver Lake Park's management hired a crew to move the former Randolph/Glens pavilion across a frozen Silver Lake to the park's eastern shore, where it would become Silver Lake's new bathhouse. (Cuyahoga Falls Historical Society.)

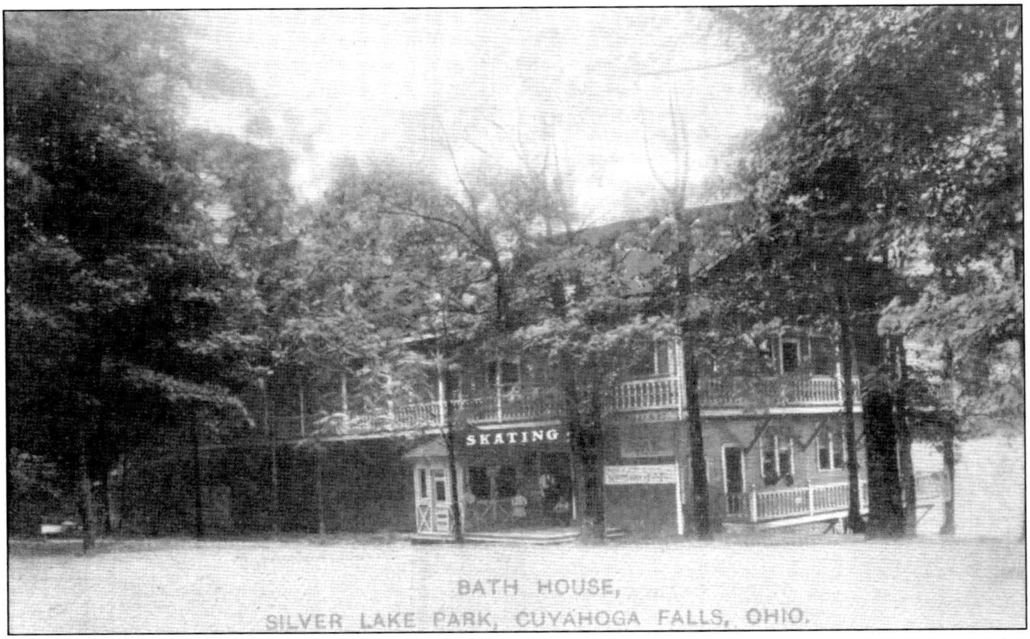


Unfortunately, after the 175-ton pavilion began its trip across the lake, it was left to rest on the ice overnight. When crews returned in the morning, the pavilion had broken through the ice and was partially submerged. The building was eventually brought to shore, where it was rebuilt and turned into a bathhouse at Silver Lake Park. (Author's collection.)

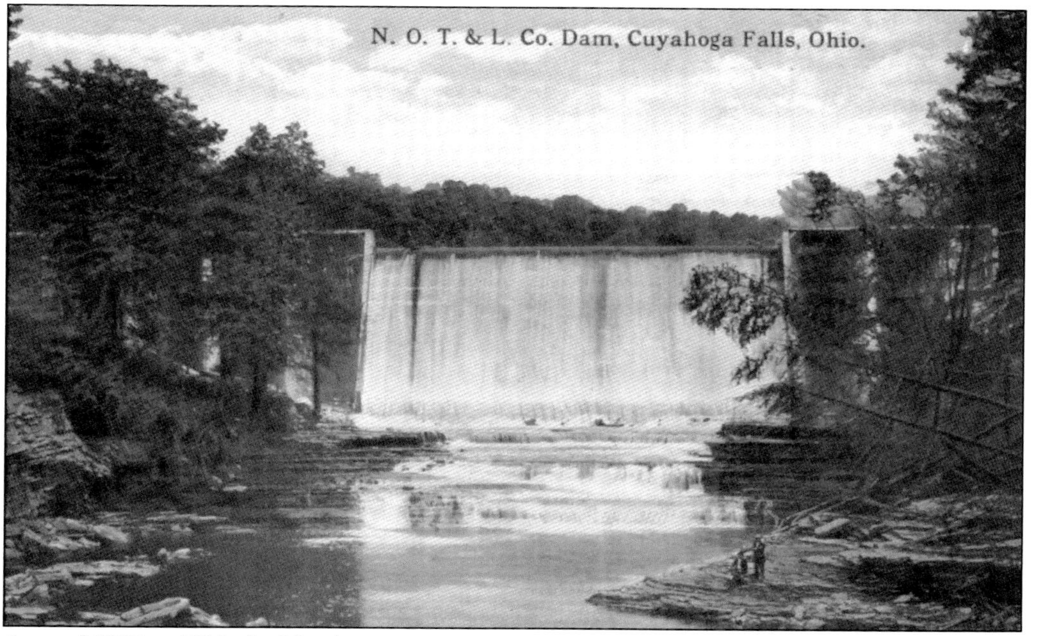


Around 1912 or 1913, the Northern Ohio Traction & Light Company built a dam on the Cuyahoga River, south of the Glens, in the Gorge. Although historians conceded that the dam and power plant were needed to provide power for nearby Akron's growing neighborhoods and trolley systems, they mourned the fact that creation of the dam backed up the level of the Cuyahoga River several feet and flooded portions of the Glens. Following the construction of the dam, the original Big Falls—the namesake of Cuyahoga Falls—also disappeared from view. (Author's collection.)

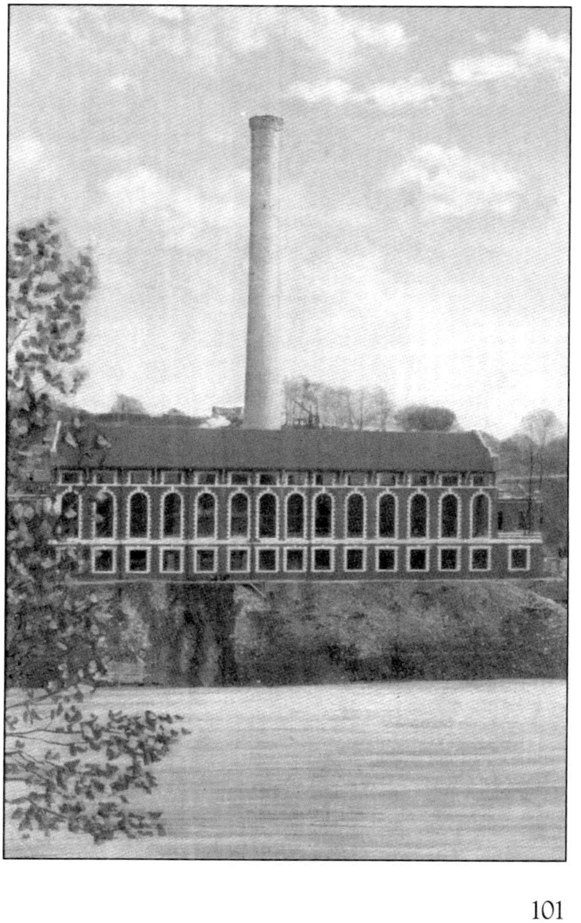

The Gorge Power House served area residents for several years. Many locals fondly recall seeing the plant lit up in the evening or watching trainloads of coal being delivered to fuel the plant's boilers. The plant was eventually demolished, beginning in 2008. (Author's collection.)

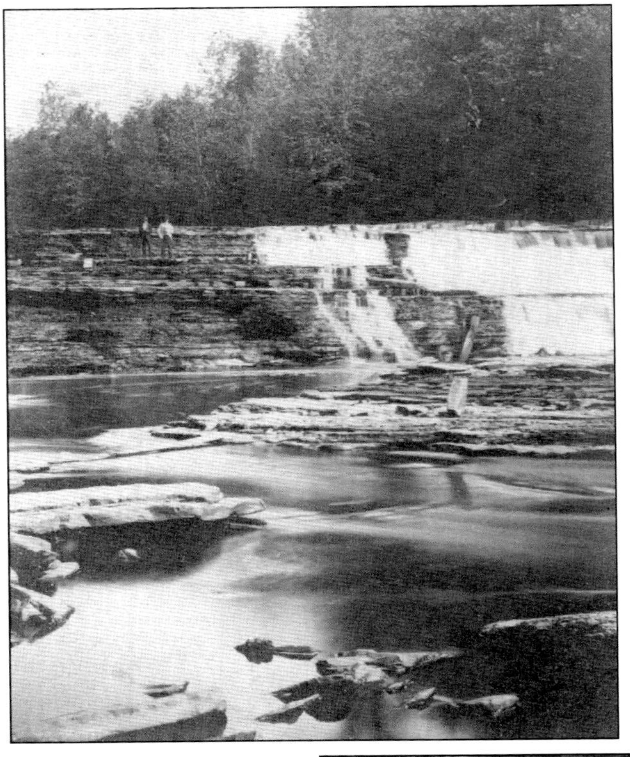

After the construction of the Gorge dam, views of the Big Falls disappeared. According to technical journals from the era, the Gorge power station replaced a number of other stations at Akron, Silver Lake Junction, and Bedford, Ohio. Note the people posing on the upper left side of the Big Falls prior to construction of the dam. (Cuyahoga Falls Historical Society.)

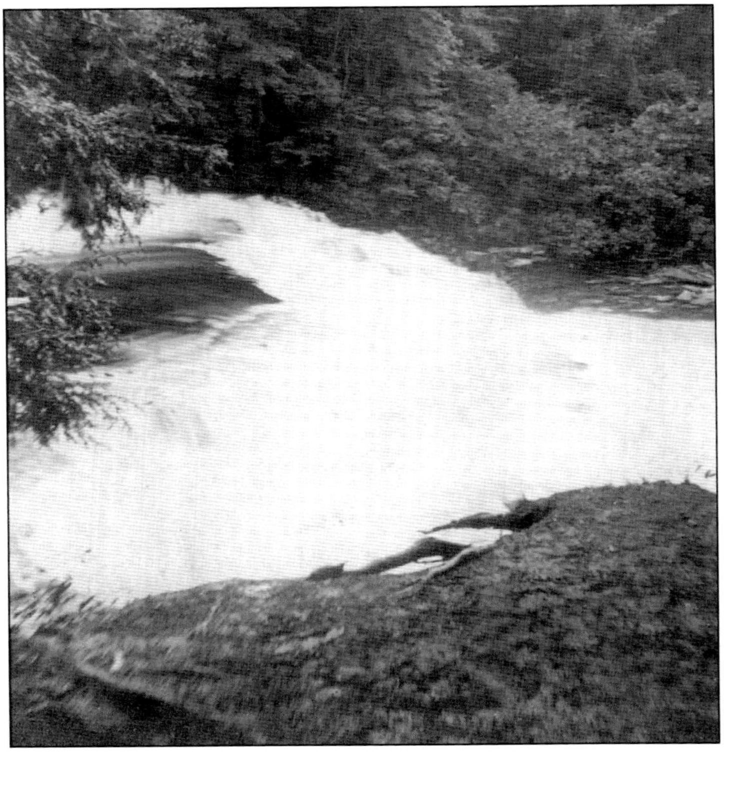

Local photographer H.L. Shumway captured this rare view looking across the Big Falls. Various organizations are working with the Environmental Protection Agency and other governmental entities to explore the possibility of removing several dams along the Cuyahoga River, leading area residents to wonder whether the Big Falls of the Cuyahoga will again be seen. (Eric Thompson collection.)

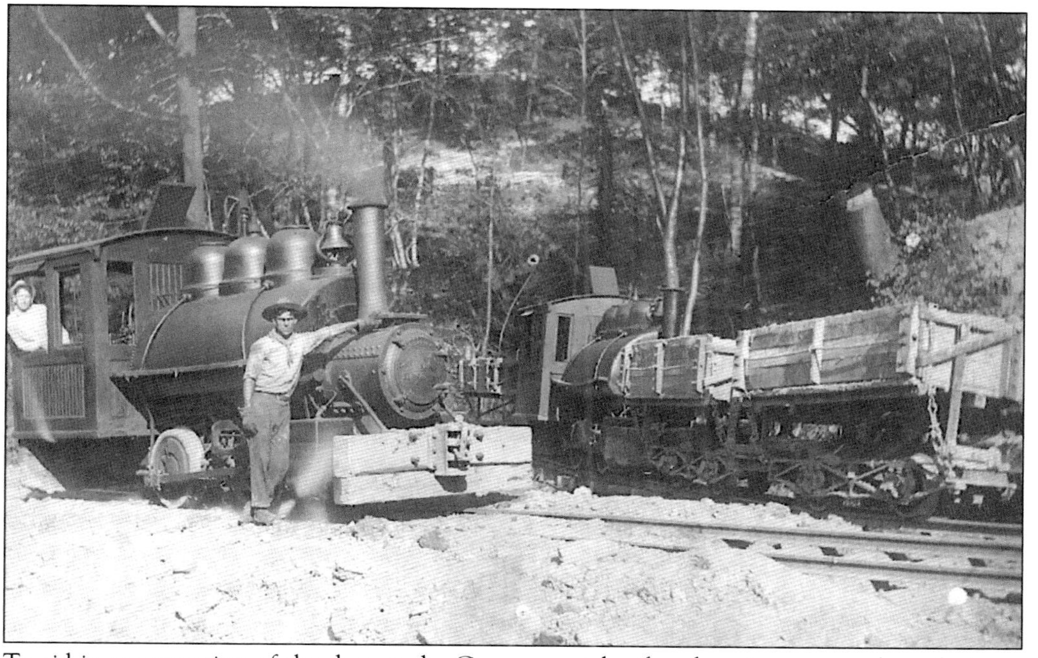

To aid in construction of the dam at the Gorge, special railroad equipment was brought in to transport materials. John D. Phillips, the grandfather of the man who donated the use of this photograph, is pictured in the cab of the engine. (John Phillips collection.)

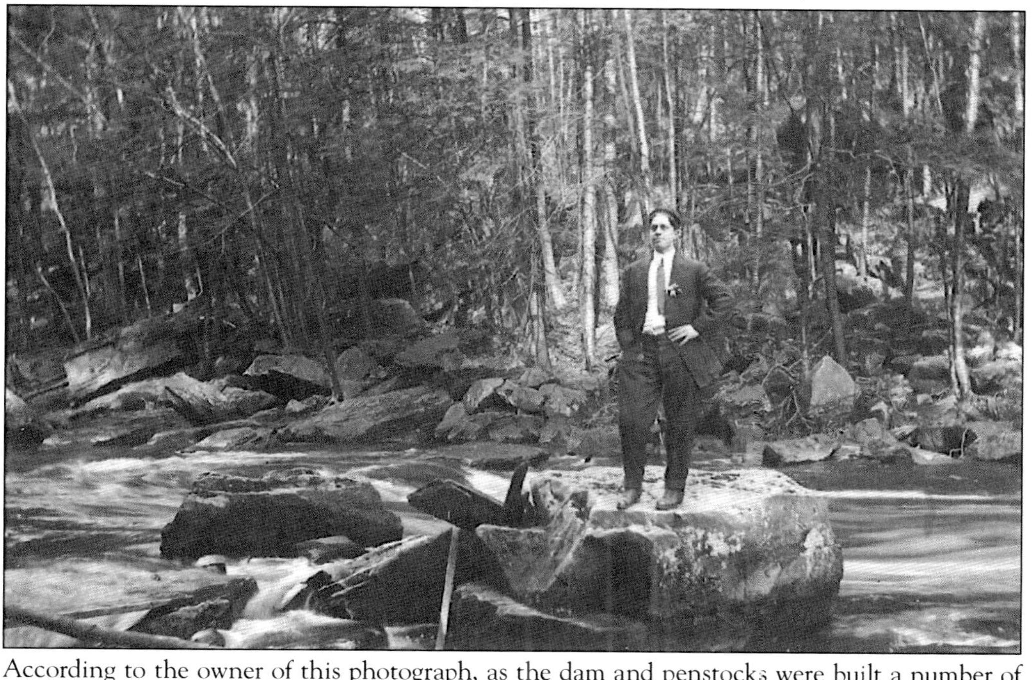

According to the owner of this photograph, as the dam and penstocks were built a number of trees were cleared from the banks of the Cuyahoga River in anticipation of flooding from the new dam. A man identified as Elmer Chamberlin poses here along the river before the deforestation. (John Phillips collection.)

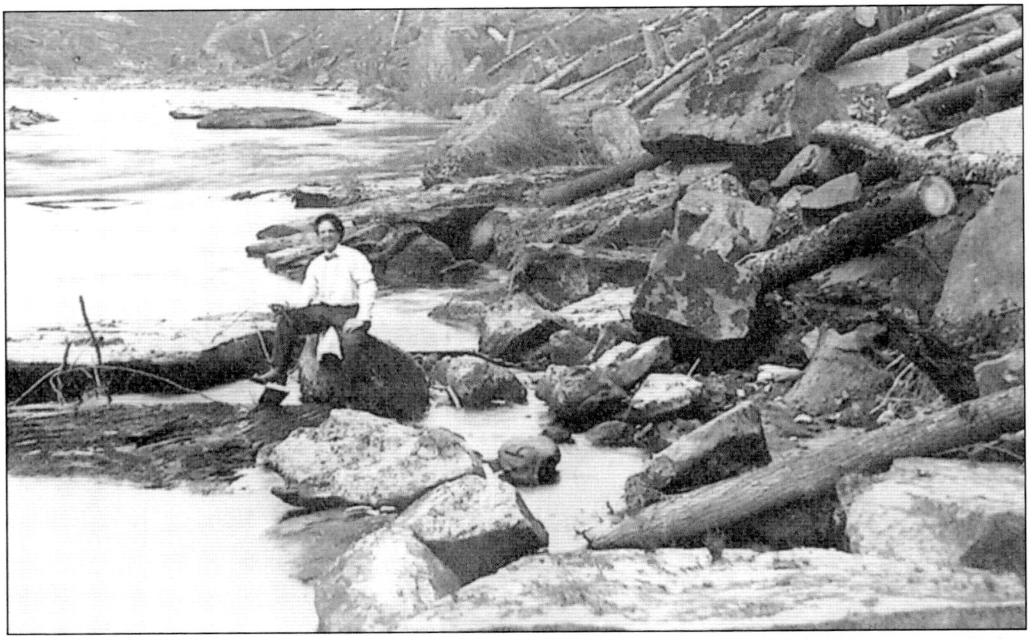

In a later photograph, Oscar Chamberlin poses among the rocks and fallen trees. (John Phillips collection.)

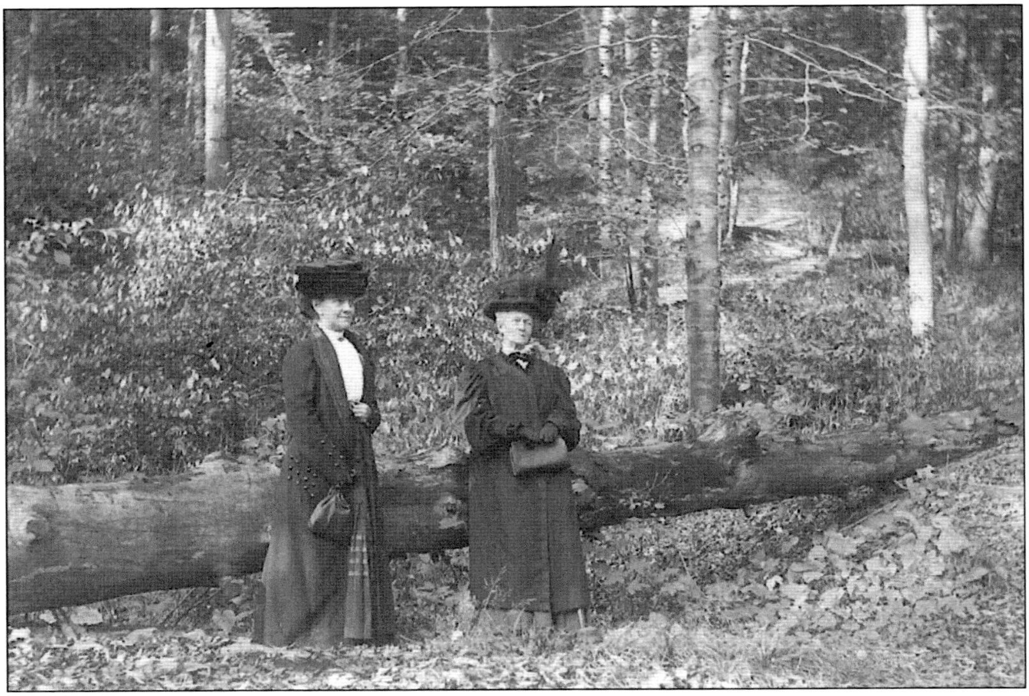

While modern-day hikers choose to wear comfortable attire, Mrs. Brown and Lisa Richards are seen here wearing stylish outfits to the Gorge in the early 1900s. (John Phillips collection.)

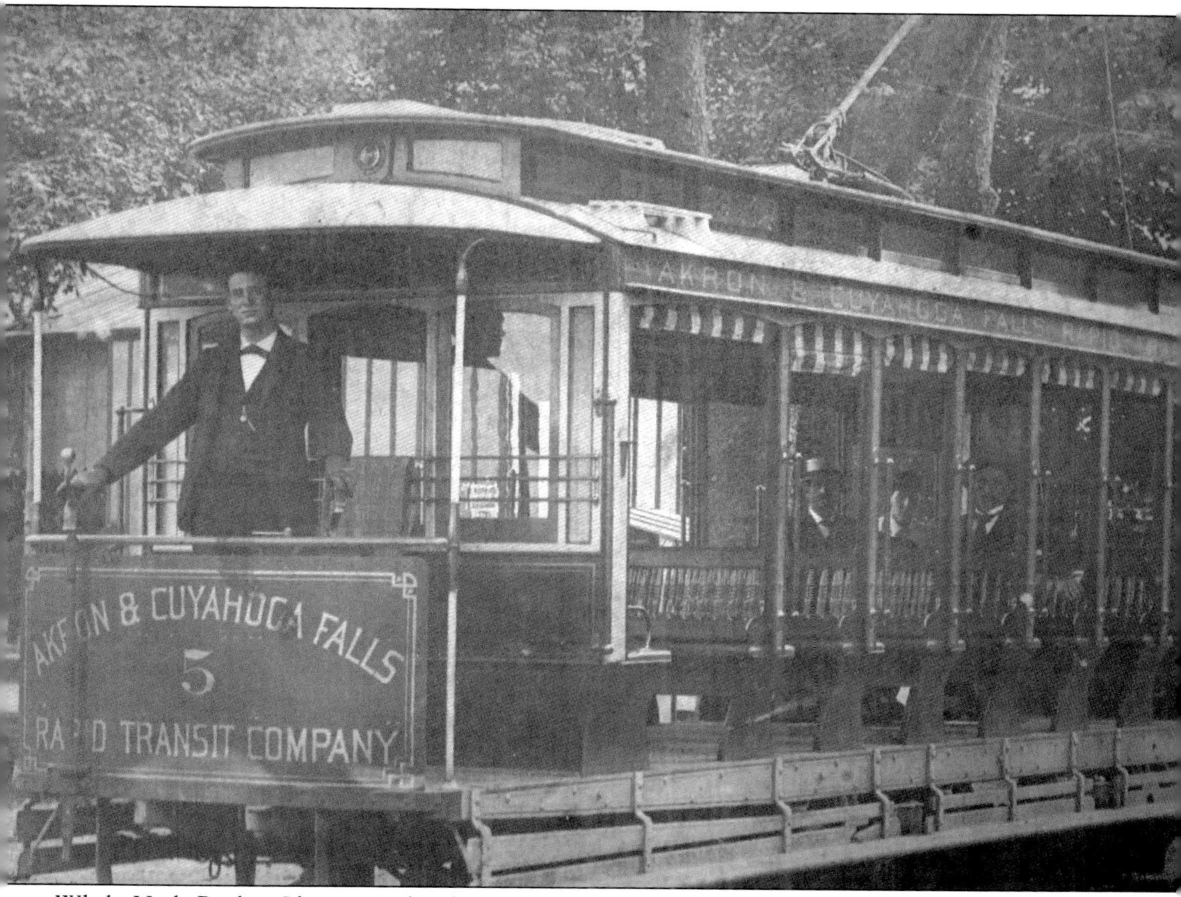


While High Bridge Glens was, for the most part, the scene of many happy memories, it was also the location of several tragic accidents. In 1918, several years after the original park had closed, the High Bridge at Front and Prospect Streets (or Glens Bridge as it was sometimes called) was the scene of a horrific trolley-car accident. (Note in the photograph on page 106 how the shape of the High Bridge changed from the original arch-shaped bottom to a rectangular construction designed to accommodate heavier trolley traffic.) The Akron & Cuyahoga Falls Rapid Transit Company was one of two trolley-car lines that served Cuyahoga Falls. (Cuyahoga Falls Historical Society.)

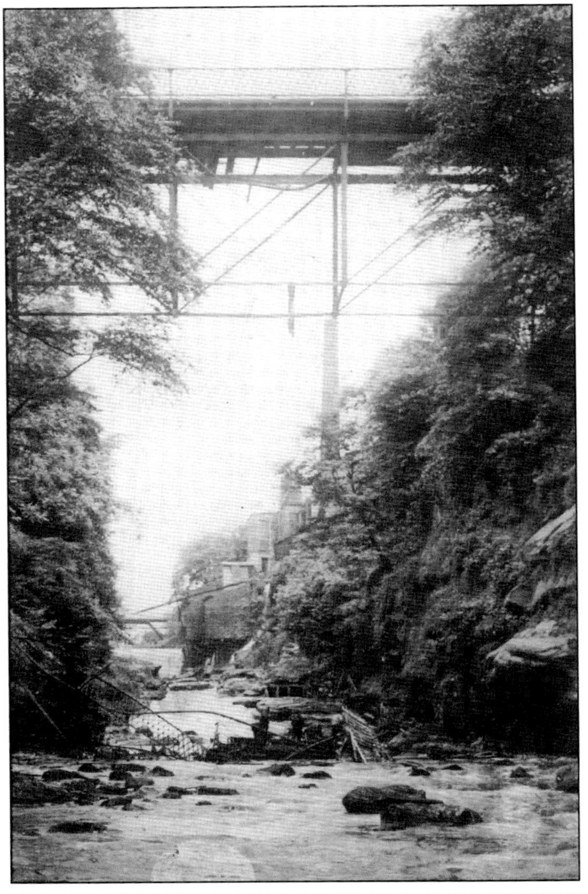

On June 11, 1918, at approximately 4:10 p.m., the Northern Ohio Traction & Light Company's Mountain Line trolley started to cross the High Bridge, heading from the eastern side toward Front Street, when the trolley suddenly came off the tracks, crashed through the bridge's north railing, and fell 90 feet down into the Cuyahoga River. (Cuyahoga Falls Historical Society.)

Rescuers rushed to the scene, and crowds waited breathlessly to learn the fate of loved ones. Initially, all the passengers and crew were feared dead, but miraculously motorman Leroy Bessemer and passenger Henry VanLoosen survived, though they were initially placed on the "dead wagon." O.D Gilmore, Emory Prior, Charles Hoy, and Liuzzi Peligione lost their lives in the accident. The rescue scene was full of tension and high drama. According to various accounts, as VanLoosen was being lifted from the river by rope, the knot on the rope loosened and he almost fell into the river for a second time that day. VanLoosen was eventually brought to safety, much to the relief of onlookers. (Cuyahoga Falls Historical Society.)

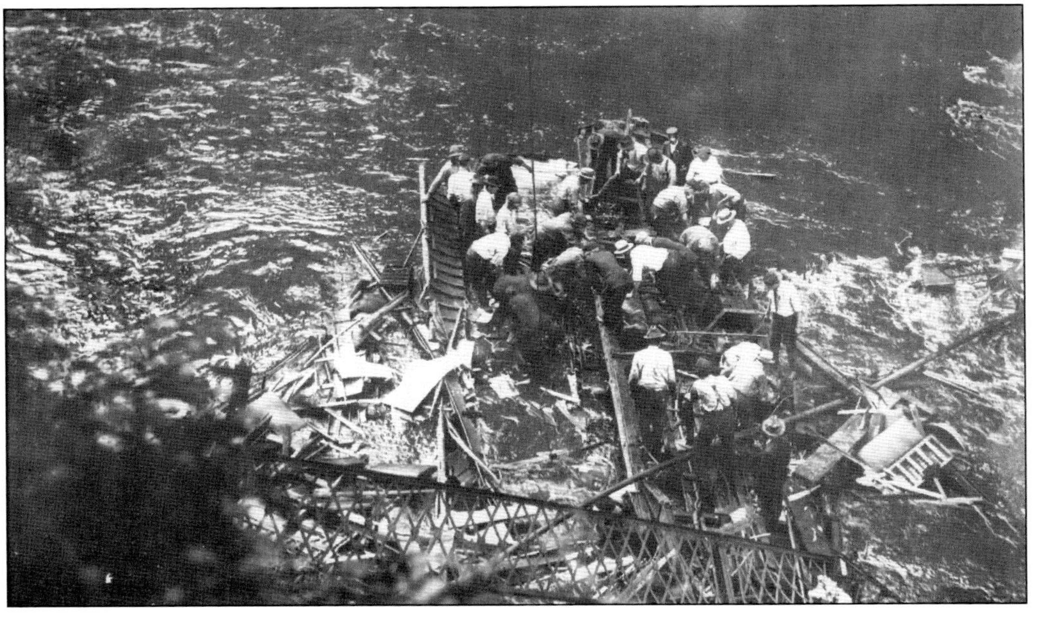

# *Seven*

# THE GLENS REMEMBERED

## SOUVENIRS OF THE PAST

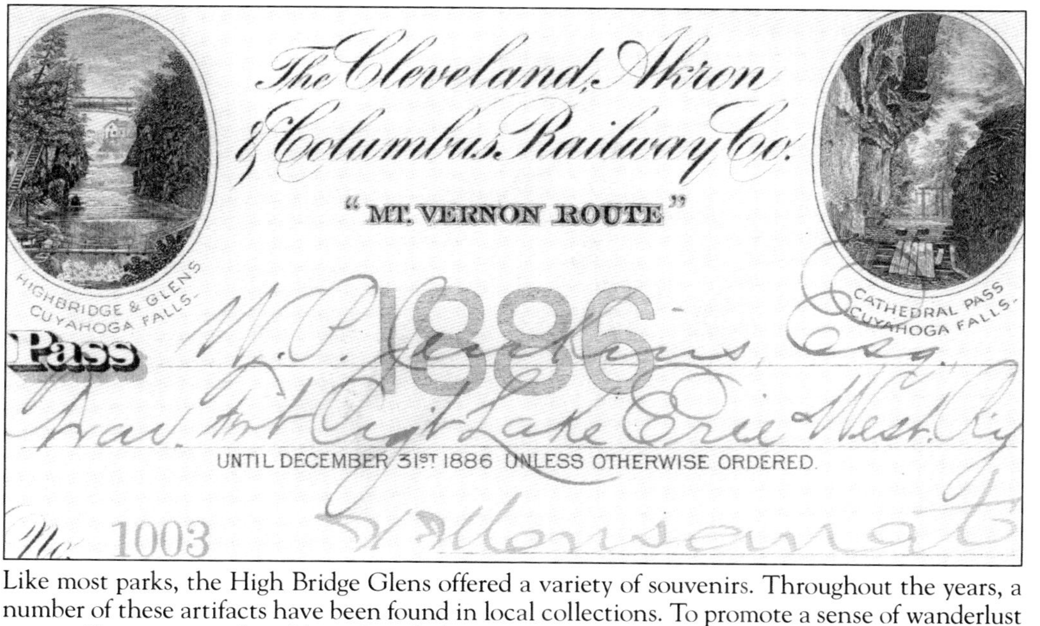


Like most parks, the High Bridge Glens offered a variety of souvenirs. Throughout the years, a number of these artifacts have been found in local collections. To promote a sense of wanderlust among Victorians, railroad lines hired photographers and artists to produce scenes of various attractions along their routes. This railway pass included engravings of the High Bridge and Cathedral Pass at High Bridge Glens. (Author's collection.)

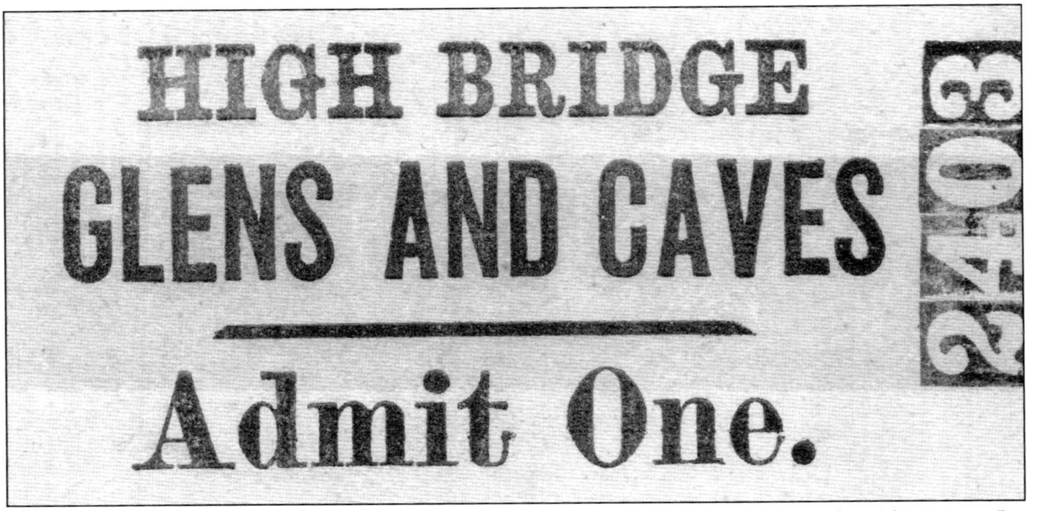


This rare ticket from the park is dated 1894 on the back. Admission to the Glens was 5¢. (Author's collection.)

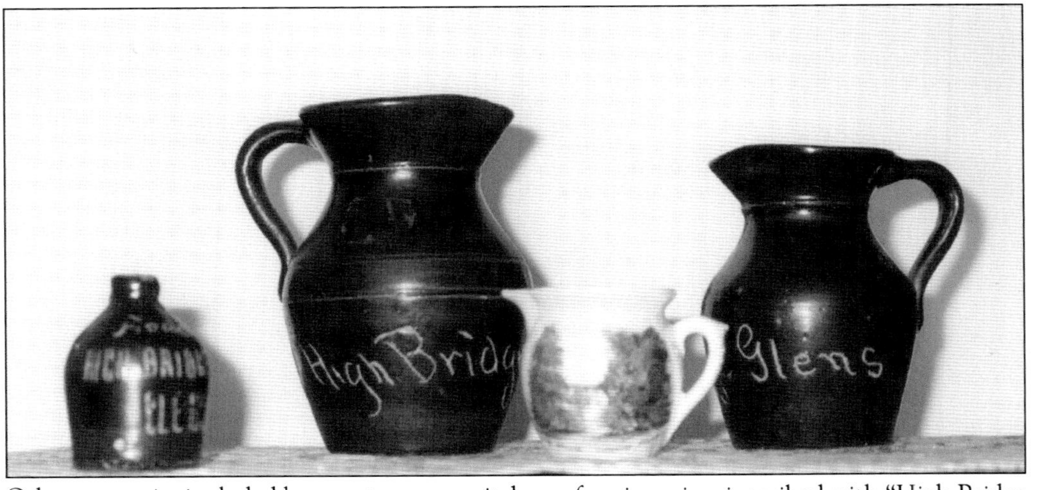


Other souvenirs included brown stoneware pitchers of various sizes inscribed with "High Bridge Glens." It is not known which factory supplied these items, but at least one local historian has speculated that the Thomas brothers, who operated a pottery business in Cuyahoga Falls, may have produced the pitchers. The small white pitcher, with the transferware image of the High Bridge, was produced by Wheelock for Loomis Hardware. (Author's collection.)

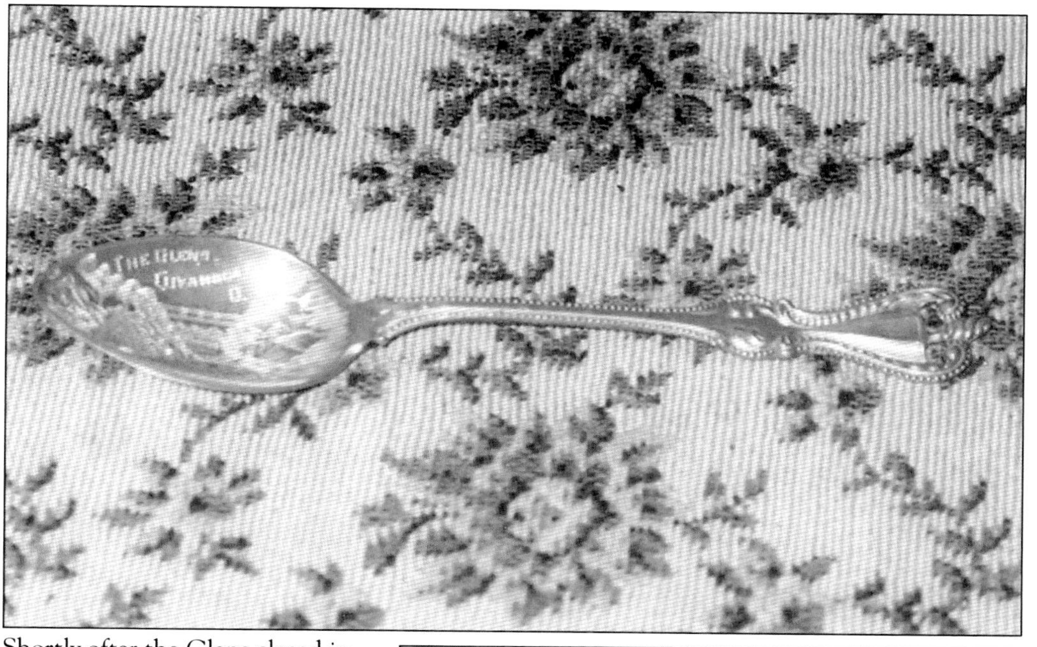

Shortly after the Glens closed in 1895, local jeweler B.F. Phillips had a souvenir spoon produced to commemorate the High Bridge Glens. The spoons were available from his shop on Front Street. A variety of scenes are depicted on different spoons, including the river, High Bridge, and Grand Pavilion. (Author's collection.)

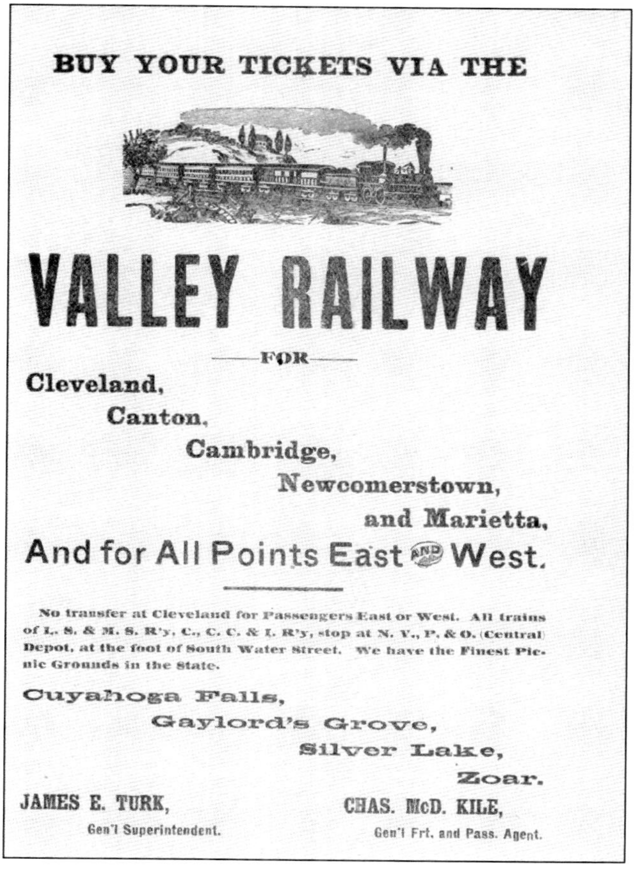


According to an 1883 High Bridge Glens poster, a variety of railway lines served the park, including the Cleveland, Akron & Columbus Railway; Pittsburgh & Western; and the Valley Railway. This Valley Railway handbill advertises routes serving Cuyahoga Falls and nearby parks at Silver Lake and Gaylord's Grove. (Author's collection.)

*A Beautiful Summer Resort.*

# High Bridge Glens and Caves,

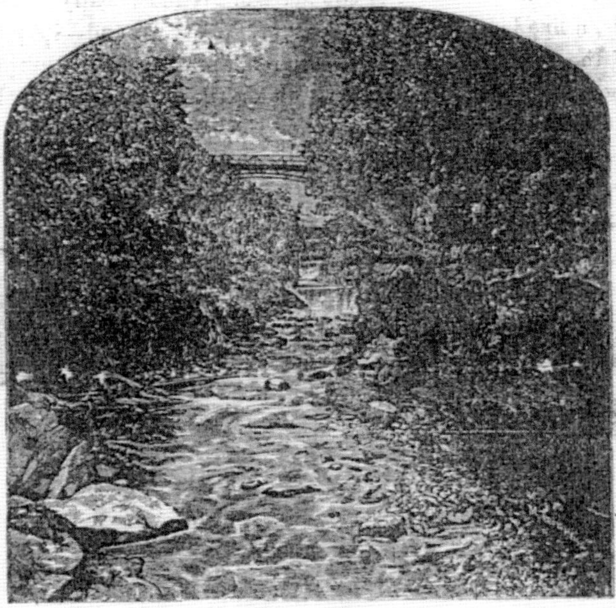

High Bridge from Grand Promenade.

## CUYAHOGA FALLS, OHIO.

The great success attending last year's venture of the proprietors of the High Bridge Glens, in fitting up and preparing these famous grounds to be used as a pleasure resort, has encouraged them to invest largely in additional buildings and facilities, in the hope that the patronage bestowed upon their enterprise this year will be equal to their desires.

The park became so successful that for the 1880 season the owners of High Bridge Glens produced a multipage brochure describing the many features and attractions added to the park, including the acquisition of the Glen House hotel. H.H. Hoover of New Jersey joined Loomis as a partner in the Glens for several years. (Cuyahoga Falls Library.)

The HIGH BRIDGE GLEN Co., Messrs. L. W. Loomis of Cuyahoga Falls, and Mr. H. H. Hoover, formerly of New Jersey, have determined to cater to the wants of pleasure seekers, and seeing the necessity for first-class boarding accommodations, have purchased the commodious and elegant residence, directly joining their property and formerly owned by J. Hinde, Esq., and now invite the inspection and attention of parties seeking a pleasant, comfortable and convenient summer residence. GLEN HOUSE stands in the centre of two acres of grounds, neatly laid out with shade trees, orchards, a fine lawn, and with pleasant scenery around—its proximity to the attractions of the Glens—make its peculiar adaptation for the purpose of a home boarding house easily seen. The house is under the immediate supervision of Mr. Hoover, who will do everything possible for the accommodation of guests, and at moderate rates. Among the improvements made on the grounds is the enlargement of the Pavillion, which is now double its former size. The Restaurant has increased facilities for supplying the wants of visitors, and can now afford accommodations to a large number. The addition of a two story building with large balcony around it, furnishes a capacious room that can be used by parties for social gatherings, and affords a splendid view of the scenery that surrounds it. The points of interest are numerous, and we mention among others the following:

## *Lovers' Retreat,*

Which is easily accessible, is a broad ledge of rocks shaded by trees and shrubs where one can have a grand view of the Glen below.

## *Fern Cave,*

A large subterranean cavity in the solid rock, 35x54 feet in dimensions, in which seats are arranged and ornamental shrubs and plants lend effect to this noted cave.

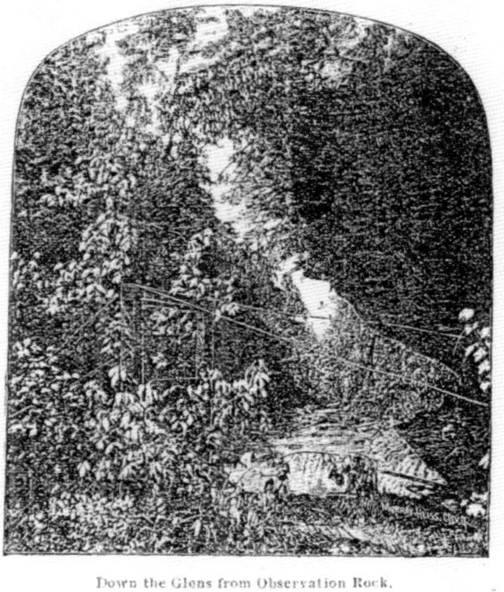

Down the Glens from Observation Rock.

The High Bridge Glens brochure featured engravings based on popular images of the park. This page highlighted two popular areas: Lovers' Retreat and Fern Cave. (Cuyahoga Falls Library.)

## *Observation Rock*

Is a high stone of 100 tons weight or more, upon which visitors can stand, and obtain a fine view of the Cuyahoga River, its numerous falls, and wonderful scenery; alſo, of High Bridge, about 100 feet above.

## *Doves' Retreat*

Is almost directly under Fern Cave, and is a large cavern with roof overhanging, 25 feet above.

## *Suspension Bridge*

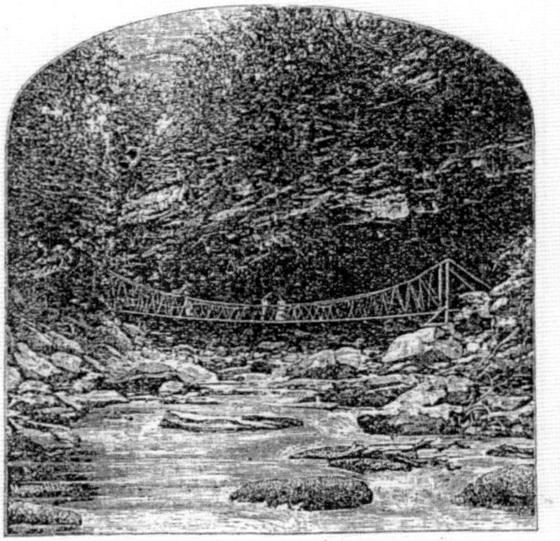

SUSPENSION FOOT BRIDGE.

Is built below the rapids and above high water mark, is a well built structure supported by strong rods of iron reaching across the chasm, and imbeded firmly in huge boulders on each side, with hand rails for protection, making it a perfectly safe bridge to gain the path leading to

## *Cascade Point,*

A lovely retreat under WEEPING CLIFF, from which we enter the

## *Grand Promenade,*

A mile in length, shaded on the one side by the overhanging rocks and on the other by the trees on the banks of the river. Springs of purest water abound along the entire walk, swings and croquet grounds have been arranged, and nature and art combined make this a beautiful, cool, and pleasant resort.

The above are some of the attractions offered. Six trains pass daily, on the Cleveland, Mt. Vernon & Columbus R. R., and for pic-nic parties or Society excursions, will stop within five rods of entrance to grounds. Special arrangements for large parties or picnics can be made by letter or personal application to the proprietors,

LOOMIS & HOOVER,

*CUYAHOGA FALLS, OHIO.*

N. B.—Of the many places of interest in and about Cuyahoga Falls, the Glens are the most centrally located, being only about ten minutes walk from the business part of town.

The park's other attractions are outlined on page three of the brochure. Many Victorian visitors thought High Bridge Glens was more beautiful than Niagara Falls or other "beauty spots" across the United States. One popular newspaper article, believed to have been written by the publicity agent for the railroad line serving the park, told the tale of three Columbus, Ohio, bachelors who were seeking one final vacation before returning to college. After rejecting the first two options—a trip to Alaska or the Himalayas—the bachelors made the next logical choice . . . a trip to Cuyahoga Falls to see the High Bridge Glens. (Cuyahoga Falls Library.)

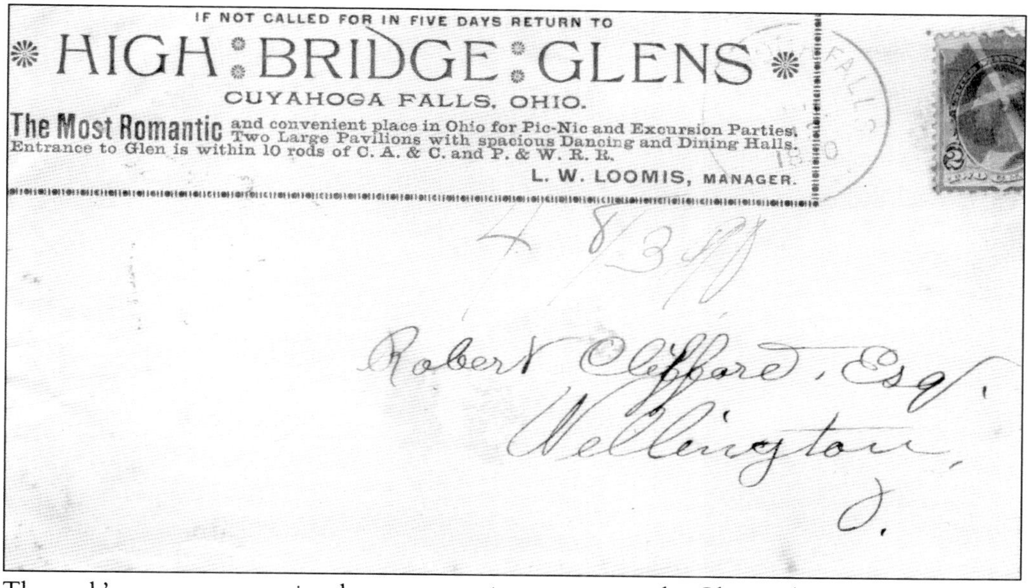


The park's owners never missed an opportunity to promote the Glens. This business envelope advertises the park as the "most romantic spot" in the state. Railroad lines serving the park also hired artists and photographers to create materials encouraging people to visit. (Author's collection.)

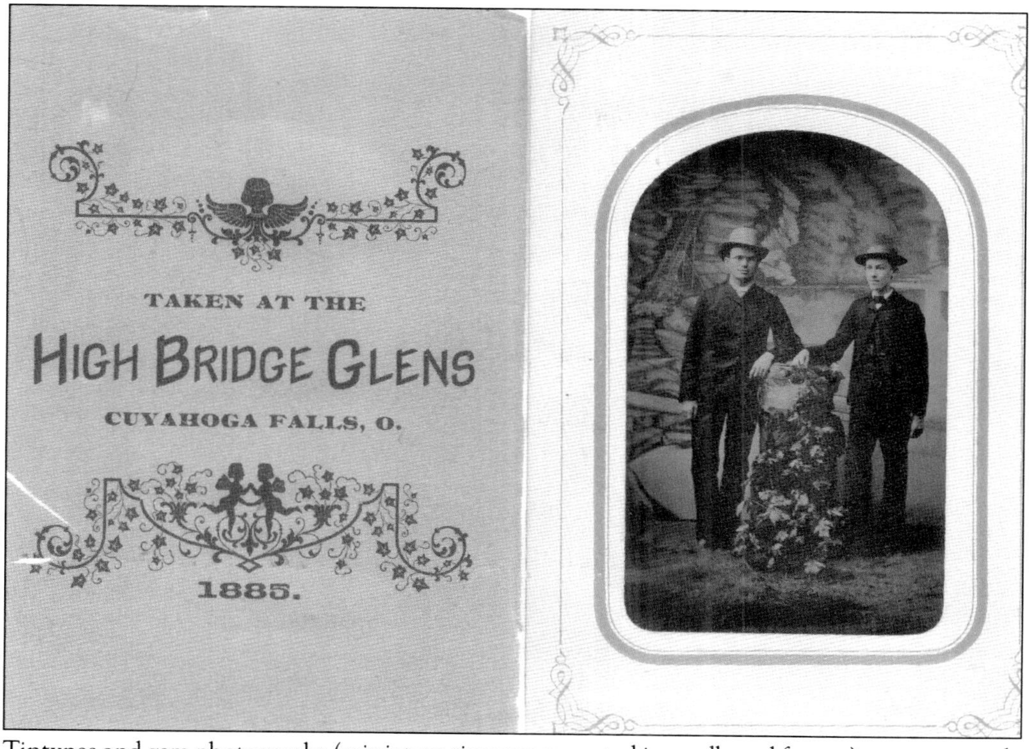


Tintypes and gem photographs (miniature tintypes mounted in cardboard frames) were extremely popular souvenirs; this tintype is dated 1885. Souvenirs from the park have been found across the country—from California to Rhode Island. (Author's collection.)

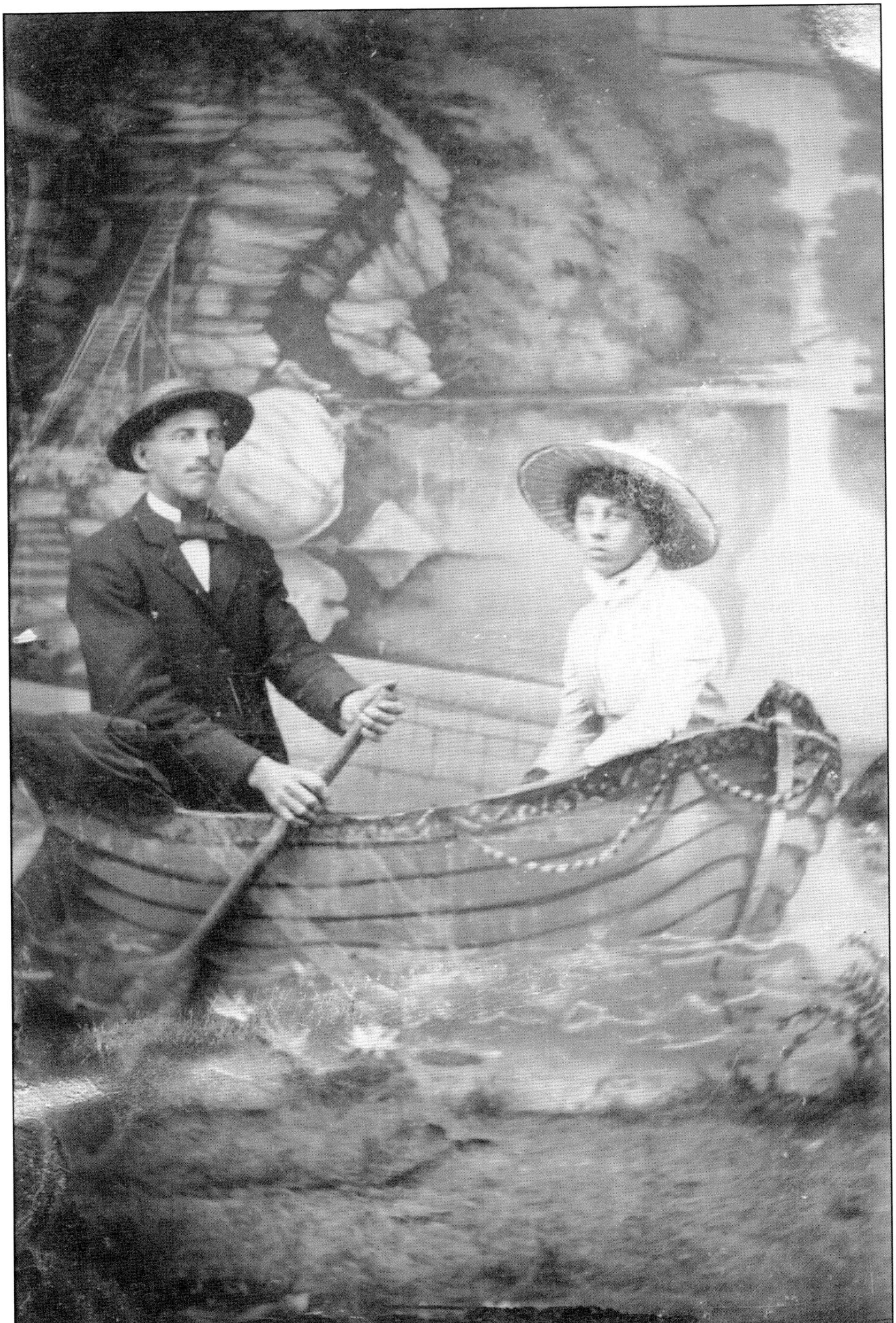

Several photography studios located in or near the Glens produced mock rowboat scenes like this one. Early photographers working in or near the park included George Hitchcock and Henry C. Mansfield. (Author's collection.)

# *Eight*

# THE GLENS REBORN

## THE NEW PARK

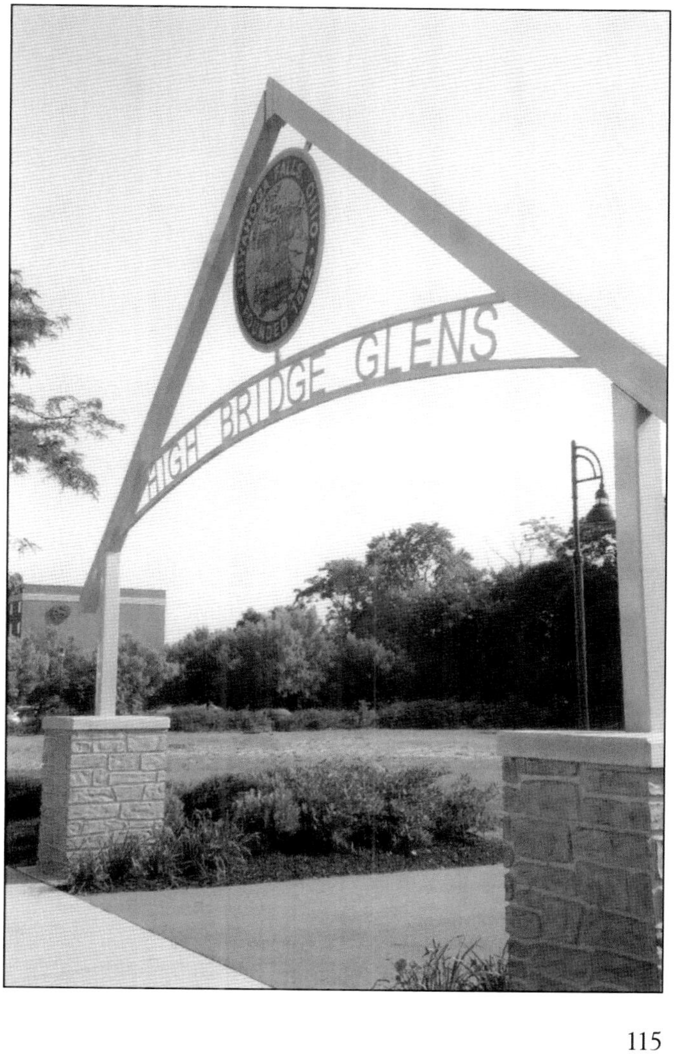


After the original Glens park closed, area residents continued to hike the trails in the Glens for a number of years. Eventually, land around the park reverted to residential and manufacturing uses. However, in recent years, the City of Cuyahoga Falls has been working to redevelop the area of South Front Street where the original High Bridge Glens park was located. To attract more families and retail establishments to the area, the city established a new two-acre urban park on the site of the former Glens. The new High Bridge Glens is located at 1817 Front Street, a few hundred feet south of the intersection of Front and Broad Boulevard. Like its predecessor, the new park has a high arching sign at the entrance. (Photograph by author.)

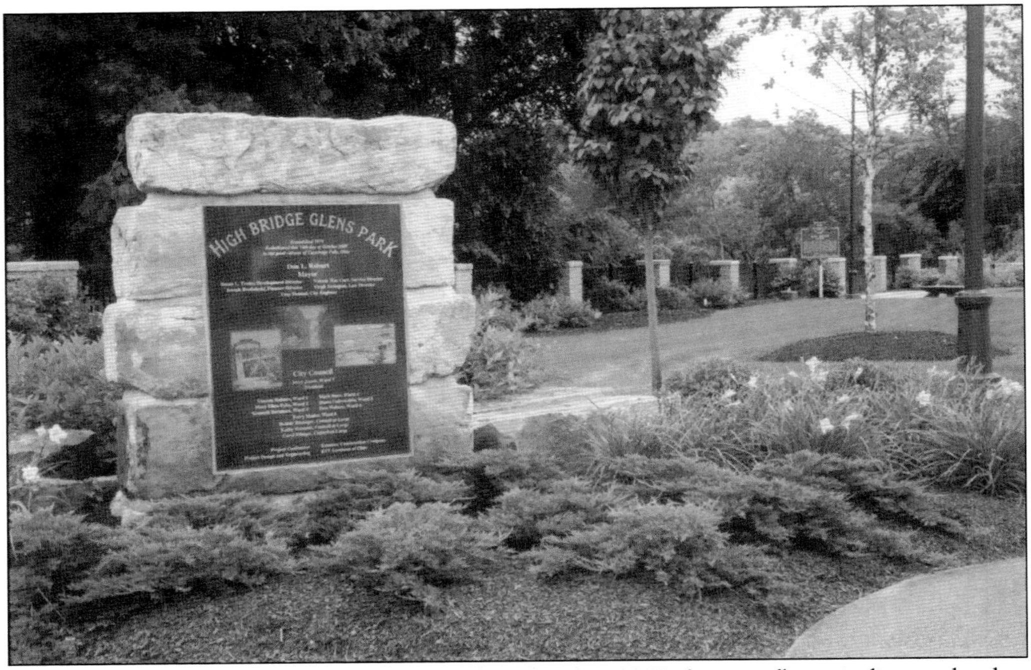


The new High Bridge Glens Park, dedicated in October 2009, features flat, winding paths that lead visitors to a variety of scenic overlooks. The park also has a sign with laser-etched images of the original High Bridge Glens, as well as a list of various individuals associated with the development of the new park. (Photograph by author.)

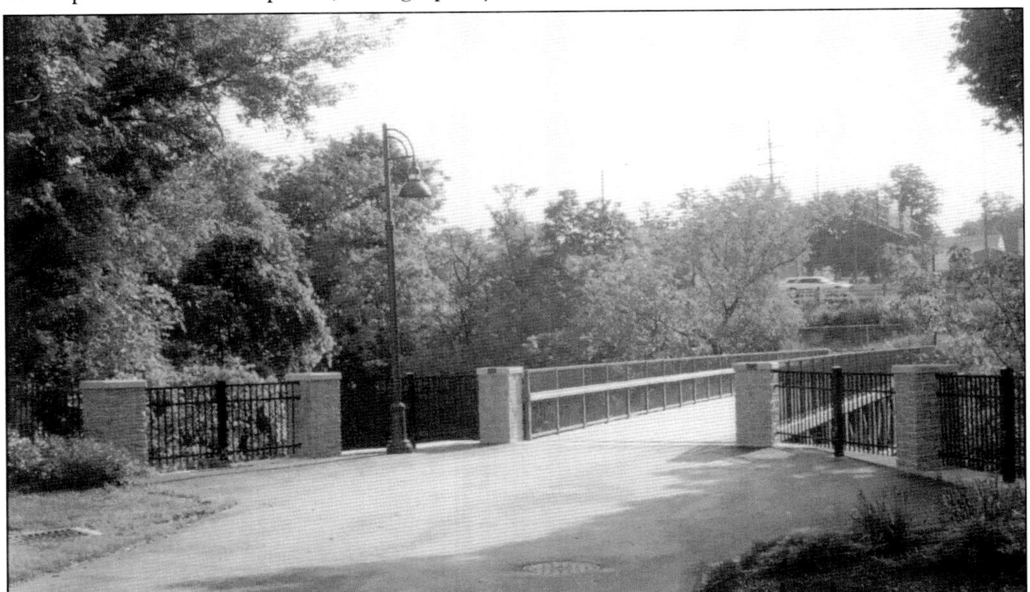

A new, safer, more attractive observation bridge was constructed on the site of the original High Bridge. From the bridge, visitors can see stunning vistas up and down the Cuyahoga River. Cuyahoga Falls is known as "the city that celebrates its riverfront heritage." (Photograph by author.)

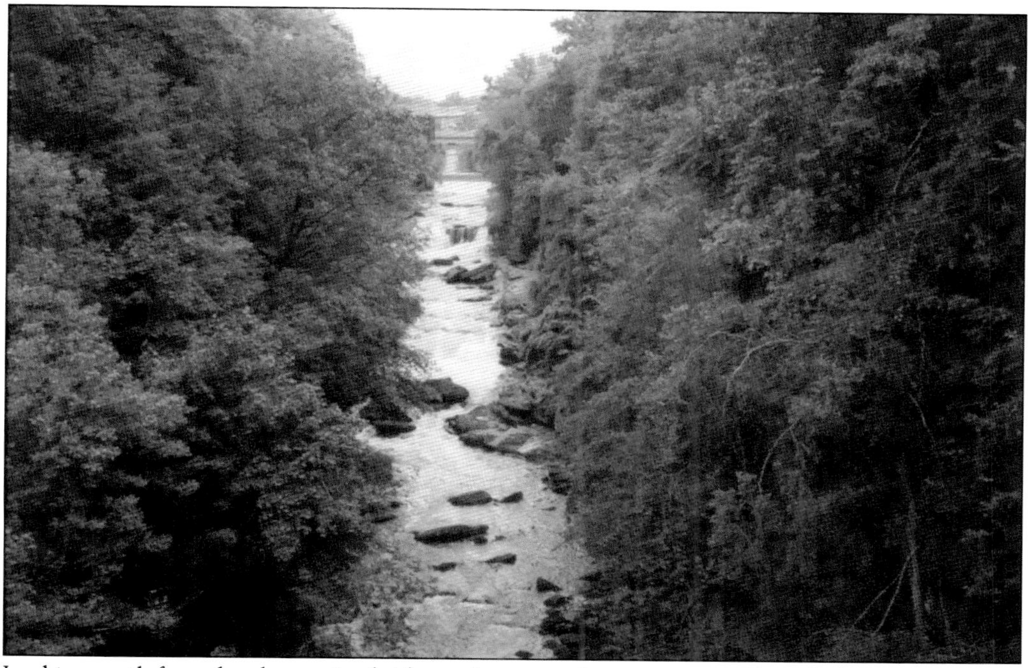

Looking north from the observation bridge at the new park, visitors can still see the beautiful cascades of the Cuyahoga River, as well as some of the dams along the river. (Photograph by author.)

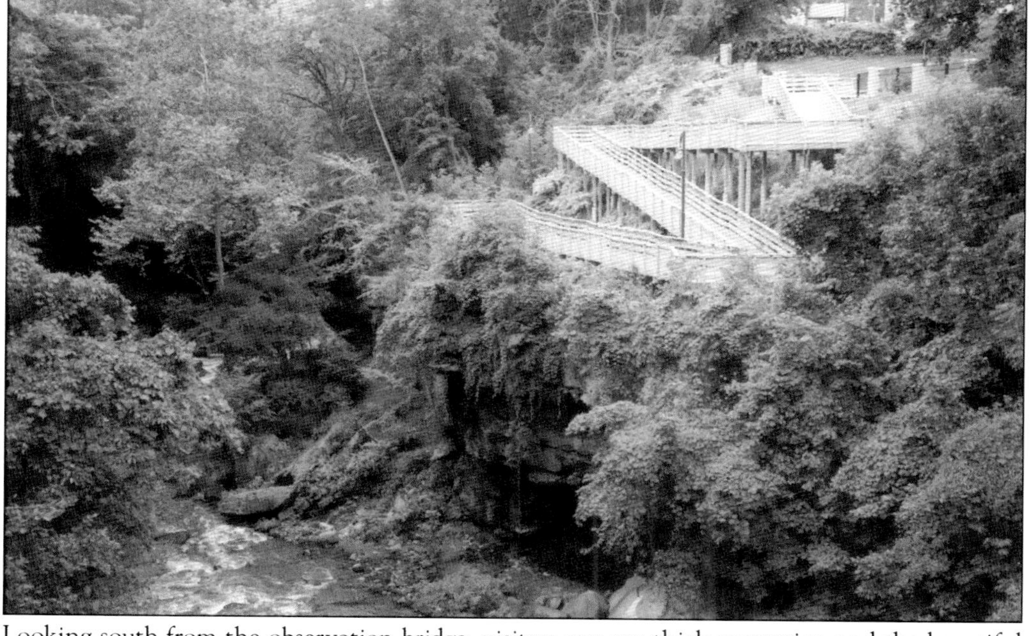

Looking south from the observation bridge, visitors can see thick vegetation and the beautiful Cuyahoga River. A three-level wooden observation deck is also visible in the distance. If modern-day visitors had been standing on the High Bridge in the late 1880s, the pavilions at the original Glens, as well as the steps leading to the park, would have in the lower right of the image. (Photograph by author.)

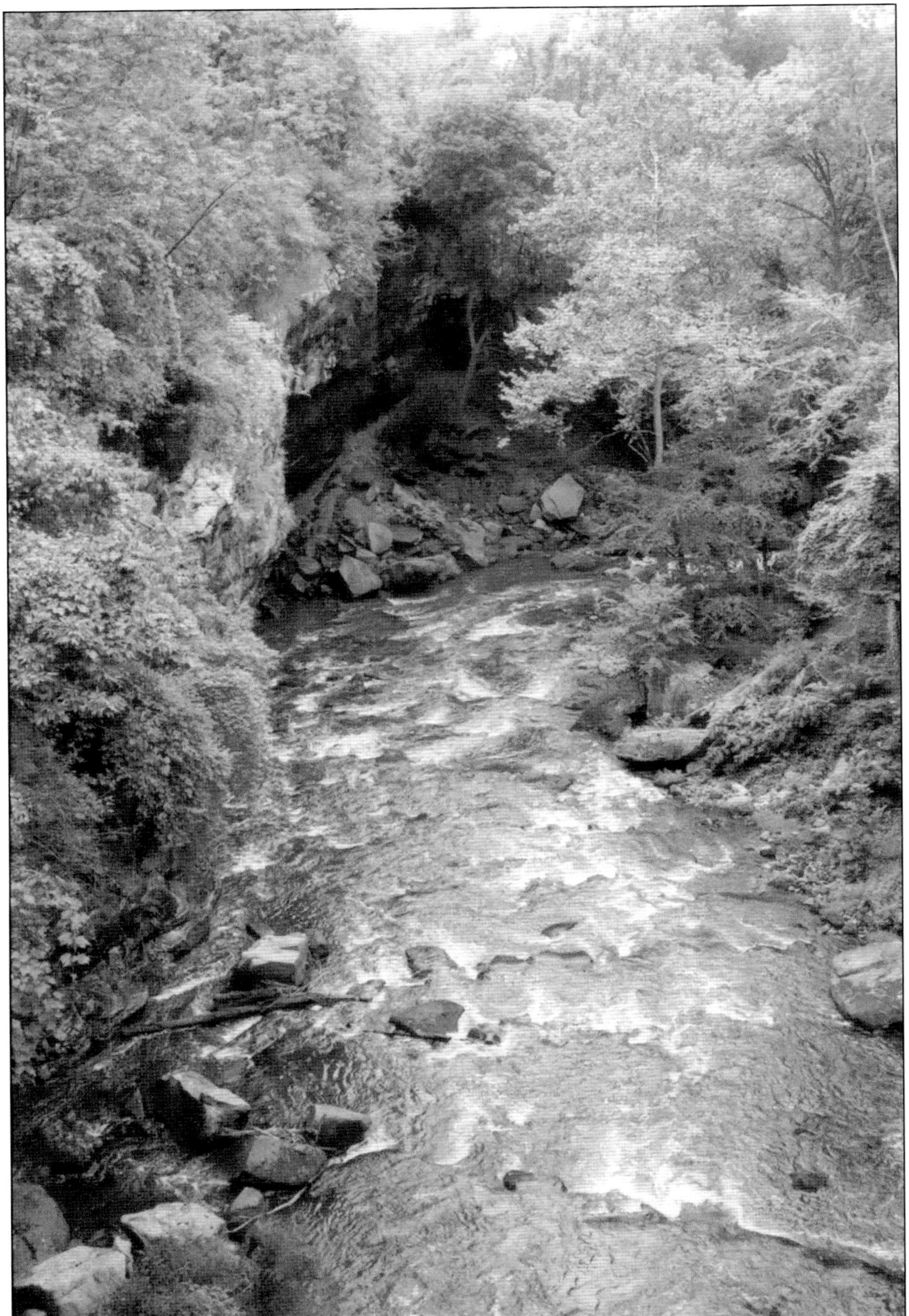

This scene, looking south from the observation bridge, shows that trees and other vegetation have overgrown many of the features of the original High Bridge Glens park. A camelback-shaped dark area is located in the top center in the background of this photograph; it is believed to be part of the former Grand Promenade. (Photograph by author.)

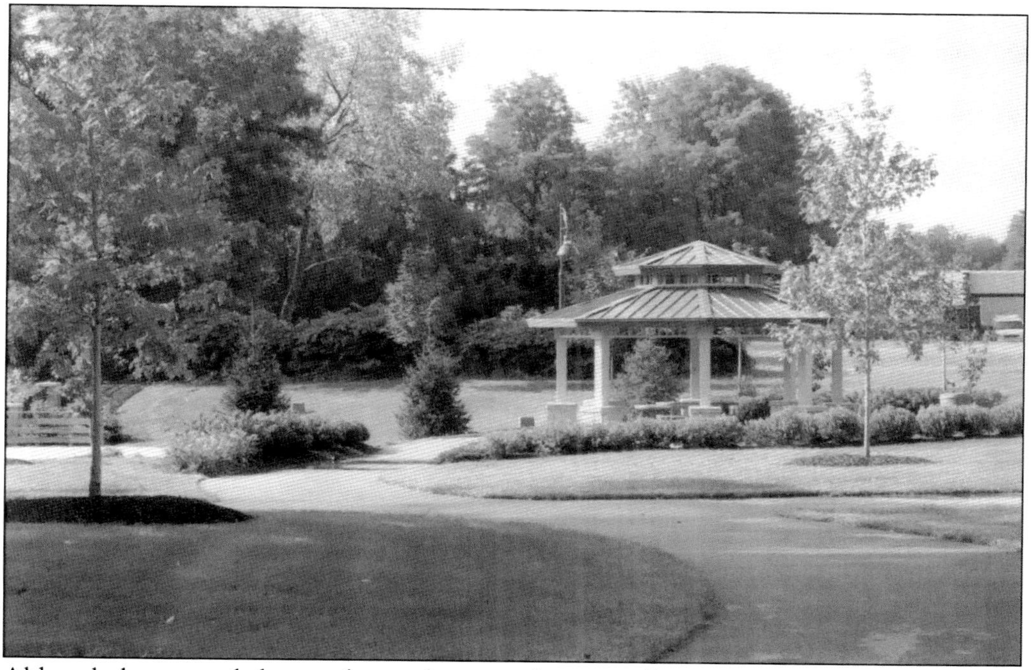

Although the new park does not have a dance pavilion or a roller coaster, it does have a number of amenities, including stunning views and a green-roofed, open-air gazebo. On weekends, the gazebo is a popular place for visitors to sit and chat or enjoy a cup of coffee. (Photograph by author.)

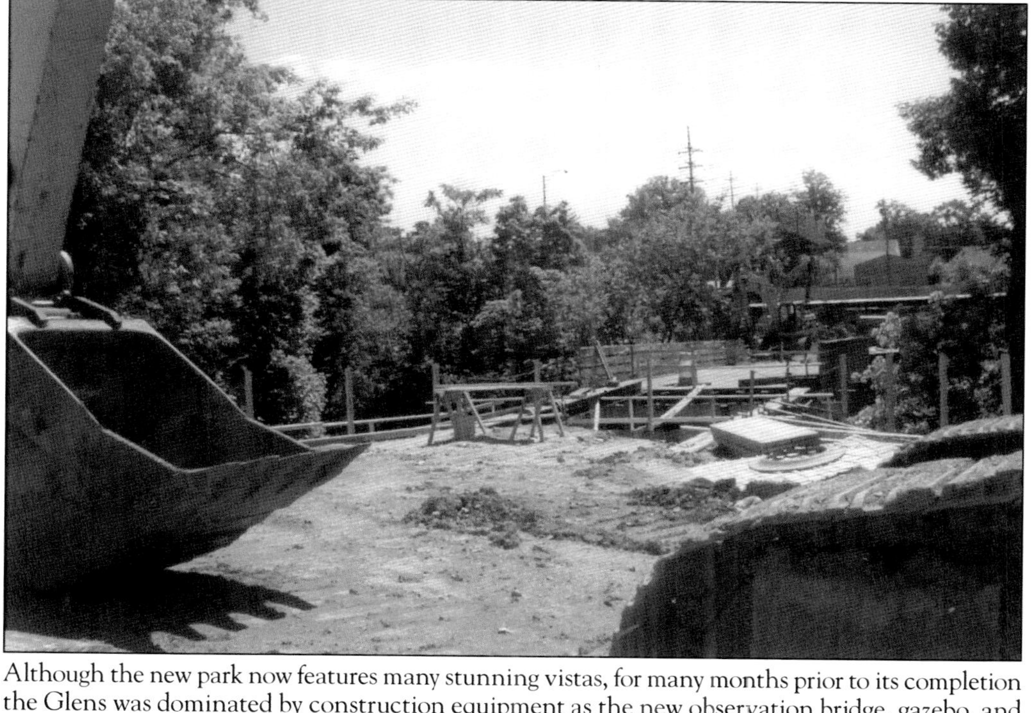

Although the new park now features many stunning vistas, for many months prior to its completion the Glens was dominated by construction equipment as the new observation bridge, gazebo, and other features were installed. (Photograph by author.)

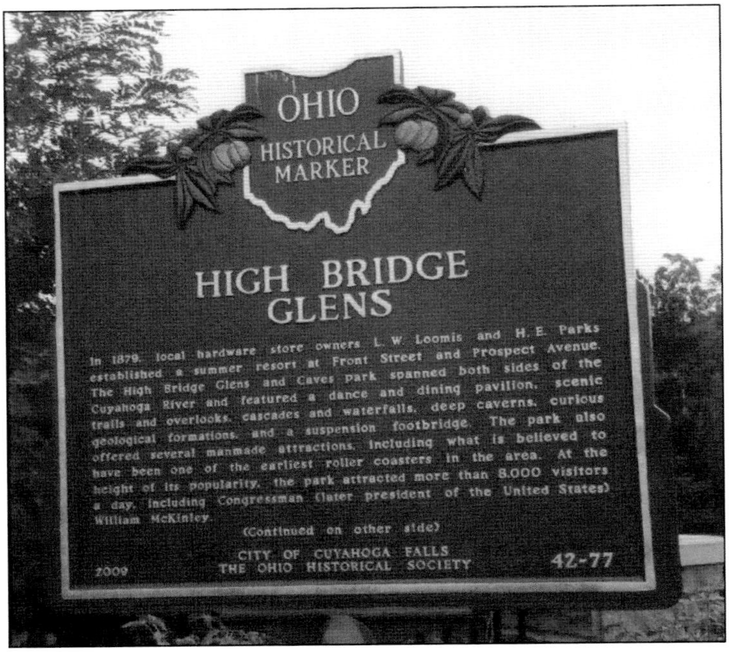


The new park is the site of Cuyahoga Falls' first Ohio Historical Marker. The front of the marker describes the history of the original High Bridge Glens and highlights its attendance figures and prominent visitors, including Ohio governor Charles Foster and Congressman (later US president) William McKinley. (Photograph by author.)

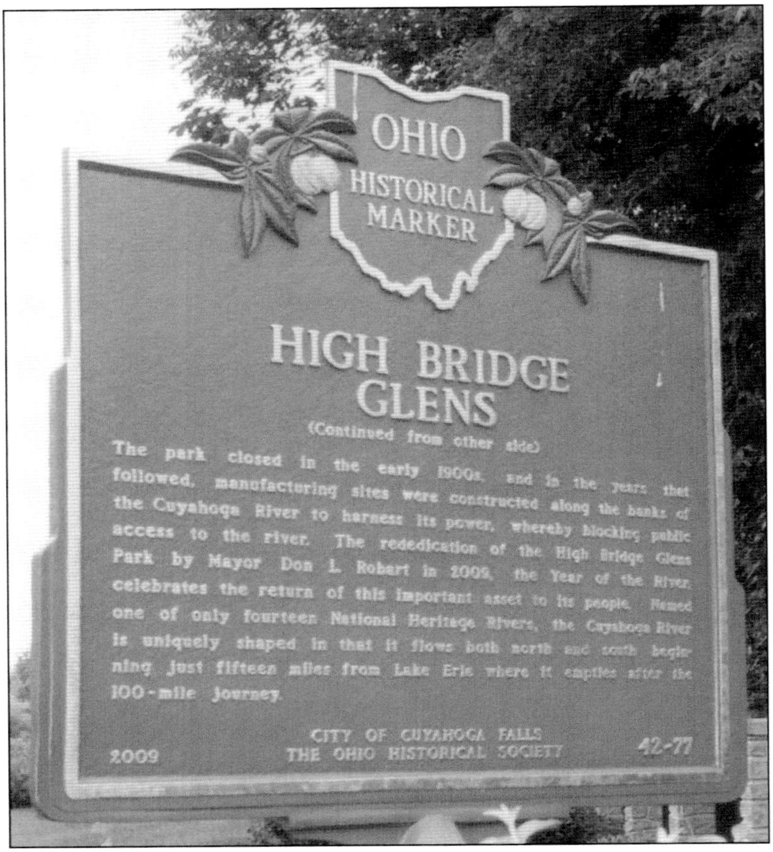


The other side of the marker describes the important role that the Cuyahoga River played in the early growth and development of Cuyahoga Falls. (Photograph by author.)

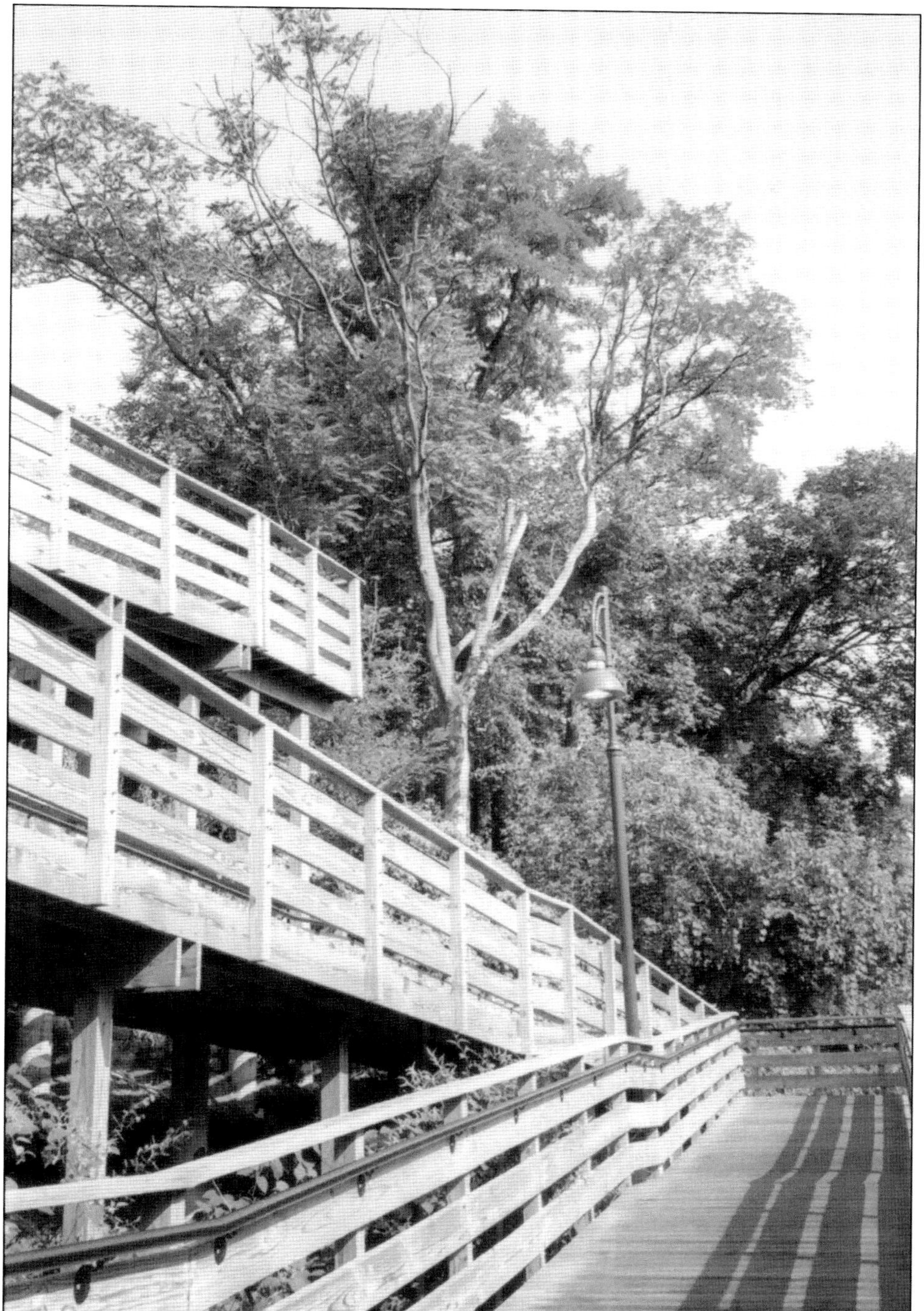

At the original High Bridge Glens, the owners placed stick fences by the edges of the trails to keep visitors from tumbling into the river below. For the new park, the city installed much more substantial railings on its three-level wooden observation deck. It also installed period-style lighting to illuminate the area at night. (Photograph by author.)

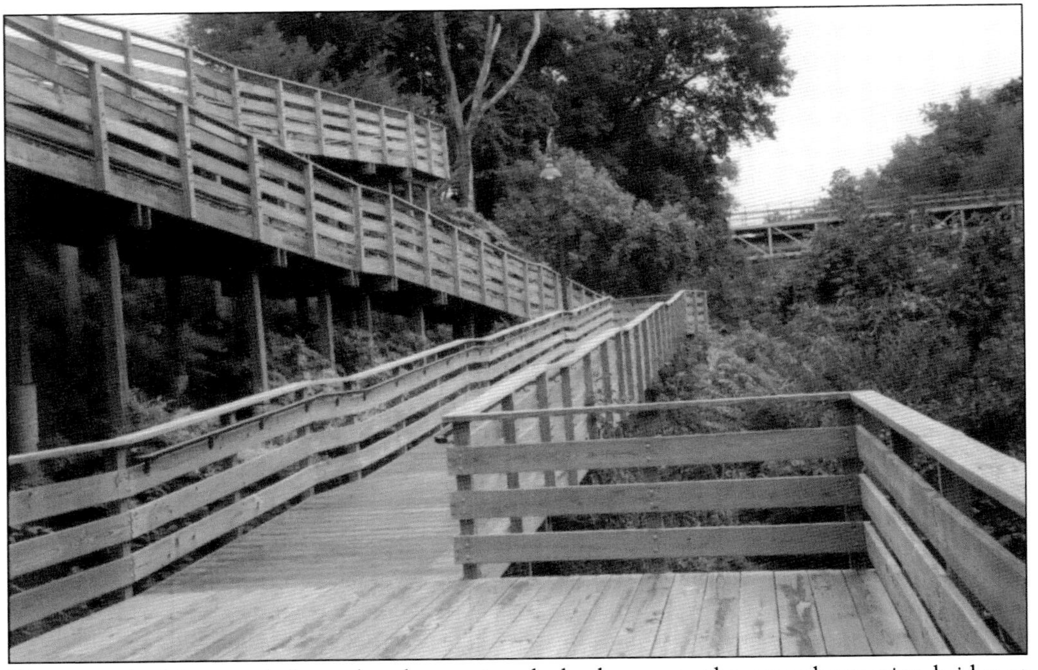

This view, looking north from the observation deck, showcases the new observation bridge at Front and Prospect Streets. (Photograph by author.)

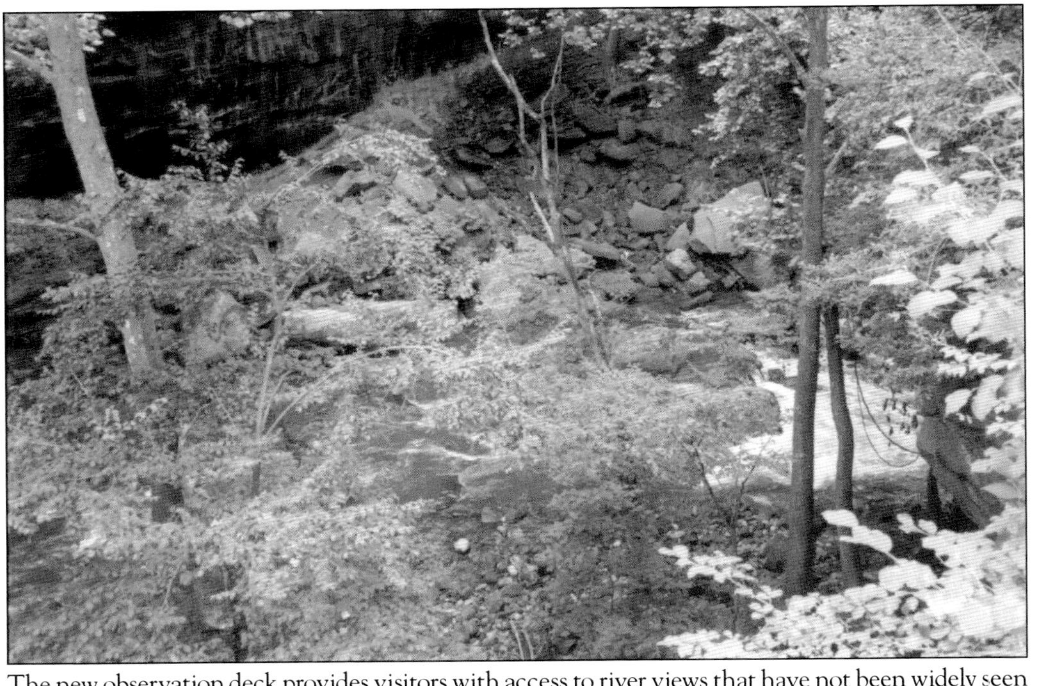

The new observation deck provides visitors with access to river views that have not been widely seen for nearly a century. Note the rocks and camelback-shaped area in the background. This is believed to be part of the former Grand Promenade on the park's east side. (Photograph by author.)

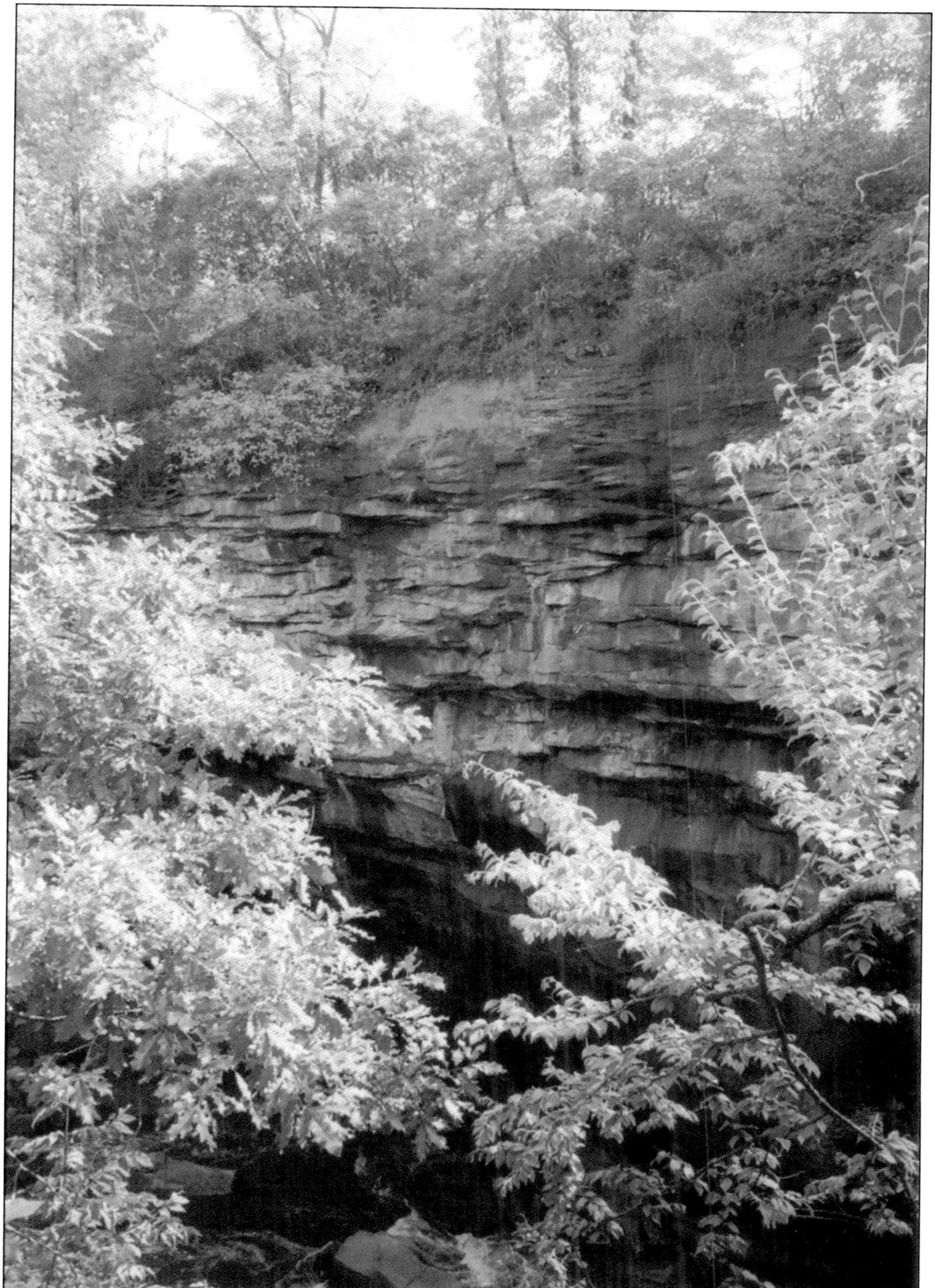

In addition to beautiful river views, visitors can enjoy the Weeping Cliffs from the safety of the observation deck. (Photograph by author.)

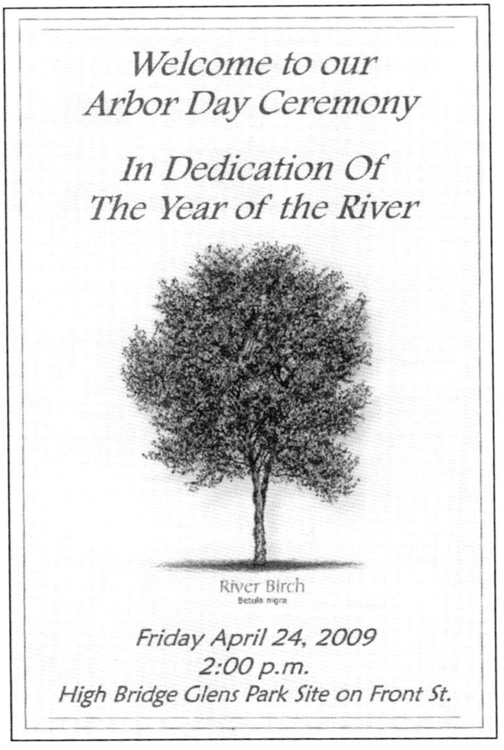


One of the first events held at the new High Bridge Glens was a 2009 Arbor Day ceremony, where a River Birch tree was planted at the park. The Arbor Day Foundation has named Cuyahoga Falls a Tree City USA community for its commitment to urban forestry. Recently, the park was the site of a nationally televised food competition. (Photograph by author.)

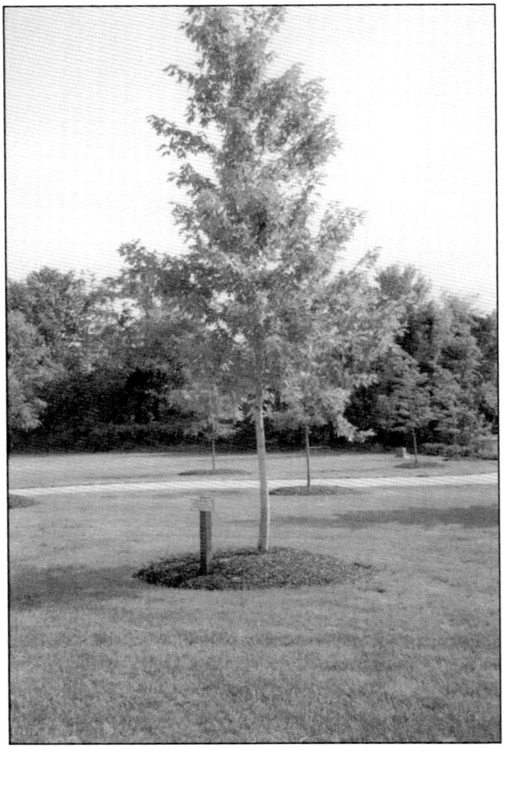

At the new park, special trees have been planted in remembrance of area residents. This tree was donated in memory of David Hunt, who was active in civic affairs and supported efforts to redevelop the South Front Street area where the High Bridge Glens was located. (Photograph by author.)

The Cuyahoga Falls Senior Strollers and the Fleming/Reinhold families donated this maple tree and a bench in memory of Dorothy Fleming. Other organizations, including a local bank and area civic groups, continue to donate trees to the park. (Photograph by author.)

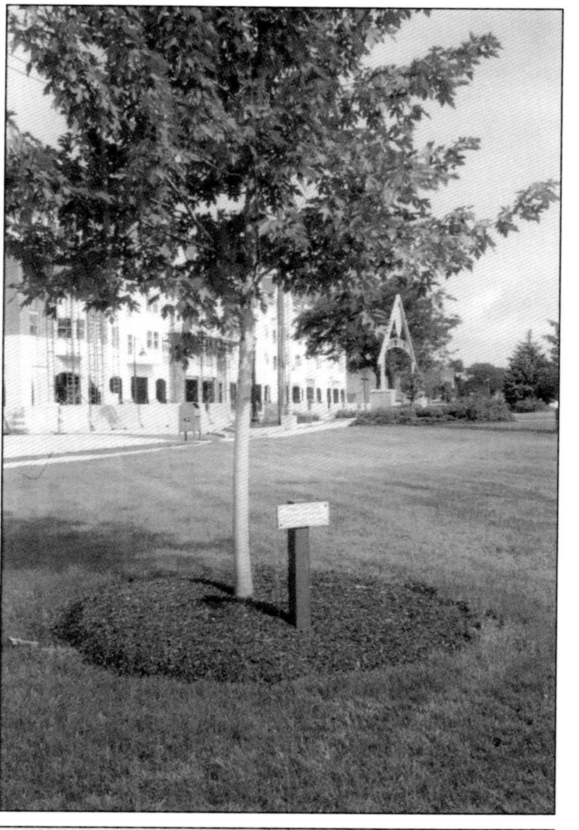

When the original High Bridge Glens opened in 1879, new businesses quickly developed around the park, including roller-skating rinks, refreshment parlors, and live animal attractions. Since the new High Bridge Glens park was rededicated, a new development called the Watermark was constructed across from the park. (Photograph by author.)

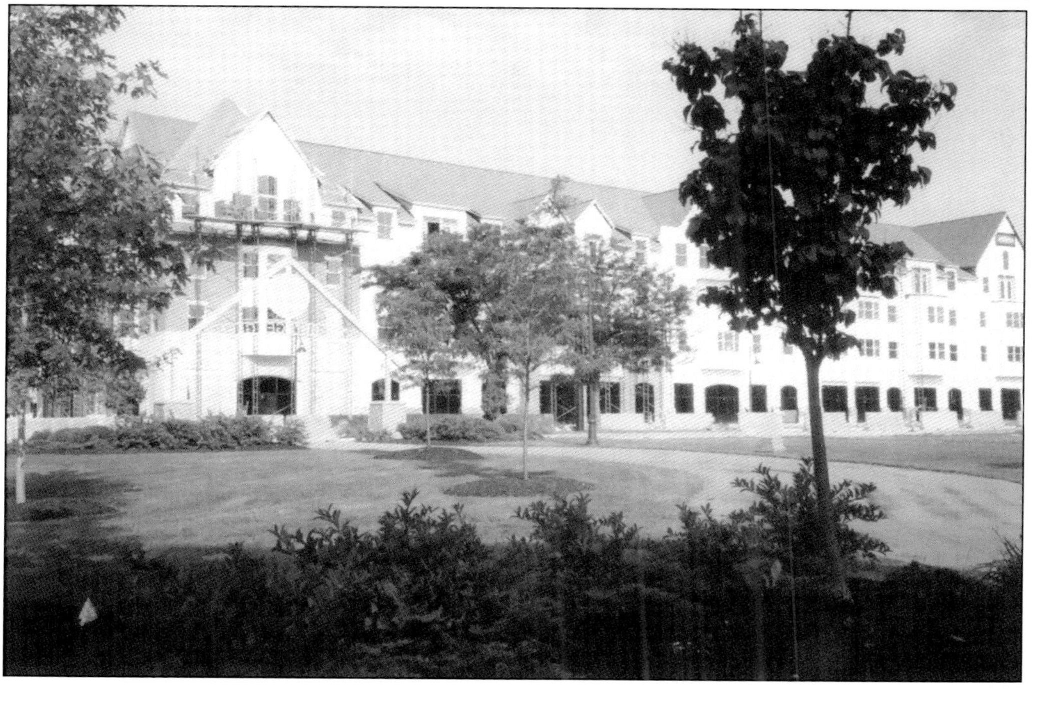

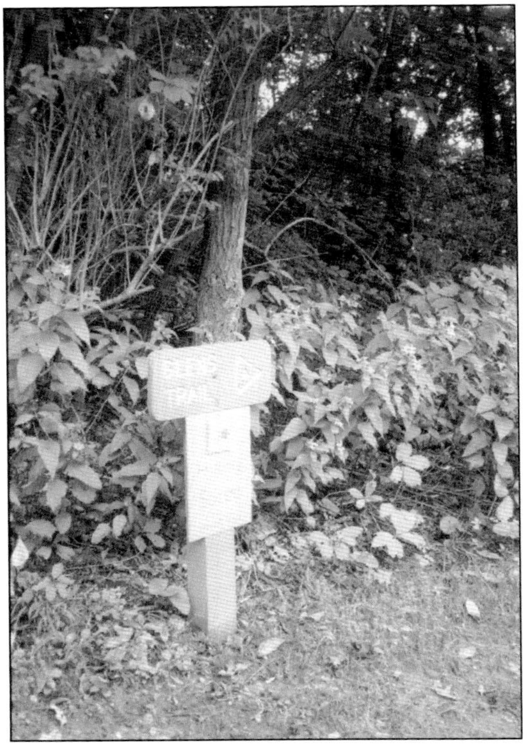

While the trail on the eastern half of the original High Bridge Glens park is no longer accessible to hikers, a portion of the trail on the western half (Front Street side) is now included in the Glens Trail at the nearby Gorge park, which is part of the Metro Parks, Serving Summit County. Looking east from the Glens Trail, modern-day hikers can see remains of the Chuckery. (Photograph by author.)

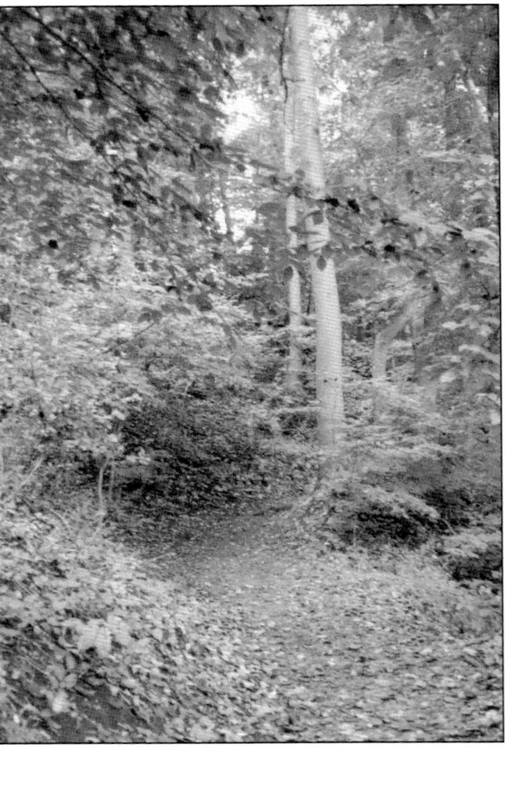

The 1.8-mile Glens Trail offers winding paths that take hikers past stunning rock formations and river views. Features in and around the Glens include ledges of Sharon conglomerate sandstone, along with the remains of the Chuckery and the former Gorge power plant. (Photograph by author.)

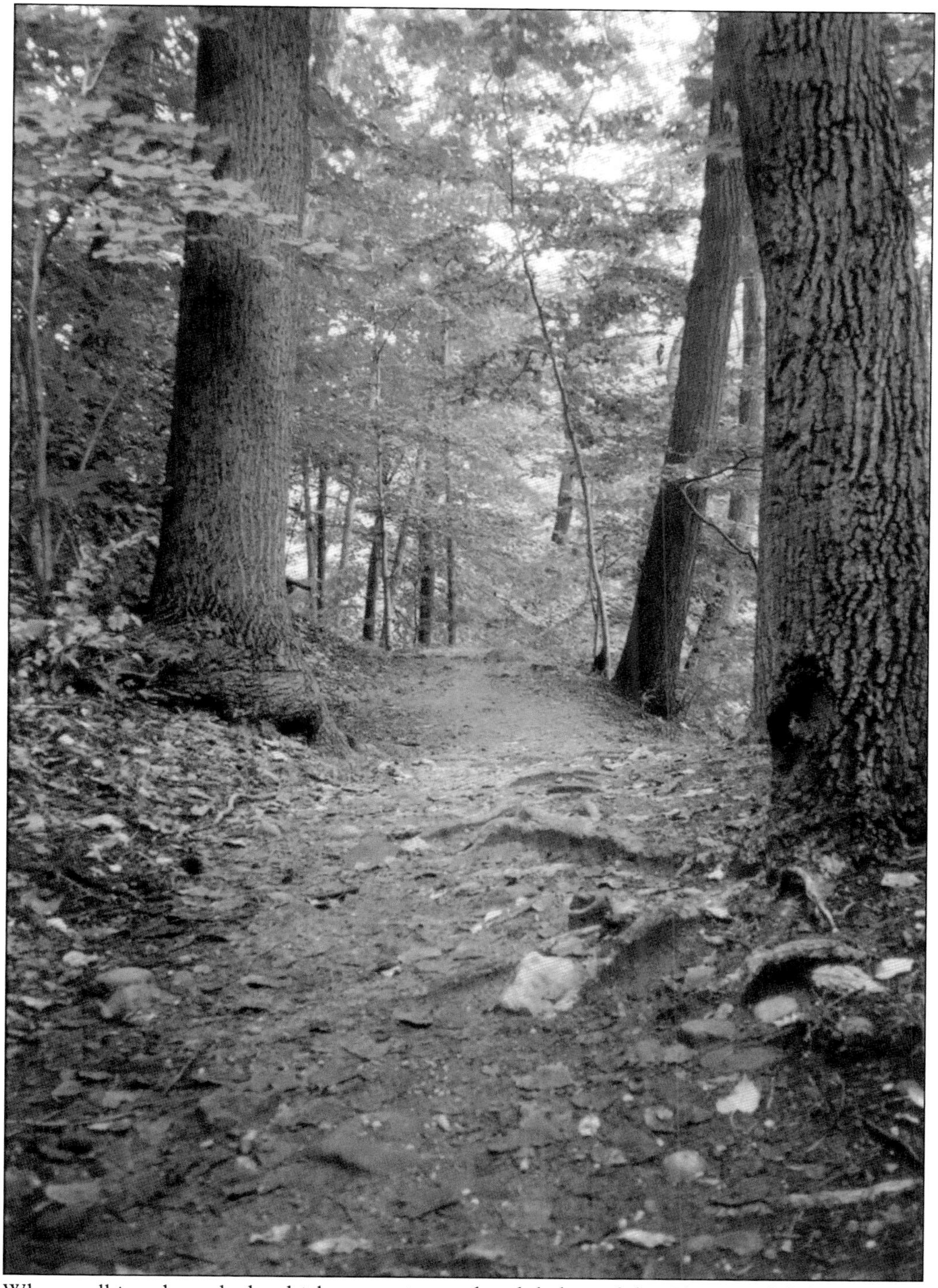

When walking through the thick vegetation and rock ledges of the Glens Trail, hikers can get the impression of being miles from civilization. In reality, the park is only minutes away from some of the area's busiest streets and expressways. (Photograph by author.)

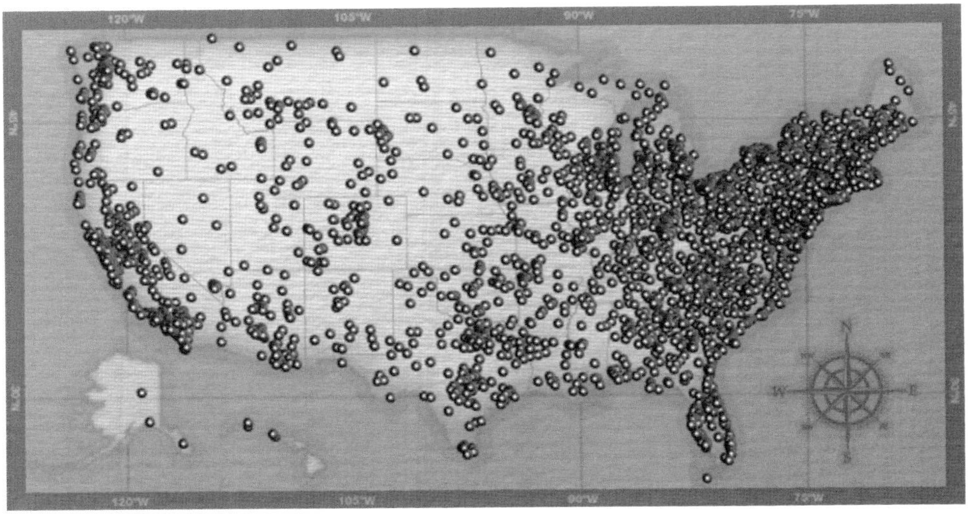